D0769013

THE MAKING OF SIR PHILIP SIDNEY

The Making of
Sir Philip Sidney

EDWARD BERRY

UNIVERSITY OF TORONTO PRESS
Toronto Buffalo London

HOUSTON PUBLIC LIBRARY

R0l2l2 74986

© University of Toronto Press Incorporated 1998
Toronto Buffalo London
Printed in Canada

ISBN 0-8020-4288-0

Printed on acid-free paper

Canadian Cataloguing in Publication Data

Berry, Edward, 1940–
The making of Sir Philip Sidney

Includes index.
ISBN 0-8020-4288-0

1. Sidney, Philip, Sir, 1554–1586 – Criticism and interpretation.
2. Self in literature.   I. Title.

PR2343.B477 1998   821'.3   C97-932559-5

University of Toronto Press acknowledges the financial assistance to its publishing
program of the Canada Council for the Arts and the Ontario Arts Council.

This book has been published with the help of a grant from the Humanities and
Social Sciences Federation of Canada, using funds provided by the Social Sciences
and Humanities Research Council of Canada.

To Margaret

Contents

Preface

If a good wine needs no bush, a good title probably needs no explanation. I cannot think of a better or more necessary preface to this book,
however, than a gloss on its title, which is intentionally and, I hope, significantly ambiguous.

The chief ambiguity in the title lies in the word 'making.' It refers
first to Sidney as poet, or 'maker,' the traditional term for the poet that
he himself adopts in the *A Defence of Poetry*. My concern is not with the
whole of Sidney's poetic 'making,' however, although I treat almost all of
the works, but with only one aspect of it – Sidney's creation of images
of himself, as in such characters as Astrophil, Philisides, and the intrusive
persona of the *Defence*. My primary aim in this study is to understand,
from a number of different perspectives – social, biographical, literary –
the significance of these self-representations.

Described in this way, my title also creates uncertainty about the name
'Sir Philip Sidney,' which might be taken to represent either the historical personage or an imagined self, a fictional self-representation. This
ambiguity, too, is deliberate, for I argue throughout that Sidney's self-
images are both historical and fictional, and that in mediating between
the two realms they represent a response to the Renaissance notion of
imitation, which considered the creation of imagined selves a means of
constructing real ones. The title 'Sir' adds an unavoidable ambiguity,
especially since Sidney did not receive it until very late in his career; I use
it not because my study focuses on the 'making' of Sidney as a knight but
because the use of mere 'Philip Sidney' might connote an exclusive focus
on the man rather than the public role.

A final equivocation lies in the question of agency, for the phrase 'the
making of Sir Philip Sidney' leaves open the possibility that 'Sidney'

might have been made by some maker other than the poet himself. This ambiguity, too, is intentional, for although I attribute agency to Sidney as a man and poet, this is not a study in the autonomy of art or the artist. To understand the images of the self made by Sidney, I believe that one must also understand the Sidney who made the images, an individual both conditioned and motivated by a particular society at a particular time. My study of Sidney's 'making' attempts to understand the complex relationship between Sidney's fictional and biographical selves and the relationship of both to Elizabethan culture.

In some ways this book is a study of a single device, that of persona. The term 'persona' is problematic, however, for it traditionally invites, as often in the New Criticism, a reductive separation between the author of a work and the voice or mask through which he or she speaks. The concept of persona also invites a divergent but equally reductive historicist denial of separation, an identification of author with mask as if the device were meaningless. Many studies of Sidney exist that treat such personas as completely fictitious or rhetorical characters, whose truth resides solely within the fiction. Many studies also exist that attempt to ferret out the biographical significance of personas such as Astrophil and Philisides. I depend heavily on both kinds of studies, and find much of value in them. My own study, however, attempts to understand the personas as *both* autobiography *and* fiction, and to understand the convergence of the two modes as the result of Sidney's continuing vocational crisis within a humanistic culture devoted to the idea of imitation. Throughout the book I use the terms 'persona' and 'self-representation' synonymously to represent this ambiguous rhetorical device.

Most readers of this book will recognize a debt to Stephen Greenblatt, whose fine studies *Sir Walter Ralegh* and *Renaissance Self-Fashioning* – the latter of which surprisingly omits Sidney – have been so influential. In view of this debt, I should perhaps highlight one difference between our approaches. As pursued by Greenblatt, the topic of self-fashioning is considerably broader than the topic of self-representation that I pursue in Sidney. His topic, as he describes it, is 'the fashioning of human identity as a manipulable, artful process.'[1] Although the terms 'self-fashioning' and 'self-representation' are complementary and at times difficult to distinguish, my interest is less in the fashioning of human identity than in the 'artful process' of its representation. With few exceptions, I have restricted my focus to explicit self-representations such as Philisides, resisting the temptation to pursue at length such psychologically interesting questions as the autobiographical significance of such figures as Pyrocles or Musidorus, both of whom are in some sense also authorial self-projections. I am less concerned with Sidney's 'self' in any ultimate sense, in short, than I am with the significance of his studied self-representations, his fictional autobiographies.

Any study of the representation of the 'self' in the sixteenth century is fraught with theoretical, methodological, and evidentiary problems. For better or worse, I have not anchored my approach in any particular theory of the self, although I have tried to write with an awareness of the various issues involved. Whether we possess an essential self; whether we construct our own identity, or whether society constructs it for us; whether what we call identity is something more than fiction – these are interesting and important questions, and I hope that an exploration of Sidney's self-representations might deepen our understanding of their historical ramifications. The questions, however, will remain. The Sidney who emerges in this study is one who was profoundly shaped by his familial, social, and cultural environment; who aspired to the unitary, stable, and social self implicit in the values of his time and class; and whose various self-representations reflect not a radical questioning of traditional conceptions of the self, as in Montaigne, but an anxiety about a loss of self, a psychological and social dissolution.

The chapters of this study are arranged in what I take to be roughly chronological order, although the exact dates of composition of most works are uncertain. Chapter 1 is introductory and outlines the various forces – familial, educational, cultural – that contributed to Sidney's becoming a writer preoccupied with self-representation. Chapter 2 traces the first emergence of a Sidneyan self-representation in his letters to Hubert Languet, written mainly from 1573 to 1576. Chapter 3 treats Sidney's early and unsuccessful efforts to play the role of courtier-poet at Elizabeth's court. Chapter 4 centres on the role of Philisides in the *Old Arcadia*. Chapter 5 treats the persona of *A Defence of Poetry*. Chapter 6 discusses Astrophil in *Astrophil and Stella*. Chapter 7 treats the revised figure of Philisides in the *New Arcadia*. Chapter 8, finally, concludes with some general observations on continuities among the various self-representations, and on their overall significance. Although the argument is developed chronologically, it does not depend upon specific dates of composition or a specific chronological order; Sidney's writing career was so short and his concerns so interrelated that it is difficult to speak significantly about development in any case. For 'Sidney's Life: A Brief Chronology,' I depend generally on the Oxford editors and indicate parenthetically the most likely span of years within which the works were written.

I use the Oxford editions of the works throughout: Jean Robertson, ed., *Sir Philip Sidney: The Countess of Pembroke's Arcadia (The Old Arcadia)* (Oxford: Clarendon Press, 1973); William A. Ringler, Jr, ed., *The Poems of Sir Philip Sidney* (Oxford: Clarendon Press, 1962); Victor Skretkowicz, ed., *Sir Philip Sidney: The Countess of Pembroke's Arcadia (The New Arcadia)* (Oxford: Clarendon Press, 1987); and Katherine Duncan-Jones and Jan Van Dorsten, eds., *Miscellaneous Prose of Sir Philip Sidney* (Oxford: Clarendon Press, 1973). The latter edition includes the *Discourse on Irish Affairs*, *The Lady of May*, the *Letter to Queen Elizabeth*, *A Defence of Poetry*, the *Defence of the Earl of Leicester*, and Sidney's will. Citations to these editions are indicated parenthetically by page and line number throughout the text. To avoid possible ambiguity, I have occasionally added abbreviated titles, as follows: *Old Arcadia* (*OA*), *Poems* (*P*), *New Arcadia* (*NA*), *Lady of May* (*LM*), *Letter to Queen Elizabeth* (*LQ*), *A Defence of Poetry* (*DP*), *Defence of the Earl of Leicester* (*DL*). In citing early texts, I have normalized *u*, *v*, *i*, and *j* to conform to modern practice.

The absence of a single authoritative collection of Sidney's correspondence poses special problems. The Sidney-Languet correspondence is entirely in Latin. Languet's side of the correspondence was eventually published (the first edition in 1633 in Frankfurt), but only a few copies remain; Sidney's side is represented by manuscripts still dispersed throughout Europe. My study of the letters, therefore, depends upon the various modern editions and translations that exist: Charles S. Levy, 'The Correspondence of Sir Philip Sidney and Hubert Languet, 1573–1576' (PhD diss., Cornell University, 1962); James M. Osborn, *Young Philip Sidney: 1572–1577* (New Haven: Yale University Press, 1972); Albert Feuillerat, ed., *The Prose Works of Sir Philip Sidney*, 4 vols., vol. 3 (Cambridge: Cambridge University Press, 1962); and Steuart A. Pears, trans., *The Correspondence of Sir Philip Sidney and Hubert Languet* (1845; reprint Westmead, England: Gregg International, 1971). I cite preferentially in the above order when multiple versions of letters are available.

Although I have tried to avoid gender bias in my own writing, I have reproduced it without comment in citing and interpreting Elizabethan materials; I trust that contemporary readers do not require underlining to perceive the gendered subtext of such usages as the so-called generic 'man.'

My argument incorporates revised versions of essays published elsewhere. A short section of chapter 1 first appeared in *Shakespeare's Comic Rites* (Cambridge: Cambridge University Press, 1984). Most of chapter 2 is taken from 'Hubert Languet and the "Making" of Philip Sidney,' *Studies in Philology* 85 (1988): 305–20. Chapter 6 depends heavily on 'The Poet as Warrior in Sidney's *Defence of Poetry*,' *Studies in English Literature* 29 (1989): 22–34. A section of chapter 7 appeared previously as 'Sidney's "Poor" Painter: Nationalism and Social Class,' in Vincent Newey and Ann Thompson, eds., *Literature and Nationalism* (Liverpool: Liverpool University Press, 1991).

At a very early stage in this project, I received helpful guidance from Henry Woudhuysen and Simon Adams. I am also indebted to the University of Victoria and the Social Sciences and Humanities Research Council of Canada for research support; to my colleague Terry Sherwood for his astute criticisms of the manuscript and for many lunch-time conversations; to my students of Sidney, whose enthusiasms often fired my own; to the readers for the Canadian Federation for the Humanities and the University of Toronto Press for their generous and constructive suggestions; and to the editorial staff of the Press for their attentive care. My final debt, as always, is to my indulgent and expanding family – especially to Margaret, to whom this book is dedicated.

Sidney's Life:
A Brief Chronology

1554   Born 30 November at Penshurst, Kent.
1564   Enters Shrewsbury Grammar School.
1566   Presented to the queen at Oxford by his uncle, the earl of
        Leicester.
1568   Enters Christ Church, Oxford; remains three years.
1572–5 Travels on the Continent, mentored by Hubert Languet.
1575   Returns to the court; attends Leicester's entertainment of
        the queen at Kenilworth in July. Father begins third term
        as Lord Deputy Governor of Ireland.
1576   Becomes cupbearer to the queen; accompanies the earl of
        Essex to Ireland to assist his father.
1577   European embassy February to June – meets Protestant
        princes throughout the Continent. Sister, Mary, marries
        the earl of Pembroke. Upon his return, becomes active in
        support of the Protestant cause abroad; defends his
        father's handling of Irish affairs in the *Discourse on Irish
        Affairs*.
1578   Entertains the queen with *The Lady of May* during her visit
        with Leicester at Wanstead. Continues active support for
        the Protestant cause abroad. Perhaps begins the *Old
        Arcadia* (1577–81) while visiting sister, Mary, at Wilton.
1579   August, Anjou (previously Alençon) arrives to woo the
        queen. Sidney challenges the earl of Oxford to a duel;
        probably writes the *Letter to Queen Elizabeth* (1579–80),
        advising her against the French marriage. Stephen Gosson
        dedicates the *School of Abuse* to Sidney, and Spenser
        The Shephearde's Calender. Sidney retires to Wilton, works

on the *Old Arcadia* and perhaps *A Defence of Poetry*
(1579–83).

1580   Works on the *Old Arcadia* at Wilton; returns to court.

1581   January, elected to Parliament. Penelope Devereux is presented at court and later marries Lord Rich. April, Sidney
participates in tournament, the *Four Foster Children of Desire*.
Perhaps begins *Astrophil and Stella* (1581–3).

1582   Escorts Anjou to the Netherlands. Probably begins the *New
Arcadia* (1582–4).

1583   January, knighted to stand as proxy for Prince Casimir at
installation of the Order of the Garter. Appointed to assist
the earl of Warwick, Master of Ordnance. September, marries Frances Walsingham.

1584   Probably writes the *Defence of the Earl of Leicester* (1584–5).

1585   Probably begins translating Duplessis-Mornay's *De la vérité de
la religion chrestienne*; perhaps translates Du Bartas's *La
Semaine* and begins a translation of *Psalms*. Appointed
governor of Flushing; arrives in November.

1586   Father and mother die in summer. Sidney, wounded at
Zutphen (22 September), dies at Arnhem (17 October).

1587   Buried in St Paul's Cathedral 16 February.

THE MAKING OF SIR PHILIP SIDNEY

1

Imitation and Identity

Although English autobiography did not emerge as a genre until the seventeenth century, an autobiographical impulse characterizes many writers of the Tudor period. The impulse appears not in the form of sustained and purportedly truthful accounts of individual lives, as in later autobiographies, but in the form of narrative or poetic fragments that mix biography and fiction. Thomas More, for example, includes himself among the characters of the *Utopia;* Spenser assumes the role of Colin Clout in *The Shephearde's Calender* and *The Faerie Queene*, and celebrates his own marriage in the 'Epithalamion'; Lyly identifies himself with Euphues in *The Anatomy of Wit*; and lyric poets from Wyatt to Ralegh create personas that reflect to varying degrees their actual experiences, amatory and political, in the world of the Tudor court. This widespread interest in fictionalized self-representation is a special case of the broader Renaissance phenomenon that, since Stephen Greenblatt's classic study, has been called self-fashioning.[1]

Although this tendency to create images of the self within independent works of fiction may seem modern in so far as it foreshadows autobiography, it shares much in common with at least one long-standing mode of self-representation, that of Renaissance visual artists, for whom self-portraiture was a recognized and important genre. Artists depicted themselves alone or, often, as participants in a historical or mythological narrative, a method closely analogous to that of Sidney. Ghiberti, for example, included himself among the prophets on both the North and East doors of the Baptistry in Florence, Botticelli depicted himself as a participant in his *Adoration of the Magi*, and Gozzoli portrayed himself along with members of the Medici family in his fresco of the journey of the Magi. In a way that seems hardly coincidental, the two modes of self-representation converged in England in 1576 and 1577, the years in which the court musician Thomas Whythorne wrote the first substantial English autobiography and the painter Nicholas Hilliard executed the first English self-portrait. Whythorne had his own portrait painted four times.[2] As we shall see later, Sidney was much interested in the visual arts: he chose Veronese to do his own portrait while in Venice, designed imprese for tournaments at court, included portraits of characters in the *New Arcadia*, and discussed painting with Hilliard. It is possible, therefore, that some of his interest in self-representation developed out of the visual as well as the literary tradition.

Although a heightened interest in self-representation is common to writers of the Tudor period, Philip Sidney is none the less remarkable for the number and variety of his literary self-portraits and the self-consciousness with which he cultivates his literary personas. As a very young man, in the letters to Languet, he writes from within the role of friend, modelling himself on the Ciceronean conception of friendship central to the humanist tradition. In the *Old Arcadia* he includes in the eclogues the character of Philisides, a melancholy shepherd whose biography is a fictitious version of his own. In *Astrophil and Stella*, he takes pains not only to identify the persona, Astrophil, with himself, but to identify Stella with Penelope Rich. In *A Defence of Poetry*, he uses a rhetorical form that encourages self-referentiality, the classical oration, and develops it in such a way that the character of the persona becomes itself a persuasive argument. In the *New Arcadia*, he retains the character of Philisides from the *Old Arcadia* but changes his role from that of melancholy shepherd to shepherd-knight. Throughout his literary career, in short, Sidney provides sketches towards a kind of fictional autobiography.

In *Sidney and Spenser: The Poet as Maker*, S.K. Heninger, Jr, illuminates the roles of Philisides and Astrophil in relation to the theory of imitation that Sidney develops in *A Defence of Poetry*. In Heninger's view, Sidney's inclusion of such borderline figures in his texts represents a metafictional acknowledgment of the process of artistic imitation, in which the 'world of fact and the world of fiction intersect, interact.' By imagining himself as Philisides and Astrophil, according to Heninger, Sidney was able to demonstrate for the reader both the imitative nature of his fiction and the limitations of the pastoral and Petrarchan roles played by his self-representations.[3] Heninger's observations on both characters are very instructive, and I shall allude to them in later chapters. My own focus, however, is more psychological and social than theoretical. Like Heninger, I see the idea of imitation as central to an understanding of

Sidney's self-representations; I am less concerned than he, however, with its theoretical significance than with its psychological and social effects. The doctrine of imitation taught in Elizabethan schools, as we shall see, defined imaginative role-playing not only as a means of making fictions but of making the self.

Among many courtier-poets of the Elizabethan period, the cultivation of a distinctive persona or series of personas, often both literary and social, had a clear political function. Poetry could be used to court the queen directly on occasion, as it was by such courtiers as Sir Arthur Gorges, the earl of Oxford, and Sir Walter Ralegh. It could also be used to establish in a general sense an attractive and exciting self-image; Stephen Greenblatt suggests that poetry was for Ralegh an important means of creating 'the marvelous image he presented to the court and especially to the queen.'[4] Poetry could also serve, as Richard Helgerson notes, as 'a way of displaying abilities that could, once they had come to the attention of a powerful patron, be better employed in some other manner.'[5] When Ralegh wooed the queen as Cynthia in the guise of Ocean, his fictional self, compounded of adoration, daring, and rhetorical skill, was intended to convince the queen and court indirectly that his 'real' self deserved their favour. The entire system of literary 'courtship' depended upon an assumed continuity between the literary and social persona, the success of the former bringing favour to the latter. With its identification of courtly and poetic dissembling, Puttenham's *The Arte of English Poesie*, as Daniel Javitch observes, can be read both as a treatise on poetry and as 'one of the most significant arts of conduct of the Elizabethan age.'[6]

Although Sidney may be considered a courtier-poet, his poetic roles seem not to have served a comparable political function. As an aristocrat and patron himself, Sidney did not require patronage in the way that poets of less exalted status did; nor did his obvious rhetorical and political skills require demonstration. As Katherine Duncan-Jones observes, moreover, the statesmen whose support he most needed, men such as Walsingham, were unlikely to be impressed by poetic achievement or a poetic persona.[7] Throughout his career Sidney's most compelling goal was to win the favour of the queen. Yet, with the possible exceptions of the unsuccessful court entertainment *The Lady of May* and other courtly pageants for which we have little evidence, he never used his poetry to that end. In his avoidance of what Steven W. May calls a 'utilitarian' courtly poetics, Sidney has much in common with his two close friends, the courtiers Edward Dyer and Fulke Greville, who addressed only a few poems to the queen.[8] The figure of Elizabeth haunts Sidney's works, as we shall see, but not in a way that could have served Sidney's political advancement.

If Sidney was not a 'utilitarian' courtly poet, he was also not a commercial poet. Both his words and actions reveal an aristocratic bias against the medium of print. In *A Defence of Poetry* he regrets that because poetry is despised in England only 'base men with servile wits undertake it, who think it enough if they can be rewarded of the printer' (111.3–5). In the *New Arcadia*, too, as we shall see in chapter 7, his satire upon the 'poor painter' who loses his hands in the rebellion of the Arcadian commoners implies a mockery of commercial art (282.10–20). None of his literary works, moreover, was printed in his lifetime. Sidney's failure to exploit the medium of print is sometimes explained as the inevitable result of a universal aristocratic opposition to its vulgarity. As Steven W. May has demonstrated, however, the so-called stigma of print did not prevent aristocrats, or even monarchs, from printing their works; nor were commoners precluded from circulating their works in manuscript.[9] If Sidney held a principled opposition to print, moreover, it would be difficult to explain the decision of Fulke Greville and the countess of Pembroke to memorialize him by printing his works. Sidney's bias against print, although clearly evident in his own statements, must have seemed insignificant to his executors after his death. He himself, moreover, might have conceived a new attitude had he lived to finish the *New Arcadia*. Whatever Sidney's attitude towards print, his failure to seek publication in that medium and the limited circulation of his manuscripts gave him an extremely restricted original audience. Any continuity that existed between his literary and social self-representations was shared only by the coterie among whom his works were circulated in manuscript.[10]

If Sidney's literary self-representations functioned in some sense as social roles, they did so, then, in a very restrictive sense. The public at large was denied them, since they reached the medium of print only after Sidney's death, and the queen was not courted through them. Any continuity between literary persona and social role was restricted to an audience of family and friends, an audience close enough to be invited into a kind of self-dramatization that might have had local political motives but was certainly more disinterested than the self-dramatizations of Ralegh, say, or Spenser. Even if he contemplated eventual publication in print, Sidney must have been aware that the personal immediacy of his self-images, with their oblique allusions to events known within a select inner circle, would have been lost in such a medium. Sidney's estrangement from both the world of patronage and the world of print thus accentuates the private rather than public significance of his self-representations. Sidney's motives for writing, in contrast to those of most contemporary court or public writers, were, as Richard Helgerson observes, 'private and experimental': 'More than any of his contemporaries, he was engaged as a writer in a testing of himself and literature.'[11]

Although signs of the same preoccupation with self-representation can be detected in Sidney's social behaviour – in his role as a courtier, his participation in court pageants, and his death at Zutphen – his life seems not to have been as self-consciously theatrical as that of Ralegh, for example, whose courtly self-fashioning has been so ably described by Stephen Greenblatt in *Sir Walter Ralegh*. Nor is the documentation of Sidney's social behaviour very rich or very trustworthy. The accounts we have of his most flamboyant instances of public self-dramatization, for example – his challenge to the earl of Oxford, his participation in tournaments, and his death at Zutphen – are either filtered through the romantic lenses of his friend Fulke Greville or, as in the case of the tournaments, so slight as to make more than general interpretation or speculation impossible. In interpreting the literary record, I shall attempt to include aspects of the public personas; in the absence of more trustworthy accounts of actual social behaviour, however, I shall concentrate on Sidney's written images of himself.

Broadly speaking, the autobiographical impulse in writers of the sixteenth century can be attributed to the same causes that are usually cited to explain the emergence of autobiography and self-portraiture as genres.[12] The Protestant Reformation, which emphasized spiritual self-examination rather than the performance of ritual duties and fostered, as Gary F. Waller observes, 'anxiety about the stability of the self, and the continuity of experience';[13] the prominence of humanism, which celebrated, as in Pico della Mirandola's oration, the potential of the individual to create himself; the centrality of the family, which encouraged memorials to posterity; the unprecedented social mobility of the period, which created a need to define one's social identity, especially among writers and painters, whose status was profoundly ambiguous – these are among the most common underlying forces that shaped the development of a modern conception of self-reflection. All of these forces, as we shall see, bear upon Sidney.

In the most immediate sense, Sidney's preoccupation with self-representation as a writer is more simply explained. Sidney would not have become a serious writer if his own sense of self had not been in crisis. His goal as a young man was to become a major political figure at Elizabeth's court. When in 1575 he returned to England after three preparatory years on the Continent, he was ready to assume that role, but found himself repeatedly frustrated by personal and ideological differences with the queen. His first serious writings, *The Lady of May* and the *Letter to Queen Elizabeth* on the Anjou match, were futile exercises in courtly persuasion. The former had no discernible effect; the latter only increased the queen's antagonism, which, coupled with his impetuous challenge to the earl of Oxford, resulted in Sidney's exile from court for the better part of 1579–80 and the composition of his first major work, the *Old Arcadia*. Although he returned to court in 1581 and participated as a courtier in a variety of formal and informal capacities from that point on, Sidney was never seriously employed by Elizabeth in any sustained capacity until he was sent with troops to the Netherlands in 1585. Hence all of his major works – both *Arcadias*, *A Defence of Poetry*, and *Astrophil and Stella* – are products of enforced periods of what he himself called his 'idleness.' The act of writing was thus for Sidney a symptom of a continuing struggle for self-definition.[14]

With its connotations of earnest conflict, the word 'struggle' implies a view of literary activity that is alien to Sidney and to the aristocratic culture within which he lived. As Dorothy Connell reminds us, the Elizabethan court was a highly theatrical world, and Elizabethan notions of the courtier or courtier-poet, shaped as they were by writers such as Castiglione, emphasized the values of performance and of play.[15] In such an environment, social discourse of any kind was likely to take place in an atmosphere of sophisticated self-awareness, in which artifice and wit were taken for granted. With its connotations of intellectual brilliance, cleverness, and entertainment, the word 'wit' perhaps best encompasses the qualities of mind valued in such a society. In academic writing, as will doubtless become clear, it is difficult to do justice to this paradoxical combination of attitudes. For Sidney, self-representation was a form of serious play.

The crisis that precipitated Sidney's literary self-explorations arose out of the sense of identity he developed as a young man. The failure to find employment with the queen affected him profoundly not chiefly for reasons of wealth or personal ambition, although both are relevant, but because service to the state was fundamental to his conception of the self. In order to understand how this came to be, it is useful to explore some of the familial and social forces that shaped his early development. The self-portraits in Sidney's writings do not derive from an autonomous commitment to self-fashioning, of the kind heralded by Pico della Mirandola in his celebration of Protean man; instead, they are personal reactions to a social identity shaped in large part by his family and society.

Sidney's early years have been ably documented in a variety of biographical studies, and, although many details are missing, there is substantial agreement about the nature of his family, his friendships, his education, his religious training, and his social environment.[16] Rather than attempt a summary of well-known information, therefore, I should like to focus on some documents from Sidney's early life as crystallizations of the various forces that shaped his conception of identity as man and writer. The first consists of a single letter from Henry Sidney to his son, written probably in the late spring of 1566 when Philip was an eleven-year-old student at Shrewsbury School. The letter provides a microcosm of the familial, religious, and educational environment in which Philip's sense of identity was formed. The second, to be considered in chapter 2, consists of a series of documents – the extended correspondence between Sidney and Hubert Languet, his mentor, during the roughly three years Sidney spent travelling on the Continent, preparatory to his assumption of an adult role at court. Since this correspondence not only illustrates various pressures brought to bear on Sidney's early sense of identity but represents his first sustained effort at literary self-representation, it provides important insights into his later development of a self as a writer.

Henry Sidney's letter to his son is printed in full in Malcolm W. Wallace's biography.[17] It is considered at some length in Richard Helgerson's excellent account of the familial and educational pressures brought to bear on young men of Sidney's generation.[18] For Wallace the letter, which includes a postcript from Philip's mother, suggests a 'family relationship' the 'beauty' of which is 'perhaps unique in the sixteenth century.' In his dismal characterization of family life in the period, Wallace anticipates Lawrence Stone, who concludes that relationships between parents and children in the period were generally distant, formal, and rigidly hierarchical.[19] In its social context, it is true, Philip's relationship with his parents seems to have been exceptionally close and affectionate, not only at the time of this letter but throughout his life. In some respects, however, that very affection may have conspired against him, increasing the coercive appeal of the family's high expectations.

Although personal, Henry Sidney's letter is also perfectly conventional. The epistolary genre of advice to a son was popular in the period, and this letter itself was printed in 1591. The general drift of such letters is acutely parodied by Shakespeare in *Hamlet*, in Polonius's parting advice to Laertes, which is neither heard nor acted upon. Although advice of this kind is not without individuality, it tends to express the values of a particular social class at a particular time. Henry Sidney's letter is striking not because of its originality but because the young Philip, unlike Laertes, seems to have taken these values to heart. His entire later development suggests that, to an extent exceptional among courtiers of his generation, he internalized the expectations of his elders.

Although the letter in question is too long for full quotation, its very length suggests something of its importance and probable psychological impact; hence I have extracted the most significant parts of its major sections:

Son Philip:
I have received two letters from you, one written in Latin, the other in French; which I take in good part, and will you to exercise that practice of learning often; for that will stand you in most stead in that profession of life that you are born to live in. And now, since this is my first letter that ever I did write to you, I will not that it be all empty of some advices which my natural care of you provoketh me to wish you to follow, as documents to you in this your tender age.

Let your first action be the lifting up of your mind to Almighty God by hearty prayer; and feelingly digest the words you speak in prayer, with continual meditation and thinking of Him to whom you pray, and of the matter for which you pray ...

Apply your study to such hours as your discreet master doth assign you, earnestly; and the time I know he will so limit as shall be both sufficient for your learning and safe for your health. And mark the sense and the matter of that you do read, as well as the words; so shall you both enrich your tongue with words and your wit with matter, and judgment will grow as years grow in you.

Be humble and obedient to your masters, for, unless you frame yourself to obey others – yea, and feel in yourself what obedience is, you shall never be able to teach others to obey you.

Be courteous of gesture and affable to all men, with diversity of reverence according to the dignity of the person. There is nothing that winneth so much with so little cost.

Use moderate diet ... Use exercise of body ... Delight to be cleanly. ...

Give yourself to be merry; for you degenerate from your father if you find not yourself most able in wit and body to do anything when you are most merry. But let your mirth be ever void of all scurrility and biting words to any man; for a wound given by a word is oftentimes harder to be cured than that which is given by the sword.

Be you rather a hearer and bearer away of other men's talk than a beginner and procurer of speech; otherwise you shall be accounted to delight to hear yourself speak ...

Above all things tell no untruth; no, not in trifles ... For there cannot be a greater reproach to a gentleman than to be accounted a liar.

Study and endeavour yourself to be virtuously occupied. So shall you make such a habit of well-doing in you as you shall not know how to do evil, though you would. Remember, my son, the noble blood you are descended of by your mother's side; and think that only by virtuous life and good action you may be an ornament to that illustrious family. Otherwise, through vice and sloth, you may be counted *labes generis,* one of the greatest curses that can happen to man.

Well, my little Philip, this is enough for me, and too much, I fear, for you. But if I find that this light meal of digestion nourish in anything the weak stomach of your capacity, I will, as I find the same grow stronger, feed it with other food.

Commend me most heartily unto Master Justice Corbet, old Master Onslow, and my cousin, his son. Farewell! Your mother and I send you our blessings, and Almighty God grant you His, nourish you with His fear, govern you with His grace, and make you a good servant to your prince and country!

Your loving father, so long as you live in the fear of God,

H. Sidney

Lady Sidney's postcript follows:

Your noble, careful father hath taken pains with his own hand to give you, in this his letter, so wise, so learned, and most requisite precepts for you to follow with a diligent and humble, thankful mind, as I will not withdraw your eyes from beholding and reverent honouring the same – no, not so long as to read any letter from me. And therefore, at this time, I will write unto you no other letter than this; whereby I first bless you, with my desire to God to plant in you His grace, and, secondarily, warn you to have always before the eyes of your mind these excellent counsels of my lord, your dear father, and that you fail not continually, once in four or five days, to read them over.

And for a final leave-taking for this time, see that you show yourself as a loving, obedient scholar to your good master, to govern you yet many years, and that my lord and I may hear that you profit so in your learning as thereby you may increase our loving care of you, and deserve at his hands the continuance of his great joy, to have him often witness with his own hands the hope he hath in your well-doing.

Farewell, my little Philip, and once again the Lord bless you!

Your loving mother,

Mary Sidney

The parental roles that characterize this letter are conventional but played with a sensitivity and grace that individualizes them. Henry Sidney is very much the lord and master, his advice a series of almost Mosaic commandments. Yet his comments on merriness reveal a quite unconventional psychological insight, and he is capable of tempering his admonitory tone, at least momentarily, with some good-humoured sympathy for his reader: 'Well, my little Philip, this is enough for me, and too much, I fear, for you.' Mary Sidney, in contrast, is the gentle and self-effacing helpmeet of her authoritative husband, suppressing her own desire to write in the interest of allowing his words more time to penetrate. While her tone is more affectionate than admonitory, she not only blesses her son but 'warns' him to keep the words of her 'lord' and his 'dear father' always before him – a warning that may have served not only to support her husband's authority but to caution her son not to belittle the importance of the letter he had just received.

To understand the psychological significance of this letter, for all of the parties involved, it helps to keep in mind the precarious situation in which the Sidney family found itself during Philip's early years. As a young man, Henry Sidney had been 'henchman' for the boy king Edward VI, who died in his arms. Although Henry had managed the transition from Protestant to Catholic monarch unharmed, even securing Philip II of Spain as godfather for his young son, his wife's family had not been so fortunate. The Dudleys had been shattered by the plot to put Lady Jane Grey on the throne. Mary's father, John Dudley, duke of Northumberland, her brother Guilford, and his wife, Lady Jane Grey, had all been executed for treason less than a year before Philip's birth. At the time of his birth, Philip's two uncles, the future earls of Leicester and Warwick, were still attainted for treason. Eleven years later, when Henry Sidney wrote his letter of advice to his son, both families showed every sign of prospering under the new regime; their family histories, however, not to mention the volatility of court life in general, must have given cause for considerable anxiety. As heir to their combined fortunes, Philip carried the destiny of both the Sidney and Dudley families in his hands. In 1566, the year of Sir Henry's letter, the earl of Leicester, after taking pains to see that Philip was properly outfitted, took his nephew and heir to Oxford for several weeks, to present him for the first time to the queen.

What is most striking about Sir Henry's letter, in the context of the young Philip's sense of identity, are the assumptions about Philip's role that underlie it. His position in life is not something he must seek out or define; it was given at birth. He is a gentleman. All of the virtues that his father commends to him are important to him in relation to that preordained social role. Piety, knowledge, obedience, courtesy, moderation, carefulness in speech, honesty – each of these attributes is essential not as a general human virtue but as a distinctive mark of a gentleman: 'There cannot be a greater reproach to a gentleman than to be accounted a liar.' Years later, when Philip himself played a parental role in advising his brother Robert on his foreign travels, he stressed that Robert's purpose must be that of 'a Gentleman borne, to furnish your selfe with the knowledge of such thinges, as maie be serviceable to your countriee, and fit for your calling ...'[20]

Philip was not merely born a gentleman, however; he was born the hope of the Sidney family and, to a certain extent, that of the earls of Leicester and Warwick, his uncles, both at that time without an heir. His father is pleased by his son's progress in Latin and French, not because he takes a disinterested joy in the mastery of the languages, or because they are simply the mark of a gentleman, but because they are the tools of a statesman 'that will stand you in most stead in that profession of life that you are born to live in.' The young Philip must 'feel in [himself] what obedience is' because he is born to rule, to 'teach others how to obey [him].' For Henry, moreover, as for most members of his social class, being born to rule was not merely a matter of social status or breeding but of blood. Implicit in his comments on merriness is the notion that his son must be urged to fulfil the conditions not only of his family and class but of his heredity: 'you degenerate from your father if you find not yourself most able in wit and body to do anything when you are most merry.' The son must remember, too, 'the noble blood you are descended of by your mother's side.' Blood, family history, social rank, religious duty – all are taken by Henry to lead to a single destiny, articulated in the climactic final sentence of the letter: 'Your mother and I send you our blessings, and Almighty God grant you His, nourish you with His fear, govern you with His grace, and make you a good servant to your prince and country!' Service to prince and country is to be Philip's vocation.

To modern sensibilities, this sense of identity as predetermined by birth, as something one does not make but none the less defines the essential self, is difficult to come to terms with. Even more striking, however, is the subtle psychological coercion by which the doctrine is enforced. Not only do Philip's parents take it for granted that his future is determined by his birth; they see their love as conditional upon his success in making that future come about. Lady Sidney expresses the hopeful and positive side of this psychological blackmail in urging her son to be an obedient scholar so that she may 'hear that you profit so in your learning as thereby you may increase our loving care of you.' The hidden, dark side of her exhortation is that failure would lessen both love and care. It is left to Sir Henry, however, to paint the terrifying consequences of failure, which he chooses to do emphatically, in his final words: 'Your loving father, so long as you live in the fear of God, H. Sidney.' Philip is to live in the fear of God in a very special sense: he is to be a good servant to his prince and country, a worthy member of the Sidney and Leicester families, a worthy vessel for his father's blood. Such is the will not only of Henry Sidney but of God. The 'profession of life' that Philip was 'born to live in' is not merely a question of occupation, social class, or family but of religious calling. Philip himself acknowledges this in the opening of *A Defence of Poetry* in his rueful admission that poetry has become his 'unelected vocation.' It was certainly not a vocation in the mind of Philip, his father, or his mother at the time of this letter.

The psychological coercion practiced by Sir Henry and Lady Sidney was by no means unique but reflected conventional attitudes towards child-rearing and education. The Calvinistic conception of original sin, coupled with the humanistic conception of education, created a vocabulary describing early development in which ideas of strict control and rigorous training predominated. In such a climate, young people were to be moulded into a preconceived form, not encouraged to discover or invent their own sense of identity. In one of his tracts on education, for example, Erasmus addresses a father on his responsibility towards his son. 'Nature,' he says, 'in giving you a son, presents you, let me say, a rude, unformed creature, which it is your part to fashion so that it may become indeed a man. If this fashioning be neglected you have but an animal still: if it be contrived earnestly and wisely, you have, I had almost said, what may prove a being not far from God.'[21] Any ideas of 'self-fashioning' Sidney may have entertained, either as youth or adult, occurred within the constraints of such a familial and social environment. In such an environment, as Richard Helgerson observes, Polonius's advice, 'to thine own self be true,' assumes a self that is identified with a social role.[22]

Nearly everything in Philip's early education reinforced the values and goals expressed in his first letter from his father. Shrewsbury School was dedicated to the training of a social élite, and the humanistic education he received there served that end. The essential means was good Latin, with the attendant exposure to rhetoric and moral philosophy; the essential end was the service to prince and country proclaimed in Sir Henry's letter. Underlying the educational system were the sentiments expressed by Cicero, among others, that being 'drawn by study away from the active life is contrary to moral duty. For the whole glory of virtue is in activity.'[23] When Sidney himself defined the end of 'earthly' learning as 'virtuous action' in *A Defence of Poetry*, he remained true to the central impulse of his own education.

Essential to this system of education was the doctrine of imitation, a doctrine so pervasive and wide-ranging in its implications that, as Thomas M. Greene observes, the Renaissance as a whole might be called 'an era of imitation.'[24] The importance of imitation in Elizabethan culture does much to explain not only the psychological pressures brought to bear on the young Sidney but his later attraction to literary self-representations. In its simplest form the doctrine was applied to the learning of Latin and involved a method whereby students progressed from copying original compositions to imitating and finally emulating them. In its most complex form the doctrine was applied not only to the development of literary style but to that of the self, as in the humanistic penchant for imitating epic heroes, such as Aeneas, or in the Christian effort to imitate Christ. Although we do not know the specific method by means of which imitation was developed at Shrewsbury School in Sidney's time, the pedagogic and psychological assumptions underlying the practice were common to the schools of the period, so a general account of the phenomenon is likely to shed light on Sidney's own development.

As Walter J. Ong has shown, Renaissance schooling was essentially a male puberty rite: learning took place in a world set apart from women; involved severe physical trials (the infamous flogging) and occasional bouts of lawlessness; provided the initiated with a 'secret' language, Latin; and gave access to the specialized and esoteric lore of the society.[25] Essential to this process was imitation, through which adolescent males defined their identities by imagining themselves in another role. W.B. Yeats admired Renaissance culture because it was based, as he asserts, not on self-knowledge 'but on knowledge of some other self, Christ or Caesar, not on delicate sincerity but on imitative energy.' 'Saint Francis and Caesar Borgia,' according to Yeats, 'made themselves over-mastering, creative persons by turning from the mirror to meditation upon a mask.'[26] Yeats's observation provides a profound insight into Elizabethan culture. His opposition between self-knowledge and knowledge of some other self is misleading, however, for the idea of imitation was to make knowledge of another a means of self-knowledge; meditation upon a mask was a mode of self-reflection and self-creation.

Renaissance schooling developed the natural tendency towards imitation in children. 'Boys are naturally apes,' says Vives, 'they imitate every-thing and always, especially those whom they consider worthy of imitation on account of their authority, or because of the faith they place in them, such as parents, nurses, masters, and schoolfellows.'[27] Not all theorists were as sanguine as Vives about these natural imitative tendencies. Eras-mus, for example, fears the susceptibility of youth to bad models: 'Nature has made the first years of our life prone to imitation – though perhaps it is easier to that age to copy evil than good.'[28] It is this concern with imita-tion as the basis not only of literary style but of behaviour that prompts Roger Ascham's long lament in *The Scholemaster* that there are so few 'faire examples' at court for young gentlemen to follow.[29]

The reasons for this anxiety about imitation become clear if we exam-ine the process as it applied to the earliest stages of learning Latin. Although the ultimate destination was originality, the road was long and laborious; one began by merely copying. In *The Scholemaster*, for example, Ascham recommends his method of double translation. His pupils first parse a Latin passage thoroughly, then translate it into English, and finally back into Latin. They then compare their final version to the origi-nal. Ascham praises the child who does well, 'either in choosing, or true placing of Tullies wordes.'[30] The aim is thus replication: the ideal student is the one who so assimilates Cicero's style that his own translation repro-duces it. It is no accident that the model is Cicero, for it is vital that the child be exposed only to the best. Underlying the entire process is the assumption that imitation is partly unconscious and therefore dangerous. 'The pure cleane witte of a sweete yong babe,' says Ascham, 'is like the newest wax';[31] it will take the form of whatever impresses it. Similar assumptions are implicit in Erasmus's impatience with the rote learning of rules. We learn not by rules, he argues, but by 'copious readings of the best authors.' Because this is in part an unconscious, assimilative process, teachers must 'choose such works as are not only sound models of style but are instructive by reason of their subject-matter.'[32] At the earliest stages, then, imitation effaces identity, sometimes with unconscious effect.

Anxieties about the consequences of imitation surface in Elizabethan attitudes towards acting. Although schoolboys were encouraged to act out dialogues and whole plays to sharpen both their Latin and their rhetori-cal skills, the imaginative adoption of a dramatic role was viewed as poten-tially dangerous. The plays of Terence, for example, which were often acted, were models of chaste Latin but unchaste behaviour. Quintilian, whose *Institutio Oratoria* was highly influential, warns against allowing schoolboys to act undesirable roles: 'For I do not of course wish the boy ... to talk with the shrillness of a woman or in the tremulous accents of old age. Nor for that matter must he ape the vices of the drunkard, or copy the cringing manner of a slave, or learn to express the emotions of love, avarice, or fear. Such accomplishments are not necessary to an orator and corrupt the mind, especially while it is still pliable and unformed. For repeated imitation passes into habit.' Quintilian even warns against students imitating themselves. They should not commit their own compositions to memory, he says, but only those of the best models, for they will 'unconsciously reproduce the style of the speech which has been impressed upon the memory.'[33]

The Puritan hostility towards acting rests upon similar assumptions. In Th'overthrow of Stage-Playes (1599), John Rainolds points out the terrible effects that immoral roles have upon those who act them on stage: 'the care of making a shew to doe such feates, and to doe them as lively as the beasts themselves in whom the vices raigne, worketh in the actors a marvellous impression of being like the persons whose qualities they expresse and imitate: chiefly when earnest and much meditation of sundry dayes and weekes, by often repetition and representation of the partes, shall as it were engrave the things in their minde with a penne of iron, or with the point of a diamond.'[34] The positive side of this coin, which Rainolds does not acknowledge, is that the habitual imitation of good models can make one good. In either case one becomes what one plays. In this sense, conventional roles create the self.

Despite the dangers, Elizabethan schoolboys and university students acted regularly, even the roles of lovers and tyrants. Sidney's headmaster at Shrewsbury, Thomas Ashton, seems to have been well known for his encouragement of dramatic performances. The school's ordinances, written in 1578, require the students in the highest form to 'declaim and play one Act of a Comedy' every Thursday. The performances were held in an abandoned quarry, the outlines of which are still visible today. In 1566, the same year in which Sidney's father sent him his first letter, Queen Elizabeth went on progress as far as Coventry in order to see one of Ashton's plays, said to have been Julian the Apostate, but she arrived after the performance had already ended.[35]

As Elizabethan schoolboys matured, the practice of imitation became more conscious and creative. Ascham, for example, encourages the advanced student to choose, within limits, his own model or models, selecting or adapting them to his own purposes. He recommends that students learn to imitate in the same way that Virgil followed Homer, treating dissimilar material with a similar style or similar material with a dissimilar style. To learn this method, he suggests comparing parallel passages of Homer and Virgil or Demosthenes and Cicero.[36] Having practised this method, the student could apply it to his own compositions. Although the process is still rather mechanical – the creativity consists in selecting and arranging a set body of themes and styles – it is less so than copying. The student is beginning to select an identity rather than to have it impressed upon him.

The final, truly creative stages of imitation are those of the mature writer. Perhaps the best contemporary description of this kind of imitation is that of Ben Jonson. The description is noteworthy not only because it defines imitation but because it does so in a way that is itself imitative, for its style and dominant image are classical:

> The third requisite in our poet, or maker, is imitation: to be able to convert the substance or riches of another poet to his own use: to make choice of one excellent man above the rest, and so to follow him till he grow very he, or so like him as the copy may be mistaken for the principal – not as a creature that swallows what it takes in crude, raw, or undigested, but that feeds with an appetite, and hath a stomach to concoct, divide, and turn all into nourishment; not to imitate servilely, as Horace saith, and catch at vices for virtue, but to draw forth out of the best and choicest flowers with the bee, and turn all into honey, work it into one relish and savour, make our imitation sweet, observe how the best writers have imitated, and follow them: how Virgil and Statius have imitated Homer; how Horace, Archilocus; how Alcaeus and the other lyrics; and so of all the rest.[37]

The image of the bee making honey, which appears in Seneca and other classical authors, conveys more precisely than any other the extent to which mature imitation was considered a free and creative act. Although it originates in the flowers of the ancients, the honey that comes forth is truly the poet's: it is the poet who chooses the flowers, gathers the pollen, and transforms it, turning 'all into nourishment.' Unlike the schoolboy copyist, who passively becomes his model, taking its impress like sealing wax, the mature poet devours it, converting the 'substance or riches of another poet to his own use.' The latter metaphor reveals the competitive and even aggressive tendencies, by no means uniquely Jonsonian, that characterize the advanced stages of a process that begins with abject self-effacement.

These aggressive tendencies were encouraged in the schools in the form of emulation. Erasmus, for example, urges teachers to arouse 'the spirit of emulation in the class,'[38] inciting boys to imitate and finally surpass the efforts of their peers. As the child matured, he gradually directed his emulation to higher models, aspiring not only to copy Cicero but to outdo him. 'If you take all of Cicero and him alone for your model,' says Erasmus's representative in *Ciceronianus*, 'you should not only reproduce him but also defeat him. He must not be just passed by, but rather left behind.'[39] It is not hard to find in the psychology of this process signs of the puberty rite that Ong describes. Bearing the impress of Cicero upon his mind and, through the strokes of the master, upon his back, the student could eventually avenge himself by devouring and converting to his own nourishment the source of both his pain and aspirations. Having thus defined and asserted his identity, the student, as Vives makes clear, would become a man: 'That a boy should imitate is honourable and praiseworthy; that an old man should do so, is servile and disgraceful. It is meet that a boy should have a master and a guide, whom he should follow; but not so, an old man. For this reason when you have had sufficient exercise on the racecourse (so to speak) of this imitation, begin to emulate, and to compare yourself with your guide, to see where you can approach nearer to him, and how far you are left in his rear ... Try to attain to his great beauties, and afterwards even to excel them.'[40] This general psychology of emulation, in which a beloved model is first absorbed and then overcome, has been explored in many studies by René Girard, for whom mimetic rivalry lies at the centre of human conflict.[41]

The effects of this subtle and complex doctrine of imitation upon Elizabethan adolescents in general and Sidney in particular are naturally difficult to demonstrate. They would be difficult to distinguish, moreover, from other, complementary influences upon the development of adolescent identity. As Thomas van Laan has shown, the notion of offices, or duties, appropriate to each station in society gave to social life a theatrical dimension, making it a matter of playing roles.[42] Contemporary faculty psychology, too, allegorized individuals into fixed types or roles, much as Jaques does in his account of the seven ages of man in *As You Like It*. The doctrine of imitation is thus part of a complex set of interrelated cultural assumptions and practices that affect not only literary composition but actual behaviour.

The imitative process seems particularly important as a context for Sidney's self-representations because it conceives of education as an act of imagination, in which the student assumes an alien identity in order to more fully understand and develop the self. Sidney's conception of poetry in the *Defence*, as we shall see, assumes the centrality of imitation, with the poet imitating ideals to be imitated by readers who may themselves become objects of imitation. Fulke Greville's biographical account of Sidney falls within the same tradition. In his description of the battle of Zutphen, for example, Greville develops Sidney himself as a heroic model and even takes pains to dissociate his actions from the dangerously aggressive motives inherent in the psychology of imitation. When Sidney follows the marshall of the camp in taking off his thigh armour, thus exposing the very part of his body in which he will be shot, he does so, according to Greville, not as an act of foolish bravado but of 'unspotted emulation': 'meeting the marshall of the camp lightly armed (whose honour in that art would not suffer this unenvious Themistocles to sleep), the unspotted emulation of his heart to venture without any inequality made him cast off his cuisses, and so, by the secret influence of destiny, to disarm that part where God, it seems, resolved to strike him.'[43] Greville not only converts Sidney's actions into models for emulative readers but anchors them in an imitative tradition that includes previous military heroes, such as Themistocles.

As is clear from Sir Henry's letter, the young Philip was expected to follow in the path of his father and uncles, whose blood and rank determined his own destiny: 'Remember, my son, the noble blood you are descended of by your mother's side; and think that only by virtuous life and good action you may be an ornament to that illustrious family.' Implicit in this expectation is a notion of familial imitation, later applied by Sir Henry to Philip himself, who had become by 1579 a model for his younger brother, Robert. In a letter to Robert, then travelling abroad, Sir Henry urges him to imitate Philip: 'Follow the direction of your most loving brother who in loving you is comparable with me or exceedeth me. Imitate his virtues, exercises, studies and actions; he is a rare ornament of this age, the very formular that all well-disposed young gentlemen of our Court do form also their manners and life by. In truth I speak it without flattery of him or of myself: he hath the most rare virtues that ever I found in any man.'[44] This is an extraordinary statement from a sixteenth-century father and suggests the extent to which, by the age of twenty-four, Philip had become a model for the entire court. The father's idealization of Philip must have had considerable psychological impact on both brothers, placing the burden of imitation on Robert and the burden of the model on Philip, who had been told twelve years before that his father's love depended upon his own great achievements.

This notion of familial imitation recurs in the memorial that Sir
Henry's secretary, Edmund Molyneux, wrote in Holinshed's *Chronicle*
upon his death. Molyneux's relationship with Philip seems to have been
problematical; at least he once received a letter from Philip threatening
to thrust his dagger into him if he ever again read one of his letters to his
father without his or his father's consent.[45] None the less, Molyneux lavishes praise upon Philip at the end of his celebration of Sir Henry, commenting particularly on the manner in which the young man has imitated
his father. He is described as 'most like to proove a famous, great, and
rare personage for the service of his countrie and commonwelth,' a per-
petuator of his father's glory who may even 'surpasse his fathers worthi-
nesse, fame, and vertues' and, it is to be hoped, 'he may in time succeed
him in his offices, or if it please God in some better and greater.' For
Molyneux, the young man's early diplomatic experience has been training for such a succession. To the attaining of such an office, according to
Molyneux, 'he is thus farre in good degree alreadie advanced (imitating
therein his fathers perfect paterne) that he hath bin imploied ambassador to the emperor when he was not above one and twentie yeeres old (as
his father at like age was to the French king) ...'[46] The imitating of the
father's 'perfect paterne' thus extends not only to his general virtues but
to the progress of his career.

In various ways, then, the doctrine of imitation shaped not only
Sidney's notion of literary composition but his sense of himself and his
familial and social roles. His preoccupation as a writer with imaginative
role-playing, as when he portrays himself in the characters of Astrophil
and Philisides, is in part a response to literary pressures, the imitation of
literary models, but it is also a response to psychological and moral pressures that translate a linguistic model of development into a more generally moral and psychological one. The imitative process provided a means
of self-definition that mediated between fact and fiction, art and life.

A concrete Sidneyan instance of the convergence of schoolboy educational models with the theory of imitation is provided by Xenophon's
Cyropaedia, a work in the curriculum at Shrewsbury that exerted a powerful effect on the mature Sidney. The *Cyropaedia* was an ideal schoolboy
text because it provided instruction not only in Greek but in the virtues
appropriate to governors. The hero of the work, the young Cyrus, is
shown in the various activities that prepare him for his later role as king;
he demonstrates, among other virtues, his wit at court, his rhetorical powers before his troops, and his heroism on the battlefield. He is shown in
all the postures of a model prince, correcting his occasional adolescent

errors, such as pursuing game too rashly in the hunt, upon the advice of his elders.

Something of the spirit in which the young Sidney must have read the *Cyropaedia* is conveyed by an early translator, William Bercker, who dedicated the 1567 edition to Philip, earl of Surrey, the son and heir to the duke of Norfolk. In his address to the young earl, Bercker stresses the moral value of the work. Observing that it demonstrates 'what a noble man by good education may prove unto,' he recommends it as a model for the young man's future service to his own prince: 'I shall desire your lordship, whan you reade it to thinke the time will come, whan you shalbe called of youre prince to take such jornies as you shall see that Cyrus appointeth to such as you are, and to do such services as youre most noble progenitours have don by the commaundement of theire princes, whose great glory shall ever so shine before youre eyes, as you must nedes forsee youre selfe to folow the same to the contentation of youre prince, the benifite of youre cuntry, the joy of youre parentes, and comforte of all youre frendes and servauntes ...'[47] To read such a work as a young man was to become potentially engaged in multiple acts of imitation: to emulate Cyrus, whose virtues are a model of noble behaviour; to emulate Cyrus's nobles in their duty to their prince; and to emulate one's progenitors in their former service. Such a conception of the self bonds it indissolubly to family, state, and cultural tradition.

Sidney includes Cyrus in *A Defence of Poetry* among the epic heroes to be imitated (98.1) and refers repeatedly to the *Cyropaedia* as an example of the superiority of fiction to history and philosophy as a source of virtuous action. Xenophon's 'feigned Cyrus,' he argues, is not only 'more doctrinable' than the 'true Cyrus in Justin' (88.16–17, 89.9–35) but superior to any 'philosopher's counsel' to direct a prince to goodness (86.32–3). In Sidney's scheme, the poet imitates virtue in conceiving the character of Cyrus, and the reader becomes another Cyrus, by imitating that virtue through the medium of the fiction. Although it originates in a fiction, the process is 'not wholly imaginative, as we are wont to say by them that build castles in the air; but so far substantially it worketh, not only to make a Cyrus, which had been but a particular excellency as nature might have done, but to bestow a Cyrus upon the world to make many Cyruses, if they will learn aright why and how that maker made him' (79.11–16). As in Bercker's preface, Sidney's imitative cycle is potentially endless, for the fictional Cyrus imitated by the author creates 'real' Cyruses whose own heroic actions may likewise be imitated. In defending his 'unelected vocation,' poetry, Sidney returned to a doctrine and text that he had first encountered at Shrewsbury School when pursuing his elected vocation of servant to the state.

The religious overtones in Sidney's allusion to poetry in *A Defence* as his 'unelected vocation' call attention to another dimension of his training for a career as a statesman. As his father's letter makes clear, Philip's 'profession of life' is defined within a Christian framework. The first action of every day is prayer, and God Himself is invoked to make the young man 'a good servant to [his] prince and country.' Philip's headmaster at Shrewsbury, Thomas Ashton, was well-known as a Calvinist. Although we do not know exactly how Ashton's Calvinism shaped the curriculum, there is no doubt that it did, and in ways that are likely to have complemented Sir Henry's fusion of Christianity and career. Sidney's later commitment to the Protestant cause in Europe, which he shared with his father and uncles, Leicester and Warwick, would have been anticipated at Shrewsbury by not only a humanistic but a Calvinistic conception of service to the state.[48]

Central to this Christian conception of public service was the doctrine of vocation to which Sidney alludes in the *Defence*. The language of vocation pervaded social discourse in the period. It is found, for example, not only in the Calvinist William Perkins' *A Treatise of the Vocations or Callings of Men* but in Shakespeare's *1 Henry IV*, a play that centres upon notions also developed by Perkins – notions of service, of time, of keeping accounts, of constancy, of idleness, of vocations, of calling. ''Tis no sin,' says Falstaff, preparing for robbery, 'for a man to labor in his vocation.'

The biblical foundation of the doctrine of vocation is Paul's exhortation in his letter to the Corinthians, 'Let every man abide in that calling, wherein he was called' (1 Cor. 7.20). For Perkins, a vocation is '*a certain kind of life ordained and imposed on man by God for the common good.*'[49] God is the author of every calling, therefore, and the community the beneficiary. There are two kinds of vocation: the first is the general calling of Christianity, common to all members of the church; the second is a special calling, such as that of magistrate, master, child, or subject. It is the duty of parents to choose the callings of their children, with regard to their inclination and natural gifts, but it is also the duty of every person to choose 'a fit calling to walk in.'[50] Within the framework established by Perkins, the 'profession of life' that Sidney was 'born in' was more than a matter of career or status in society; it was a calling from God, endorsed by his parents, which he was bound to answer. The public impact of that calling becomes clear in Arthur Golding's praise for the manner of Sidney's death, in which he is said to have received 'manly wounds ... in the service of his prince' while defending 'the only true, catholic, and Christian religion.' For Golding, such a death was 'the honorablest death that could be desired and best beseeming a Christian knight, whereby he hath worthily won to himself immortal fame among the godly and left example worthy of imitation to others of his calling.'[51]

For Sidney and his peers, the Christian idea of vocation was buttressed by the classical conception of duty articulated above all by Cicero in *De Officiis*, a book that Sidney would have studied at school and that he recommended highly to his friend Edward Denny as part of his educational program.[52] As Helgerson observes, 'a central tenet' of the upbringing of gentlemen of Sidney's generation 'was the notion that duty properly defines the self.'[53] In the *Offices*, a work itself composed as a letter of advice to a son, Sidney would have encountered all of the moral duties that were to govern his life and define his essential self; he would have learned as well that the 'most important activities, those most indicative of a great spirit, are performed by the men who direct the affairs of nations.'[54] Lord Burghley carried the *Offices* in his pocket.[55]

It is clear, then, that Philip was being groomed for a specific social role, one that was reinforced by religious, educational, and familial conceptions of the self as identified with that role. In this he was not exceptional. To varying degrees, similar pressures were exerted upon most gentlemen of his generation, as Helgerson and others have shown. Sidney's position was exceptional, however, for two reasons. First, none of his contemporaries had his combination of great literary abilities and great social status; as heir to the earls of Leicester and Warwick, he was for a time potentially the most powerful man in England. Secondly, few of his peers seem to have assimilated the values of their elders so completely. Although rebellious energies run through the literary works, as Richard C. McCoy has demonstrated in *Sir Philip Sidney: Rebellion in Arcadia*, there is no evidence in Sidney's behaviour of the overt rebelliousness of the earl of Oxford, say, or the earl of Essex. Fulke Greville's comment that he knew Sidney as a child yet 'never knew him other than a man'[56] is supported by everything that we know about his relationship to his family. As he matured, Sidney not only pleased his father, as his mother had encouraged him to do in her postscript, but became his father's model of a gentleman.

If one looks beneath the surface of this early education, one can find the seeds of many potential conflicts and tensions – between the humanistic idealization of public service and the actuality of life at court; between the Spartan study of Xenophon at Shrewsbury School and attendance on the queen in full regalia at Oxford; between the moral earnestness of Henry Sidney and the moral ambiguity of the earl of Leicester; between an educational system that valued poetry in the teaching, as a source of moral education, but dispraised it in the making, as a mere recreation for ladies. These and other conflicts find indirect expression in Sidney's later writing and will be dealt with at a later stage. Sidney's ironic mode of writing, moreover, makes it likely that he did not take his early training entirely at face value. Sidney's reading, too, in Sannazaro, Petrarch, Heliodorus, took him into imaginative worlds that were scarcely recognized in the realm of humanist pedagogy. There is no evidence, however, that either the tensions within his early social experience or an innate sense of ironic detachment inhibited Sidney's early commitment to his destined social role. Nothing in his early years signals his later commitment to the role of poet, and this commitment was itself broken in mid-sentence before the completion of the *New Arcadia*. During his early years Sidney's sense of vocation seems to have been clear and unequivocal. He was being trained, and training himself, for a significant political role at court.

Although Sidney was chronologically part of what Anthony Esler has called the aspiring generation,[57] his aspirations were contained within the conservative framework of his family and social class. The familial and social pressure brought to bear upon Sidney was extraordinary, not the least because of the uncertainty of the family's own position within the volatile world of the court. Beleaguered by debt, by the wavering support of the queen, by a vexed and dangerous past, the Sidney family itself epitomizes in many respects the forces that created what Lawrence Stone describes as a crisis of the aristocracy.[58] One response of the family to this persistent sense of crisis, it might be said, was to invest in Philip their greatest hopes for the future, making him all the more vulnerable to a crisis of identity when those hopes could not be achieved.

In the chapters that ensue, we shall explore, through the medium of Sidney's self-representations, the onset and development of that crisis. We shall begin with Sidney as a very young man, seventeen years old, developing an epistolary identity in his correspondence with his mentor, Hubert Languet, while travelling on the Continent. We shall then explore his unsuccessful attempts to fashion a role for himself at court, which culminated in the withdrawal that initiated his 'unelected vocation' as a writer. In the remaining chapters – on the *Old Arcadia, Astrophil and Stella, A Defence of Poetry,* and the *New Arcadia* – we shall examine in roughly chronological order the evolution of Sidney's self-representations as he sought to define a self within a variety of fictive and rhetorical worlds. Many of

these self-representations, as we shall see, place Sidney in the various roles
that he was called upon to play, or slipped into, at court – among them,
the roles of friend, courtier, lover, poet, and warrior. The recurrence of
such roles suggests the urgency of Sidney's need to explore in autobiographical writing the meaning of his ongoing experience.

Although each of these roles is important to Sidney's evolving conception of his identity, one in particular has perhaps not received the kind of
attention it deserves, that of soldier. Throughout his short career, as we
shall see, Sidney repeatedly sought military service. The motives behind
this desire were complex. As a supporter of a militant foreign policy
against Spain, Sidney found himself necessarily advocating military intervention abroad, as in the Netherlands. Viewed from this perspective,
military service is simply one necessary manifestation of the role of a
statesman for which he was being trained. More immediately personal
motives, however, were also involved. Sidney expressed the desire to
prove himself in combat in the early correspondence with Languet, and it
is clear from Languet's unsympathetic response that he distrusted Sidney's aggressive impulses and those of other young aristocrats. From this
perspective, Sidney's quest for military action seems part of an adolescent
initiation rite, a quest to prove himself a man, and his death at Zutphen
becomes tinged with tragic irony. Whatever the ultimate origin of this
preoccupation with war, it becomes an important motif in Sidney's self-
representations, appearing most prominently in the letters to Languet, *A
Defence of Poetry*, and the *New Arcadia*.

Despite their autobiographical immediacy, Sidney's literary roles are
not mere reproductions but self-conscious displacements of experience.
Hence we shall deal with them not merely in relation to Sidney's personal
experience but to the literary worlds in which they occur. The literary
framework for each of these self-representations, as we shall see, is crucial
to its meaning. In imagining a self, Sidney places that self within an imagined world. In the earliest exercises, the letters to Languet, Sidney's treatment of that imagined world, the world of epistolary friendship, is
relatively uncritical and naïve; the generic framework and all its implicit
values are taken for granted. In the later works, however, Sidney's explorations of the self implicate the framework for the self – a framework provided not only by the shape of the individual work but by its sources and
genre. Hence we shall be concerned not only with the relationship
between Sidney's roles and his 'real' experience but between the roles
and, in a broad sense, their literary environment. Sidney's playful search
for a self is also a search for literary form.

In *Literature as System*, Claudio Guillén defines genre as 'an invitation to form' or, more precisely, as 'a problem-solving model on the level of form.'[59] For Guillén, genres stimulate authors into dialogue with their time and culture, enabling them to match their own experience to existing form in a creative and exploratory way. Sidney's remarkable generic range suggests that in his mature works he responded to the challenge of genres in just this way, testing them not only against his own experience but against each other as problem-solving models. The sheer difficulty critics experience in providing precise generic labels for his works testifies to the restless energy that he devoted to generic exploration. Through his self-representations, then, Sidney was not merely recreating a self in relation to his social experience but in relation to his literary imagination, testing the capacity of the self to live up to pre-existing forms and the capacity of those forms to meet the experiential needs of the self. The generic complexity of the individual works and the rapidity of change from one genre to another throughout Sidney's career both suggest that Sidney felt a need to define his self not merely in relation to the court but in relation to the conventional yet imaginative ways of perceiving the self provided by genre. With each experiment in generic form, Sidney was at pains to place a version of his self inside the form, as if to experience vicariously the implications of the problem-solving model he was testing. His first, naïve gestures towards this sophisticated mode of self-representation occur in the letters to Hubert Languet.

2

Friend to Hubert Languet

As part of his training for a public role, Sidney was expected to travel on the Continent, furthering his knowledge of languages, developing contacts among his Continental peers, and acquiring an understanding of political affairs that would advance his career as a statesman. Such travels were conventional among young Elizabethan aristocrats and gentlemen. The roughly three years that Sidney spent abroad are important for many reasons: they encouraged his commitment to court service; they enhanced his expectations of a major future role; they took place at a crucial time in his development, the transitional phase between adolescence and adulthood; and they involved him in one of the most significant friendships of his career, that with the humanist Hubert Languet. Sidney's correspondence with Languet during that period, moreover, gives us our first sustained contact with Sidney as a writer. The persona he develops in those letters, written from the age of seventeen to twenty-one, represents his first exercise in the development of a literary persona and establishes a pattern of self-representation that recurs in different forms throughout his later works.

On 25 May 1572 Queen Elizabeth granted Philip Sidney, then seventeen years of age, licence 'to go out of England into parts beyond the seas ... for his attaining the knowledge of foreign languages.'[1] One day later Sidney's uncle, the earl of Leicester, wrote to Francis Walsingham, Elizabeth's ambassador in Paris, commending Sidney to his care. 'He is young and raw,' observed Leicester, 'and no doubt shall find those countries and the demeanours of the people somewhat strange unto him; and therefore your good advice and counsel shall greatly behove him for his better direction ...'[2] Sidney remained in Europe for three years, continuing his studies, travelling widely, immersing himself in political affairs, and earning the friendship and respect of many of Europe's leading aristocrats and intellectuals. In May 1575, no longer 'raw,' he returned to England eager to assume an important role at court.

For a 'Gentleman borne,' as Sidney himself explained to his brother Robert when he was about to take his own tour abroad, the purpose of such travel was 'to furnish your selfe with the knowledge of such thinges as maie be serviceable to your Countriee and fitt for your calling.'[3] In the case of both of the brothers, the 'calling' was that of political leadership. Sidney's letter to his brother provides the orthodox rationale for such trips and was itself widely circulated and printed as early as 1633.[4] He stresses the knowledge of history, geography, political affairs, the nature of peoples, languages, the establishment of personal relationships, and the like. He says nothing, not surprisingly, about the study of such things as poetry or art. Sidney's correspondence with Languet during his own trip abroad shows that he acted on his own advice.

Although the contemporary rationales for such tours abroad tend to focus on limited utilitarian objectives, one can recognize within them the contours of a traditional male initiation rite. While in Europe these young men acquired knowledge and skills essential to their adult roles, indulged in periods of carnival release, encountered tests imposed by the hazards of travel, and looked for opportunities to initiate themselves into the rites of war. Upon their return to England, they were incorporated into adult roles, often including marriage or the consummation of a marriage that had been arranged before their departure.[5] Sidney's father tried to arrange a marriage with the daughter of Burghley shortly before Philip departed, but the plan collapsed. In his autobiographical account in the *Old Arcadia*, Philisides, Sidney's persona, sees the experience in initiatory terms: it occurs at a time when 'I was thought able to be mine own master' and is arranged so that 'by the comparison of many things I might ripen my judgment' (334.30–2).

The potential for various kinds of adolescent escapades in such foreign sojourns was relatively high, as is illustrated by the spending habits of the earl of Oxford, Sidney's contemporary and rival. The earl travelled on the Continent for fourteen months during 1575 and 1576 and was sent a total of £4,561, an amount that, according to Lawrence Stone, made him the 'greatest spendthrift tourist' of the era.[6] Although Sidney's correspondence while abroad offers only a selective account of his experiences, he seems to have been as conscientious and dutiful as Oxford was rebellious.

An appreciation of the initiatory context of such trips is helpful for an understanding of the intensity of Sidney's relationship at this time with the noted humanist and diplomat Hubert Languet. The contact was presumably made through Walsingham, who had been asked by Leicester to look after the 'raw' young traveller. On the face of it, the arrangement seems likely to have been a relatively formal one, with Languet agreeing to serve as a kind of mentor during Sidney's stay abroad. Young Elizabethans on such tours generally travelled with a tutor. The formality of the relationship is particularly likely because of the vast difference in age between the two. Languet was fifty-three at the time, ten years older than Sidney's own father. Sidney himself was seventeen. Very quickly, however, the relationship became emotionally intense, particularly on the side of Languet.

Languet had been educated in France, Padua, and Wittenberg, and had travelled widely throughout Europe in the service of various German princes. He had once travelled to England. At the time of his meeting with Sidney, he was living in Paris as the representative of the Elector of Saxony.[7] He was thus knowledgeable, experienced, and well connected in Protestant circles throughout Europe. Fulke Greville praises him as 'learned *usque ad miraculum;* wise by the conjunction of practice in the world with that well-grounded theory of books.' The relationship between Sidney and Languet, according to Greville, was that of 'an humble hearer to an excellent teacher'; it 'so equally fitted them both as, out of a natural descent both in love and plenty, the elder grew taken with a net of his own thread, and the younger taught to lift up himself by a thread of the same spinning ...'[8]

From their first meeting in the summer of 1572 until Sidney's return to England in May 1575, Languet gave direction, both literally and figuratively, to Sidney's life. Languet advised Sidney on his studies, worried about his health, promoted his interest in Continental politics and the Protestant cause, introduced him to men of learning and influence, told him where and where not to travel – served, in short, as teacher, as surrogate father, and, although his senior by thirty-six years, as friend. 'This much I confess,' wrote Sidney to Languet after nearly two years under his influence, 'and will proclaim it so long as I enjoy the light of day: that I have benefited more from my acquaintance with you alone than from everything else during my stay abroad' (4/15/74).[9]

The early letters between Sidney and Languet, written mainly during 1573 and 1574 when Sidney was travelling in Italy, have been generally ignored by literary scholars. Of more immediate interest have been the letters from 1576 to 1579, which illuminate Sidney's frustrations at Elizabeth's court; such critics as Rudenstine, Helgerson, Montrose, and

McCoy have shown how important these frustrations were for Sidney's general development as a poet.[10] The earlier letters, however, are important in several respects. Although less explicit than some later letters in revealing Sidney's attitudes, the early letters show how profoundly his relationship with Languet at this crucial, initiatory stage influenced his conception of his identity. They set the stage, therefore, for the crisis of identity that occurred to Sidney upon his return to Elizabeth's court. The letters also show, moreover, how intricately Sidney's conception of identity was bound into his development of a literary persona. They thus provide perhaps the clearest example we have for a sixteenth-century English writer of the humanistic theory of education being put into practice.

As a courtier and diplomat committed to the Protestant cause in Europe, Languet had a very specific interest in Sidney, whose abilities and social status made him a promising future leader of the cause. Languet therefore ensured that Sidney was provided with the knowledge, skills, and contacts necessary for such a role. This specific role, however, represented merely a focusing of the broad aspirations towards political service that had been implanted in Sidney from birth and that Languet sought to cultivate. Central to Languet's vision of Sidney was the belief that political leadership was not merely a career but a vocation, to which Sidney had been called by God, nature, social position, family, and education. Sidney's years abroad, according to Languet, were to be devoted to activities that would prove directly useful to that end. Although he occasionally encouraged relaxation in his pupil, since Sidney was somewhat weak in health and prone to melancholy, Languet never encouraged an exploration of ideas or modes of life that could not be justified on utilitarian grounds; time was short, and Sidney had to devote himself to the rational pursuit of broad but precisely defined educational goals. Languet's aim, in short, was to complete in a European context the humanist program that Sir Henry Sidney had in mind when he concluded his first letter to his young son with a prayer that God 'make you a good servant to your prince and country!'[11] The values inculcated by this program – duty to parents, service to the state, a thrifty use of time, a preference for moral philosophy and history over poetry, truth to one's self – are all reflected in Languet's letters to Sidney.

Although Sidney did not always accept Languet's advice – he balked at learning German, for example, and desired more geometry and Greek than Languet felt he needed – there is no doubt that it influenced him profoundly. More subtly persuasive than overt advice, however, and probably more subtly coercive from a psychological point of view, must have

been Languet's incessant praise of his pupil. The correspondence over-
flows with references to Sidney's natural virtue, his intelligence, his devotion to goodness, and his potential greatness. In his first preserved letter
to Sidney, Languet attributes his anxiety about Sidney's welfare to his
desire to see the 'glorious blossoms' of his 'noble character' bring forth
'the delightful fruits of [his] many virtues' (9/22/73); in his second, he
reminds his pupil that his father has 'centered all his hopes' on seeing
the 'ripe fruits' of his 'many virtues' (11/19/93). A few months later he
prays to God that 'your virtue may prove the salvation of you and your
country' (3/5/74). Still later he writes, 'God has bestowed mental powers
on you which I do not believe have fallen to anyone else I know, and he
has done so not for you to abuse them in exploring vanities at great risk,
but for you to put them in the service of your country, and of all good
men' (6/11/74).

The reasons for this consistent and hyperbolic praise are no doubt various. One can attribute it to Languet's affection or desire to please, to Sidney's very real abilities, or to the customary rhetorical inflation of
humanist discourse; probably all three motives are at work. The most
important explanation, however, probably lies in the humanist paradigm
of imitation explored in the previous chapter, by which pupils were
encouraged to model themselves on ideal patterns of conduct in order to
shape their own identity. Languet's idealizations of Sidney, like Ben Jonson's later and less successful efforts with King James, were celebrations
of the heroic self he could become. At its best this idealization encouraged in young men the pursuit of their highest potential. The method,
however, is not without obvious shortcomings. The discovery of one's
inability to fulfil such high promise could produce tremendous guilt,
resentment, and disillusionment. Or, in contrast, a natural confusion
between the actual and potential self could engender arrogance of the
worst kind, such as that which lies behind King Lear's pathetic cry, 'they
told me I was ague proof.' Sidney, who seems to have been encouraged
towards high moral aspirations by this celebration of an ideal self, seems
also to have been afflicted with its attendant problems: a proud bearing, a
hot temper, and writings that betray deep feelings of guilt and resentment at his lack of success at Elizabeth's court.

For Sidney to read his letters from Languet, then, was to see himself
destined for a heroic future. His true self, he was told, was the ideal self
that Languet saw within him, the heroic potential that God had
implanted in him and that his education would bring to harvest: 'My dear
boy, as long as you do not swerve from yourself, nowhere will you be with-

out good men to show you affection and courtesy. And if in early manhood your virtue bears such sweet fruit, what do you think will happen
after twenty or thirty years, if you adhere steadfastly to your excellent
intentions?' (2/26/74). Steadfastness, or constancy, is a goal to which
Languet alludes repeatedly, as in a letter of 4 December 1573, in which he
urges Sidney not to 'swerve from yourself or become a different man.' In
Languet's formulation, there is no middle ground; Sidney is either true
to his ideal or he loses his self. In this regard the correspondence con-
firms Richard Helgerson's observation that the 'threat of a Circean transformation, of a metamorphosis from the self decreed by duty, haunted
the mid-century humanists.'[12]

The conception of the self held by both Languet and Sidney was on the
conservative side of sixteenth-century thought. In the context of their
correspondence, the self was identified with the mind or soul, as opposed
to the body, and was therefore incapable of change without destruction
or loss. To some extent, the conception is neoplatonic, but it shares none
of the excitement in metamorphosis that one finds, say, in Pico della
Mirandola's celebration of man as a chameleon by nature. The ideal is
not change or fluidity of self but constancy. One's self is one's essential
being, given by nature and by God, and one's vocation is the fulfilment of
that self. Such a doctrine leads almost necessarily to a conservative conception of human nature, with unchanging virtue as the goal, and to a
conservative conception of society, with each self relegated to its appropriate station or calling.

Since Languet's idealization of Sidney fit within the humanist program,
Sidney may have experienced something like it in his earlier education,
although his Calvinistic headmaster at Shrewsbury School might have had
less faith in human capacity than Languet. Whatever Sidney's earlier
exposure to the idealization of himself, that of Languet must have been
particularly seductive, for he played the role not merely of mentor or surrogate father but of friend. To be fully understood, Sidney's relationship
with Languet must be viewed in the context of the 'cult' of friendship
that so powerfully affected both literature and life in the period.
Although the ideals of friendship derived from a wide variety of sources,
Languet and Sidney seem to have been influenced primarily by Cicero's
classic statement in *De Amicitia*. In view of the importance of Cicero's letters to epistolary training in Elizabethan schools, it is not surprising that
Sidney's early letters imitate Ciceronean values.[13] The central idea of *De
Amicitia* is that true friendship, which, significantly, does not depend on
closeness of age, can only be based on the love of virtue.

The way in which Sidney and Languet wove this literary ideal into the language of their correspondence can be seen by comparing Laelius's account of the origin of friendship in Cicero's dialogue with Languet's account of his first meeting with Sidney. In Laelius' account, friendship is the natural result of the recognition of virtue in another person: 'But since ... virtue knits friendship together, if there should be some exhibition of shining virtue to which a kindred spirit may attach and adjust itself, then, when that happens, love must needs spring forth.'[14] In his account of his first meeting with Sidney, Languet too bases his affection on his recognition of Sidney's virtue: 'As long as I live, I shall consider the day I first saw you a happy one, for the innate virtue which shines forth in your face, in your discourse, and in your every action, immediately made me very eager to form a friendship with you' (5/1/74). Although based on the same conception of friendship, the two accounts contain subtle differences. In Cicero, the exhibition of virtue implies the passage of time in the development of love. Languet too implies a temporal process, for at his first sight of Sidney he could not have experienced his virtuous discourse or actions. His emphasis upon their first meeting, however, and upon the light of virtue that shone in Sidney's face, gives a Petrarchan twist to the Ciceronean conception, as if the experience were one of friendship at first sight. As we shall see, Languet returns to such language at other moments in the relationship.

The significance of Languet's friendship in shaping Sidney's conception of his identity becomes clear in their first exchange of letters, an exchange that establishes the main patterns of the entire correspondence. In his letter dated 19 November 1573, Languet reproves Sidney for not writing, expresses his fears that this might signify a loss of affection, and advises him strongly not to allow his 'eagerness to learn' to lead him into danger in Italy, especially now that the political situation in France and the Low Countries has worsened. To endanger himself, Languet argues, would be offensive not only to Sidney but to his father, who 'expects to see the ripe fruits of the many virtues of which your character gives us all great promise.' The letter concludes with praise of the historian Pietro Bizzarri, an example of whose style Languet encloses so that Sidney might 'cull some flowers from it.' Reproaches for not writing, anxieties about Sidney's affection, moral and educational advice, badinage, political news – these are the characteristic motifs of Languet's correspondence.

Sidney's reply, written on 5 December 1573, is his first preserved letter to Languet and shows him very much the student, struggling with a rhetorical exercise in a foreign tongue. He assures Languet that he failed to write only because he met no one to carry a letter; he quotes Ovid to display his sensitivity to Languet's concern – 'I well know how "full of anxious fear love is"' (*Heroides* I.12). He counters Languet's anxieties about the strength of his affection by asserting, 'I am not so full of childish stupidity, womanly fickleness, or brutish ingratitude as not eagerly to seek the friendship of such a man, once having acquired it not to cultivate it, and, having cultivated it, not to show myself thankful for it.' The conventional epithets and careful syntactical balance betray the artificiality of the exercise, which Sidney himself calls attention to: 'O that I had skill enough in Latin, or you in English! Then you would see what a scene I would have made about those doubts of yours.' Later in the letter Sidney comments on the epistle of Pietro Bizzarri, saying that he has 'culled some flowers from it, which I imitated since I could not readily improve on them.'

Although the letters in this initial exchange are simple and straightforward, they none the less reveal the complicated psychological, moral, and literary demands the relationship placed on Sidney. The role he was assigned, and which he willingly accepted, was that of friend to Languet, a man who was at the same time expected to be his teacher and mentor, and whose age, social background, and experience were dramatically different from his own. To reciprocate this friendship, Sidney had not only to express his affection but to perfect himself in virtue, to fulfil his true self, as was expected by Languet and, as Languet kept reminding him, by his father. Central to these expectations, and in many respects the foundation of any future political role, especially on the Continent, was a mastery of Latin style. To reciprocate Languet's friendship, then, was to become a writer: to quote Ovid, to cull 'flowers' from Bizzarri, to consider his letters creative acts ('what a scene I would have made'), to imitate the ideal of friendship as embodied in Cicero's *De Amicitia*, and to cultivate in his epistolary style the graceful wit and polish of a gentleman born. As both a personal and literary ideal, friendship with Languet thus involved Sidney in a complex and intertwined series of imitations: of his own 'true' self, as articulated by Languet; of Languet and his father; of Latin styles; and of the ideal of friendship as expressed by Cicero. Sidney's first sustained literary persona was that of friend to Languet.

From the point of view of their friendship, Languet's reply to Sidney's first letter is among the most significant in the correspondence. In this letter, written on 24 December 1573, Languet calls Sidney 'son' for the first time, but his expressions of love go beyond paternal affection:

My very dear son (for I am now pleased to call you by that name), thus far I have coveted no riches and have taken no trouble to acquire any besides the friendship of those in whom I have seen the eager desire for virtue flourishing; and I have not failed in this, for I have formed very rewarding and gratifying friendships with more than a few persons. But my affection for you has entered my heart far more deeply than any I have ever felt for anyone else, and it has so wholly taken possession there that it tries to rule alone, and, as it were, to practice tyranny. Therefore do not let it surprise you that I am distressed if I am given even the slightest reason to suspect that your good will toward me has at all abated. If you had come upon a jewel of such value that you believed the greatest part of your wealth lay in it, would you not be justified in fearing that someone might steal it from you?

As Languet himself points out, the strength of his love exceeds that of a conventional friendship; the metaphors of tyranny and treasure are not those of Cicero's *De Amicitia* but of Petrarchan poetry.

The letter Languet wrote one week later, on 1 January 1574, speaks with less passion but is also revealing. Responding to some annoyance from Sidney at his reproaches for not writing, Languet insists that these are a customary mark of affection and do not reflect a lack of faith in his 'steadfastness.' Assuring Sidney that he will not be spared such complaints in the future, Languet informs him that he intends to apply a rule he has used with other friends. This rule is 'that I may freely jest with you, admonish you, reproach you, argue with you, or write you whatever comes to my mind.' So far this might be read as a version of the Ciceronean ideal of complete freedom of expression in friendship: 'What is sweeter than to have someone with whom you may dare discuss anything as if you were communing with yourself?' (vi.22). Yet Languet departs from Cicero in suggesting how Sidney will benefit from such freedom: 'I shall now and then sport with you in such letters as the ones which aroused you, in order to give you the opportunity of exercise in writing letters of a versatile sort, as you refute my complaints or in turn make complaints about me. This kind of exercise is thought to be most beneficial.' What Languet here proposes is not the kind of freedom espoused by Cicero, which demands frankness and sincerity, but an epistolary roleplaying that creates the possibility of uncertainty and ambiguity at both ends of the correspondence.

Why did Languet make such a proposal? In part, no doubt, for the motive he mentions – its usefulness as a literary exercise. Such role-playing merely extends the imitative impulse that Sidney himself betrayed earlier when he wished he had language enough to make a 'scene' for

Languet. Sidney had been instructed in Latin at Shrewsbury School by literary role-playing and had almost certainly performed in the school productions of Latin plays for which Thomas Ashton, the headmaster, was well known. If Languet's anxiety about Sidney's affection derived from a truly 'tyrannical' love, however, as he himself suggested, then perhaps there is a deeper motive. Languet proposed the role-playing in response to Sidney's vigorous denial of his fears that the failure to write signified a loss of affection. Given their differences in age, role, social status, and cultural background, Languet must have sensed that the expression of his powerful feelings required considerable delicacy and tact. If so, the ambiguity he created could have afforded an effective emotional shield, much like that provided by disguise for Shakespeare's comic heroines. If anything he said met with Sidney's approval, it could be taken literally; if anything he said proved offensive, it could be explained as a deliberate provocation, aimed at improving Sidney's rhetorical skills.

There is little evidence of such a strategy in the letters that follow immediately, for they offer strong, direct, and occasionally effusive gestures of affection. Before Languet had received Sidney's reply to either of the two letters discussed above, he had written requesting a portrait, which he desired even though 'one is engraved upon my heart and is always before my eyes' (1/22/74). In the same letter he tells of visiting their friend Abondio, whose portrait of Sidney 'had such an effect on me that upon my return home I wrote these little verses, which I send you, although since early adolescence I have not practiced this kind of writing at all. I want to give myself to you as a morsel for mockery, and to say that these little verses do not seem inappropriate to me, and that I therefore wish them to be inscribed on the picture which you order painted, if there is room enough on it.'[15] Throughout Languet's letters during this period recurs the melancholy note that, because of the disasters in France and the Low Countries and the loss of his friends, all that sustains him is his friendship for Sidney.

Sidney's replies to Languet's passionate declarations are sympathetic but restrained. In a letter of 4 February 1574 he consents gladly to commissioning a portrait for Languet (he says he will approach Veronese or Tintoretto) but refuses to be 'so thoroughly immodest as to order the inscription of such laudatory proclamations about me.' In an earlier letter, dated 15 January 1574, he responds directly to the letter in which Languet proposed complete freedom of expression (1 January 1574) and, perhaps, unless a letter is missing or Languet's was never received, indirectly to Languet's previous letter declaring his 'tyrannical' love (24 December

1573). Although Sidney's response is affectionate and playful, it contains only one comment, and that indirect, on Languet's expressions of love. Replying wittily to Languet's mockery of 'those who think that the *summum bonum* lies in imitating Cicero and waste their entire lives doing that' (1/1/74), Sidney writes, 'I shall find the *summum bonum* (next to eternal bliss) in the cultivation of true friendship, and here you will unquestionably hold first rank' (1/15/74). If this is Sidney's reply to Languet's avowal of passionate love, it is certainly oblique. Even as a reply to Languet's letter of 1 January, moreover, which it certainly is, the letter is puzzling, for it makes no reference at all to Languet's proposal for complete freedom of expression. Given the openness and volubility of Languet's declarations of love, Sidney's polite restraint is striking.

Yet when Sidney dedicated himself to friendship with Languet as his '*summum bonum*,' he was not merely being playful. For the remainder of this stage of their correspondence, Sidney's letters not only affirm his friendship repeatedly but place it against the ideal as developed by Cicero. If Languet attempted to protect himself from possible offence by means of epistolary role-playing, Sidney, confronted with Languet's desire for a degree of emotional intimacy he could not reciprocate, seems to have protected himself by playing the role of friend. Languet's repeated demands that Sidney correspond more often, his anxiety about the loss of Sidney's affection, his Petrarchan rhetoric, his epistolary stratagems, his desire for a portrait, his writing verses for the first time since adolescence – all of these suggest a degree of emotional dependency, accentuated no doubt by conditions in France and the loss of his friends, that Sidney might well have had difficulty responding to. By dedicating himself to an ideal of friendship, he could reciprocate Languet's love in a conventional and therefore psychologically manageable way. The very language of Sidney's dedication – 'I shall find the *summum bonum* (next to eternal bliss) in the cultivation of true friendship' – suggests a conscious act of imitation, for it paraphrases the advice of Laelius in *De Amicitia*: 'all that I can do is to urge you to put friendship before all things human' (v.17).

From a post-Freudian perspective, it is easy to detect a strong homoerotic element in Languet's expressions of friendship. More problematic is the significance of such language in the sixteenth century, when the cult of male friendship made it possible, in Freudian terms, to sublimate homoeroticism within a language of spiritual union. Whether Languet's affection was overtly or self-consciously homosexual, it is impossible to say. There is no external evidence, as there is in the case of Fulke Greville, say, or James I, to suggest a tendency towards homosexual behaviour on

the part of Languet. Sidney's response to Languet's overtures is also difficult to gauge. One might be tempted to view his conventional idealization of the relationship as itself a sublimation of sexual feelings, especially
since, as Katherine Duncan-Jones observes, Sidney's most intense personal relationships throughout his life were with men – in particular, with
Fulke Greville and Edward Dyer, neither of whom ever married.[16] The
lack of evidence about the subjective side of Sidney's life, however, coupled with the difficulty of contextualizing the notion of 'homosexuality'
in sixteenth-century England, makes such a line of thought highly speculative. Whatever the exact nature of the emotional relationship between
the two men, there is no doubting its strength or the degree of pressure
Languet's feelings for Sidney exerted upon him at this crucial stage in the
development of his identity.

   From the perspective of self-representation, Sidney's translation of
these emotional pressures into epistolary form is particularly significant
because it establishes a pattern that recurs throughout his career as a
writer. By constructing an identity for himself, that of Ciceronean friend
to Languet, he was able to place his relationship within the relatively
objective sphere of a literary and moral tradition, and at the same time
respond to the immediate pressures of a complicated relationship. The
result is a persona that combines emotional engagement with ironic
detachment and literary idealization with experiential reality. As we shall
see later, similar impulses characterize Sidney's creation of more obviously literary personas, such as that of Philisides. In each case the experiential basis of the persona, which Sidney insists upon even in the most
fictional of self-representations, both shapes and is shaped by the conventional form within which it is contained.

   Sidney's letter dedicating himself to his friendship with Languet provoked a reply, dated 5 February 1574, which suggests that Languet sensed
Sidney's reluctance to reciprocate his gestures of emotional intimacy.
Languet's tone is no longer that of the lover but of the affectionate peda-
gogue. He praises Sidney for his decision to place his 'greatest happiness
(next to the worship of God) in the cultivation of friendship with good
men,' and, perhaps prompted by Sidney's paraphrase, alludes to Cicero:
'if you do this you will never regret it, because, as the speaker in Cicero
says, "Friendship is the salt and spice of life."'[17] Languet ignores completely, however, Sidney's statement that Languet himself would be his
chief friend; instead of personalizing the subject, he offers an extended
discussion of Sidney's natural ability for friendship and its advantages for
men with his prospects, who are likely to depend upon friends both

inside and outside their own country. The themes that Languet develops – the importance of making friends with 'good men,' the tendency for friendship to occur mostly with one's countrymen, the aid it may bring in adverse fortune – all appear in *De Amicitia* (v.18, v.19, vi.22). Instead of developing the unique value of their own relationship, Languet becomes the sage tutor, offering practical advice on friendship for Sidney's future. He too thus retreats into a more conventional mode.

Throughout this period Sidney's letters show him attempting to put into practice the moral and rhetorical ideal to which he had dedicated himself. When Sidney received Languet's letter of 26 March 1574, for example, a letter full of anguish at events in France and the Low Countries and at his own uselessness, Sidney attempted to console him with a formal, tightly structured argument, both political and personal; his purpose, he says, is 'to fulfill as best I can the duties, so to speak, of both a loving and a well-mannered friend' (4/15/74). This letter, which contains Sidney's assurance (quoted earlier) that he had benefited more from Languet than from anything else in his travels, provoked from Languet a passionately grateful response. In a letter of 1 May he expresses his amazement at Sidney's grasp of political affairs and his joy in their friendship, which, he reminds him, originated in 'the innate virtue which shines forth in your face'; in one of 7 May he writes that he has 'reread' Sidney's letter 'again and again' and still has not had his fill of it. The more successfully Sidney fulfilled his role as friend, the more he confirmed Languet's idealization. By shaping a literary persona based on the imitation of Ciceronean ideals of friendship, Sidney demonstrated for Languet his true self.

Two more letters written by Sidney at this stage show an even more explicit attention to these Ciceronean ideals. In a letter of 7 May 1574, Sidney, having heard of the defeat and mortal wounding of Count Louis of Nassau, expresses his fears that events in the Low Countries are tending towards a surrender of the rebels to Spain. Impressed by the significance of the problem, he considers it his 'duty' to discuss it with Languet. On occasions of such gravity, he says, friends must join together: 'For I have always considered friendship's greatest benefit the possibility of communing freely with a friend, that is with one's self, about either public or personal affairs; and this matter seems, so to speak, to demand that all of us who are imbued with the true faith abandon all other thoughts and devote ourselves to this one concern with all our hearts.' The seriousness of the occasion calls forth from Sidney a heightened style and a heightened self-consciousness about the role to which he had pledged himself. The phrasing of this role, as one might expect, recalls *De Amicitia*, in which Laelius calls a friend 'another self' (xxi.80), and someone 'with whom you may dare discuss anything as if you were communing with yourself' (vi.22).

The sense of crisis continues in Sidney's next letter, written on 28 May 1574. Opening with his usual banter, Sidney breaks off to ask, 'But, my dear Languet, what are we doing? Are we jesting in these times?' Instead of condemning humour as inappropriate to the occasion, however, he defends it: 'But this is the true spice, or rather, the true fruit of friendship: when the thought of a dear friend not only proves a great relief for all one's sorrows, but also forces one to let his soul somehow relax. Now, this spiritual recreation especially consists in the decent witticisms which are inherent in, and, as it were, engrafted upon the natures of some men, and wise men at that; for neither Socrates nor our More could resist jesting at their executions. Therefore let us jest.' The first sentence of this passage paraphrases *De Amicitia*, in which friendship is linked with relaxation (xviii.66) and with the sharing of misfortune: 'friendship adds a brighter radiance to prosperity and lessens the burden of adversity by dividing and sharing it' (vi.22). The emphasis upon wit, however, and the examples of Socrates and More show Sidney assimilating Ciceronean values into a more complex conception of his identity. Sidney's suggestion that wit is natural to him takes on special significance when we recall that his father's first letter to him at Shrewsbury School had made just that point: 'Give yourself to be merry; for you degenerate from your father if you find not yourself most able in wit and body to do anything when you are most merry.'[18] The imitation in this passage thus includes Ciceronean ideals of friendship, historical examples of the value of wit, and, implicitly, the example of Sidney's own father, who expected his own merriness to be in the very blood of his son.

Sidney's dedication to the ideal of friendship, then, provided him not merely with an epistolary theme but with a conscious role, a means of defining, in life and writing, the self. It enabled him not only to create a safe emotional framework within which to respond to Languet's desires for intimacy but to commit himself to a central ideal of humanist culture. Languet's 'tyrannical' love could be psychologically absorbed by being translated into the realm of ideal friendship, as articulated by and embodied in Cicero. This attempt to translate complex emotions into the realm of pure ideals – of love or heroism or poetry – is perhaps the core problem in all of Sidney's later works, one that is experienced both by his central characters and his own personas. Hence it is possible that the emotional pressure from Languet, occurring as it did as part of an initiatory process, set a pattern of response crucial to Sidney's development as a writer. Since patterns of idealization were central to humanistic education and training at all stages, however, it is more likely that the relationship with Languet merely focused and intensified impulses that had been ingrained in Sidney since childhood. Whatever the case, Sidney's first persona, that of friend to Languet, shares the idealizing tendencies of all those that follow.

In Sidney's later fictions, idealization almost invariably fails, a victim of the human inability to transcend what he calls in *A Defence of Poetry* an 'infected will.' Friendships, however, remain surprisingly secure. Such seems to have been the case as well with the most important friendships in Sidney's life, those with Dyer, Greville, and Languet. Although frequently interrupted for long intervals, Sidney's friendship with Languet remained firm until the latter's death in 1581. One important exchange of letters at this early stage, nevertheless, shows that Sidney's friendship with Languet gave him an early taste of the human incapacity to sustain ideals. The exchange also reveals a pattern that becomes increasingly important in Sidney's writing, the use of self-representation as a form of self-justification.

Sidney's return to England in the spring of 1575 marked the end of what one may call the initiatory phase in his relationship with Languet. In his letter of 12 June 1575 Languet notes the change by suggesting a different kind of correspondence. Recognizing that Sidney 'is now leading a far different sort of life' and that the 'court is not at all a thrifty steward of time,' Languet says he will make less insistent demands for replies and will no longer write so often or 'send you idle and jesting letters, as I used to do.' Instead, he will write informatively about 'public affairs.' Although Languet continued to write fairly often, the topic of friendship was no longer important; with one significant exception, friendship was assumed by both parties but was not a topic for discussion or literary imitation.

The exception occurred in an exchange of letters beginning on 17 March 1576, when Sidney had been in England nearly a year. During this time he had hardly written to Languet at all. On 3 December 1575 Languet had accused him of letting five months go by without a letter, and on 17 March 1576 he sent a stern and forceful protest both on his own behalf and on that of Sidney's other neglected friends:

I would write you more often if I did not gather from your persistent silence either that our letters do not please you or that you pay little attention to them.

We know that our friendship can be of no benefit to you; still, it was not like your courtesy to cast aside so quickly the memory of those with whom you acted in such a way as to show that their company did not displease you, and who love you dearly and esteem you very highly. But do not imagine that I say these things about myself alone, for the other friends you made here in Germany by your virtue and your pleasant behaviour feel the same way as I, and whenever they write me they complain that you are unexpectedly spurning friendship which, they had reason to hope, would be lasting.

Reproaches for not writing, as we have seen, are recurrent features of Languet's letters; on this occasion, however, his characteristic playfulness is replaced by a tone of marked severity.

Sidney was stung by Languet's accusation, and his reply, written on 21 April 1576, shows the extent to which he had absorbed the Ciceronean ideal of friendship.[19] Languet's charge of inconstancy, he maintains, strikes at the heart of their relationship:

I wonder what you can be thinking of, that you should put to such torment the friend who loves you more than himself. Has your heart hardened so suddenly, my friend? I would never have thought that our friendship, of which the deepest, indeed, the only foundations have been love of virtue and my admiration for you, could have degenerated to such an extent that one of us could reproach the other with bad faith. One may condemn a friend for indolence, even without hearing his defence, or for carelessness, but to cast doubt on his constancy – that is, if there is any good in him at all – what is this but to announce that you wish to terminate our sacred friendship?

Sidney's allusions to indolence and carelessness hint at his consciousness of his guilt, but he cannot accept the charge of inconstancy without admitting to a loss of virtue, without which there can be no friendship at all.

Even more serious than Languet's accusation of inconstancy, Sidney contends, are his insinuations of deceit and ingratitude:

But you not only accuse me of inconstancy towards you and of forgetting you, to which evils God forbid I should stoop, you also clearly imply, in all seriousness, that you suspect me of deceit and ingratitude. My friend, if you do not know me, I myself do not know what kind of promises I can make to defend myself; I can under no circumstances be led to believe that your hopes of me have weakened to such an extent that you imagine sins of this enormity could find any room in my heart – and yet you cannot deny that you have behaved too harshly towards a friend by heaping misery upon misery in this way. For let it be sufficient torment that I am denied your company; but now you have also deprived me of your delightful letters. You have long been punishing me in full measure by writing so rarely; but what kind of cruelty is this, that you should insult the misfortunes of a friend and at the same time add to them?

The absurdity of the counter-accusations against Languet as a correspondent at the end of this passage suggest just how deeply his attack had touched Sidney's sense of identity.

The topics of constancy, deceit, and ingratitude are all developed in Cicero's *De Amicitia*. Central to Cicero's definition of friendship is a distinction between false friendship, based on a desire for advantage, and true friendship, based on the disinterested love of virtue. By accusing Sidney of abandoning his friendships when they were of no more use to him – 'we know that our friendship can be of no benefit to you' – Languet had denied him the virtue necessary to any friendship at all. According to Cicero, moreover, both virtue and friendship depend upon the constancy of the self: 'since the effect of friendship is to make, as it were, one soul out of many, how will that be possible if not even in one man taken by himself shall there be a soul always one and the same, but fickle, changeable, and manifold?' (xxv.92). A single terse statement in *De Amicitia* suggests forcefully the link in Sidney's mind between failure to write to Languet and the loss of self: 'For on the assumption that advantage is the cement of friendships, if advantage were removed friendships would fall apart; but since nature is unchangeable, therefore real friendships are eternal' (ix.33). Beneath Sidney's anguished outrage, it seems, lay a deep anxiety about his essential nature, about the stability of his self. Having been urged by Languet throughout their correspondence to remain true to himself, and having identified that self with an ideal of friendship, Sidney was forced to confront the possibility that he had become, in the words of Languet's earlier warning, 'another person.'

Sidney's letter continues with a plea that Languet desist from such accusations, and with an attempt to deflect his anger through the use of wit:

My friend, so may God be good to me as there is no other human being for whom my love is more heartfelt than for you, and by whom I have a greater wish to be loved. So I beg you, do not torture me any further with these suspicions. As far as I am concerned, you may do anything else so long as you consent to write: say that I am lazy, idle, even stupid, if you wish; but as to my love for you, not a word! –

unless you want to stir up this hornet's nest again. You knew that I am easily provoked; in fact, I would have answered you in the high tragic style, had my vocabulary not been deficient. For this you can thank life at court, which has driven all
my Latin into exile.

This passage echoes uncannily a letter quoted above, Sidney's first preserved letter to Languet, written more than two years before (34–5). In
that letter, too, Sidney had defended himself against accusations of
inconstancy and ingratitude, disclaiming 'childish stupidity, womanly
fickleness, or brutish ingratitude,' and wishing he had skill enough in
Latin to make a 'scene.' That Sidney's pattern of response is identical in
both instances suggests a deeply ingrained habit of mind, a tendency for
feelings of guilt, anger, and resentment to demand expression and resolution in fictions – in making a 'scene' or writing in a 'high tragic style.'
   Sidney had a violent temper throughout his life and even at this early
stage was well aware of it: 'you knew that I am easily provoked.' From a
modern perspective, Sidney's pattern of response is a familiar one, characteristic of children or adolescents prone to temper tantrums or other
kinds of violent display. We use Sidney's theatrical metaphor, indeed,
that of 'making a scene,' to characterize such behaviour. Sidney's education and training, with its emphasis upon the development of identity
through imitation and role-playing, seems to have accentuated this tendency towards theatrical display and made it more self-conscious, both in
life and imagination. In the letters, however, Sidney does not throw a
temper tantrum but expresses the desire to throw one, to vent himself in
gestures of high passion. The wish is towards comedy, in short, and, more
specifically, towards burlesque, as though portraying the self farcically as
tragic victim could exorcise the anger of the moment. When one considers the autobiographical basis of Sidney's later fictions, this pattern of
response becomes especially significant. The displacement of anger into
fictions seems a recurrent impulse. In his persuasive biographical reading
of the *Old Arcadia*, for example, Richard C. McCoy discovers in its problematic ending 'a mixture of sympathy, guilt, and defiance that Sidney
could not fully articulate.'[20] In his literary personas, too, as we shall
see later, Sidney often translates his personal frustration even more self-
consciously into material for fiction, and often, as in the roles of Philisides and Astrophil, into the mode of burlesque. In their combination of
moral seriousness, high passion, and broad humour, these early letters
anticipate the distinctively Sidneyan kind of comedy that surfaces later in
such works as *Astrophil and Stella*.

When Languet replied to Sidney's angry letter, on 28 May 1576, he took refuge in the strategy he had proposed nearly two years before; claiming that he has no doubts about Sidney's loyalty, he says that he accused him of deceit and ingratitude 'in jest, to stimulate you to write.' This defence seems unlikely, especially in view of a letter from Charles de l'Ecluse to Sidney, written on 19 March 1576, which conveys Languet's complaints about Sidney's failure to write and his idleness: 'It has been a long time since we have heard any news of you, and Monsieur Languet has often complained about this to me; he tells me you have grown idle.'[21] Even if Languet had written in jest, Sidney's inability to perceive the irony would provide yet another indication of his troubled state of mind.

One reason for Sidney's quickness to anger, as I have suggested, was guilt: Sidney had been idle at court and had not fulfilled Languet's expectations either as student, courtier, or correspondent. During the summer of 1575 he participated in the queen's progress, which included two major visits: one to Kenilworth, the newly refurbished palace of the earl of Leicester, the other to Woodstock, the estate of the unsuccessful courtier who was to become one of Sidney's closest friends, Edward Dyer. Although these pageants would have enmeshed Sidney deeply in the ritualized politics of the court, they were clearly not the kind of political activity either Sidney or Languet had in mind when thinking of his vocation. In a letter of 3 December 1575, Languet had complained of the lack of news from Sidney by stating that he could have satisfied all his hungry correspondents 'by giving up one dance a month.' It might well have been during this period, as Katherine Duncan-Jones suggests,[22] that Sidney first turned to poetry, another activity that mingled pleasure with self-reproach.

Guilt combines with feelings of resentment in Sidney's absurd counter-accusations against Languet as an unfaithful correspondent. Sidney was after all powerless to change his basic condition, which depended upon the queen's will. His life as a whole, moreover, was subject not only to Languet's moralistic judgments but to the moral, political, and economic authority of his elders, particularly his father and the earl of Leicester. As Duncan-Jones suggests, the 'abundance of advice' that Sidney received as a young man from such elders probably 'contributed to a build-up of rage and frustration in a child who was unusually passionate and sensitive.'[23] The crucial underlying problem, however, and one that would plague Sidney for the rest of his life, was the failure to fulfil at court his own sense of vocation. 'We are doing nothing here,' he writes at the end of the letter in which he explodes at Languet; 'I long to live in your part of the world again.' And he then turns to his hopes of fighting in a campaign against the Turks.

Sidney's inactivity at court upon his return from the Continent produced what might be called a prolonged identity crisis, lasting to his death. His frustrations were deep because his expectations of service were high. They were also deeply ingrained. From birth he had been marked for a major position at court, and his initiatory friendship with Languet merely served to confirm the rightness of that identity. Having defined himself as friend to Languet, and having absorbed Languet's idealization of his future political role into his own conception of his identity, Sidney reacted to his failure at court with anger, guilt, and resentment. Elizabeth, Languet, and Sidney himself were all implicated: Elizabeth because she provided no outlet for his expectations; Languet because he personified the humanist education and ideals that had created them; and Sidney himself because he had failed to live up to them, failed to become his true self. The ironic or comic displacement of these frustrations, as we shall see, forms the basis of Sidney's self-representation as Philisides in the *Old Arcadia*.

In contrast to his later exercises in self-representation, Sidney's development of an epistolary persona as friend to Languet does not lead to a questioning of the values of the genre within which he writes. Throughout the relationship with Languet epistolary conventions remain intact, along with the ideal of friendship they embody. Epistolary ideals thus persist as a sturdy backdrop against the challenges of an inconstant self posed by Sidney's failures as a correspondent. As we shall see, Sidney's later self-representations always involve not only the testing of the self-image against a conventional ideal but the testing of the ideal itself against the conflicting demands of experiential reality. Not only is Astrophil found wanting by Petrarchan standards, but Petrarchan standards are found wanting by Astrophil's. The absence of ironic complexity of this sort marks the epistolary persona as the work of a young man – 'young and raw,' to use Leicester's words – and a beginning writer.

In a broad sense Sidney's early correspondence with Languet demonstrates the powerful effect of the humanist system of education; students who internalized its ideals and methods, as Sidney seems to have done, were shaped in profound and lasting ways. More particularly, the correspondence allows us a glimpse of some of the forces that shaped Sidney at his entry into manhood. Sidney's conception of his identity at this stage was in crucial ways defined by his relationship with Languet. When Sidney responded to Languet's idealizing love by dedicating himself to friendship, he not only internalized Languet's idealized image of himself but the humanist ideal of friendship epitomized in Cicero's *De Amicitia*. The test of Sidney's truth to himself, ironically, was writing; when his writing failed, the victim of life at court, not only his friendship but his very identity was called in question. To re-establish a sense of self, to explain and excuse his lapses, Sidney, true to his humanist education, was drawn to imitation, to the making of 'scenes.' With his increasing estrangement from court, such 'scenes' became the dominant motifs of his fictions. In a deep and somewhat problematic sense, then, Sidney's friendship with Languet was crucial to his 'making' as a man and poet.

3

Self-Portrayals at Court, 1575–9

From the time of his return to England in May 1575 until his 'exile' from court in the autumn of 1579, Sidney devoted himself to the role of courtier. In the summer of 1575 he participated in Leicester's lavish entertainments for the queen at Kenilworth, and he may have begun his career as a tilter before the queen at Woodstock in September. He sought military service abroad throughout this period, seizing every opportunity to press his claims upon such a role. He participated in his father's Irish affairs, representing him in England, travelling briefly to Ireland, and writing a defence of his policies. His most notable success as a courtier was his embassy to the Holy Roman Emperor, which took him to the Continent in the winter and spring of 1577, where he was celebrated as a promising leader of the Protestant cause. Shortly after his return, however, court life soured, and a series of disappointments and misadventures, culminating in the Anjou affair and the quarrel with Oxford, resulted in the prolonged stay at Wilton that enabled him to devote his 'idleness' to the *Old Arcadia*.

During these early years at court Sidney was also engaged in intellectual and poetic activities. For a time he studied 'chemistry' with John Dee and Edward Dyer, the latter of whom also worked with him to adapt classical measures to English poetry. He studied Livy with Gabriel Harvey, who presumably introduced him to Spenser. Although the dating of many of his early poems is uncertain, several of the works later included in the *Old Arcadia* seem to have originated at this time. Taken as a whole, Sidney's writing in these years is of the kind one might expect of an aspiring courtier: occasional poems for private circulation, verses composed for a tilt at Whitehall, a defence of his father's policies (the *Discourse of Irish Affairs*), an entertainment for the queen (*The Lady of May*), and a letter of advice, urging the queen to abandon the idea of marriage with the duke d'Anjou. All of this writing might be called persuasive and political, for it was designed to win the favour of the queen and to influence political affairs. Such courtly writing necessarily involved not only self-representation but self-promotion of the kind described by Castiglione in *The Courtier* and by Puttenham in *The Arte of English Poesie*. Taken as a whole, Sidney's development of personas in this period is rhetorical rather than exploratory and offers neither the introspective quality nor the literary energy of the later self-representations. During this early phase in his career, Sidney was too busy enacting the self, one might say, playing both socially and rhetorically the role of courtier, to engage in literary self-exploration.[1]

In the absence of a significant or sustained act of literary self-representation during this period, it might be useful to examine a pictorial analogue to such a work, the major portrait of Sidney executed, perhaps by Zuccaro, in 1577 or 1578 (Figure 1). The portrait was probably presented as a gift to Sidney's sister, Mary, and perhaps as a wedding gift. (The marriage took place on 21 April 1577 when Sidney was in Prague.) Sidney seems to have sat for at least six portraits during his relatively short career, a number that Roy Strong finds exceptional and that attests to his continuing preoccupation with images of himself.[2] Although not a self-portrait, the work none the less represents Sidney as he chose to be seen and illuminates some important features of the social role he played at court.

While Sidney's interest in such public images as portraits was no doubt partly social and political, his allusions to portraiture in both *Arcadias* suggests that he considered the medium an important revealer of truths of character. In the *New Arcadia*, Artesia parades the portraits of all her unsuccessful competitors, and each one is described in terms that correlate the external appearance of the sitter with her inner nature (94–8). In the *Old Arcadia*, the narrator's description of Philoclea's portrait, which precipitates Pyrocles' love, provides a lesson in interpretation that might perhaps be applied to the portrait of Sidney himself. The painting of Philoclea enables the viewer not only to appreciate the 'show of her beauties' but to 'judge even the nature of her countenance, full of bashfulness, love, and reverence – and all by the cast of her eye – , mixed with a sweet grief to find her virtue suspected' (11.28–31). Through her portrait, Philoclea conveys not only her beauty and goodness of character but an attitude, sorrow that her father's belief in the oracle has caused him to distrust her. Written only a year or two after his own portrait of 1577–8,

Figure 1: Sir Philip Sidney. Reproduced by permission of the Marquess of Bath,
Longleat House, Warminster, Wiltshire, Great Britain.

this description suggests that Sidney, too, might have intended his portrait not only to record his physical appearance, character, and social status, but to suggest an attitude or stance towards his present situation.

As the depiction of an attitude, however, Sidney's portrait seems at first glance unrevealing. Sidney's peers were often much more idiosyncratic and dramatic in their poses, more emphatic in their assertions of some aspect of their identity or of some special relationship with the queen. In 1568, for example, Sir Henry Lee was painted by Antonio Mor. The portrait is full of cryptic symbolism, some of which, as Roy Strong suggests, may allude to Lee's relationship with the queen.[3] Lee has his left hand at his breast, with the thumb slipped through a gold ring that is suspended from his neck by a scarlet cord. Two additional rings are also tied around his left arm, and his sleeves are embroidered in a pattern that includes true-lovers'-knots and armillary spheres. The significance of these emblems is heightened, although not clarified, by the fact that an identical portrait exists of Edward, third Lord Windsor. In 1580, to take another example, Sir Francis Drake had himself painted with his right hand on a globe (Pl. 126). Although portrait styles of the 1570s tend to be less personally expressive than those of the 1580s or 1590s, which occasionally featured gentlemen in the various postures of melancholy, the portraits of Lee and Drake remind us that Sidney could have chosen a far more flamboyant medium in which to assert his public self. He chose neither to celebrate ostentatiously some aspect of his personal identity nor to symbolize a relationship with the queen. Since Sidney's identity was to a great extent defined by the role of courtier at this stage, and since he later achieved a reputation for his skill at the courtly lore of imprese, the absence of courtly allusiveness in the painting is itself worthy of comment.

In contrast to some paintings of his peers, then, Sidney's portrait seems highly formal and conventional. The pose is itself very common in the period. Sidney stands turned slightly to the left, with his right hand at his waist and his left resting on the hilt of his sword. Very similar poses can be found in a great number of roughly contemporary portraits. The costume consists of matching ruff and hand ruffs in figure-eight shape, a metal gorget, a pinked and slashed doublet with a peascod belly, and bombasted and paned trunk hose. Although fashionable and ornate, it too seems calculated not to call attention to itself: there is nothing emblematic or idiosyncratic about it. One conclusion we can draw, then, is that Sidney eschewed idiosyncrasy, that he chose not a dramatically expressive portrait but one that displayed his adherence to the conventional values of his family and rank. The portrait is formal, ceremonial, restrained – the image, in short, not of a flamboyant courtier or potential poet but of a young and aspiring statesman. It is a pose appropriate to a young ambassador to the Holy Roman Emperor.

The sense of dignity conveyed by the portrait is accentuated if we relate the pose to the social status of those it was often used to characterize. Although not restricted to the higher aristocracy and royalty, the pose struck by Sidney – standing, in formal attire, left hand on the hilt of a sword – seems to have been particularly associated with men of such rank, both nationally and internationally. A survey of roughly contemporaneous portraits depicted in volume 2 of Roy Strong's *Tudor and Jacobean Portraits* yields the following nearly identical poses: Edward VI as a young man (Pls 172, 173); Robert Dudley, earl of Leicester (Pls 378, 385, 387); Philip II (Pl. 492); Robert Devereux, earl of Essex (Pls 225, 232, 233); James I (Pl. 347); and Henry prince of Wales (Pls 319, 320). Lorne Campbell's *Renaissance Portraits* includes, in similar poses, Charles IX, king of France (Pl. 131), Alessandro Farnese (Pl. 140), and Don Carlos of Spain (Pl. 217).[4] In 1572 the then duke d'Alençon was painted in the same pose, ironically, with what Sidney would doubtless have considered the foppish addition of gloves in the right hand and a feathered hat on the head.[5] At the time of the 1577–8 portrait, Sidney was a very young man and not even a knight; in such a context, the aristocratic and royal connotations of the pose suggest a rather elevated sense of social rank. The connotations of the pose seem to be confirmed by the 'arrogant' expression of the face, noted by Duncan-Jones.[6]

Both the elevated pose and the hint of arrogance in the face seem symptomatic of Sidney's conception of his role as courtier to the queen. As heir to Leicester and focal point not only for the political hopes of his family but of Continental Protestantism, Sidney seems to have approached Elizabeth with a far greater degree of independence and self-assertiveness than was sanctioned by a courtier's role. Although her courtiers achieved personal success with a remarkable variety of ploys throughout her reign, including, occasionally, imperious self-assertion, the norm was self-abasement or at least extreme deference, and departures from it were dangerous. When Sidney's friend Edward Dyer advised Christopher Hatton on methods of influencing the queen, he stressed above all the need to consider her consciousness of her own status: 'First of all you must consider with whom you have to deale, and what wee be towards her, who though she does descend very much in her Sex as a woman, yet wee may not forgett her Place, and the nature of it as our Sovraigne.'[7]

Dyer's attention to the importance of gender in relations with the queen is suggestive, for much in Sidney's attitude, as in that of other courtiers of the period, implies a patriarchal restiveness with the idea of obeisance to a woman. As Philippa Berry has shown, the practice of the so-called cult of Elizabeth often masked a struggle between male aristocrats and a female monarch over control of the royal image.[8]

The personal assertiveness of Sidney's self-representations before the queen can be seen in three major documents or episodes from this period: *The Lady of May*, the entertainment that Sidney composed for Elizabeth's visit to Leicester's estate, Wanstead, in May 1578; Greville's account of the Oxford affair; and Sidney's *Letter to Queen Elizabeth*, in which he opposed her plan to marry the duke d'Anjou. Taken as a whole, these cases suggest a convergence of social and literary personas that helps to explain why Sidney had such little success as a courtier.

As the only 'dramatic' composition in Sidney's career, *The Lady of May* lacks an explicit self-representation or persona. As I have argued elsewhere, however, the work is not truly dramatic but rhetorical, an attempt to persuade the queen towards a new conception of her relationship with Leicester and a more aggressive stance towards foreign affairs, especially in the Netherlands.[9] Sidney was himself intimately identified with Leicester at this time, and in that sense the work as a whole projects his own attitudes. Sidney's aggressive stance towards the queen becomes clear in two ways. First, he creates what amounts to a coercive theatrical form. He places the queen in the role of judge of a debate between two ostensibly legitimate claimants to the hand of the May Lady: Therion, the hunter, and Espilus, the shepherd. At the same time, however, he attempts to manipulate her judgment rhetorically by favouring the character and claims of Therion. The queen either ignored or, more likely, resisted this manipulative strategy, for she chose Espilus as the winner, marring the ending that Sidney had composed in celebration of Therion.[10] Secondly, Sidney implicitly identifies both Leicester and himself with Therion, who embodies the 'masculine' aggressiveness that both men found wanting in Elizabeth's foreign policy towards the Netherlands. On a more personal level, as we shall see, Therion's aggressiveness characterized Sidney's own desire for military combat, which was particularly strong both shortly before and after the entertainment. Sidney seems to have failed on all counts in this first attempt at the role of literary courtier, and he never again wrote an entertainment for the queen.

Fulke Greville's account of Sidney's confrontation with the earl of Oxford on the tennis court provides a social counterpart to the literary construct of *The Lady of May*. The most striking feature of this famous episode is not Sidney's heated refusal to accept Oxford's command to leave the tennis court or his subsequent challenge to a duel, but his spirited defence of his own rights before the queen. According to Greville, the queen intervened in the dispute and gave Sidney a lecture on 'the difference in degree between Earls, and Gentlemen; the respect inferiors ought to their superiors; and the necessity in Princes to maintain their own creations, as degrees descending between the peoples licentiousness and the anoynted Soveraignty of Crowns: how the Gentlemans neglect of the Nobility taught the Peasant to insult upon both.' In the context of his role as courtier, Sidney's response to this lecture is nothing less than astonishing. Although Greville states that his reply was characterized by 'such reverence as became him,' Sidney rebutted the queen's arguments, even personalizing the debate by using her own and her father's actions against her. He gave her a lecture of his own, in short, on her responsibilities as queen. He asserted that 'place was never intended for privilege to wrong,' as she herself demonstrated in her gracious behaviour; that although Oxford was a 'great Lord,' he was 'no Lord over him: and therefore the difference of degrees between free men, could not challenge any other homage than precedency'; and that by a wise and politic act of her own father, the gentry had been given 'free, and safe appeal' to the monarch 'against the oppression of the Grandees,' whose power might otherwise threaten the crown itself. Greville does not indicate what transpired next in this conversation or what role it might have played in Sidney's subsequent exile from court.

Although Greville praises Sidney's behaviour in this episode, he does so in a manner so convoluted as to betray his awareness of the outrageous breach of social decorum it involved. To conclude the story, he draws the following moral: 'This constant tenor of truth he took upon him, which, as a chief duty in all creatures – both to themselves and the soveraignty above them – protected this gentleman (though he obeyed not) from the displeasure of his sovereign; wherein he left an authentical precedent to after ages that howsoever tyrants allow of no scope, stamp or standard but their own will, yet with princes there is a latitude for subjects to reserve native and legal freedom by paying humble tribute in manner, though not in matter, to them.'[11] Although this extraordinary paragraph seems to celebrate Sidney, whose 'constant tenor of truth' protects him, and whose behaviour leaves 'an authentical precedent to after ages,' its contorted syntax reveals that the true subject is Elizabeth's astonishing magnanimity. The most crucial words in the passage are tucked into a

parenthesis: '(though he obeyed not).' Faced with the outright disobedi-
ence of her subject, Elizabeth demonstrated that she was no tyrant but a
true prince, willing to allow 'latitude for subjects to reserve native and
legal freedom.' This 'latitude' of the queen, ironically, not Sidney's pro-
vocative behaviour, is the 'authentical' precedent that Sidney bequeaths
to 'after ages.' The directness of Sidney's address, his argumentativeness,
his appeal to Elizabeth herself and Henry VIII as precedents, all suggest a
degree of familiarity and independence that were unlikely to win favour
of Elizabeth.

A final example of Sidney's apparent inability to submerge himself in
the rhetorical conventions of the courtier is provided by the *Letter to Queen
Elizabeth*. Both the Oxford affair and the controversy surrounding the marriage to Anjou, the subject of this letter, seem to have figured prominently
in Sidney's decision to absent himself from court in the autumn of 1579.
Since Oxford supported the Anjou match, moreover, the two affairs were
probably related.[12] That the letter to the queen was important to Sidney
psychologically as well as politically is suggested by the fact that he adapted
its essential arguments, as we shall see later, in the unheeded advice that
Philanax gives to Duke Basilius in the *Old Arcadia*.

Both the effect of the letter and the effectiveness of the persona are difficult to contextualize. Greville's treatment of the episode is suspiciously
equivocal. He himself raises the question 'whether it were not an error –
and a dangerous one – for Sir Philip, being neither magistrate nor counsellor, to oppose himself against his sovereign's pleasure in things indif-
ferent.' Predictably, his answer is negative, but the reason again lies more
in the magnanimity of the queen than in Sidney's behaviour: 'although
he found a sweet stream of sovereign humours in that well-tempered lady
to run against him, yet found he safety in her self, against that selfness
which appeared to threaten him in her.' As in the case of the Oxford
affair, Greville transforms Sidney's daring into a compliment to the
queen's forbearance. Although his assertion that Sidney 'kept his access
to her Majesty as before'[13] makes it impossible to argue that the episode
resulted in outright banishment, Greville's acknowledgment of the complex tensions on both sides suggests the strong possibility that both the
queen's displeasure and Sidney's frustration contributed to Sidney's decision to abandon for a time the role of courtier.

The rhetoric of Sidney's letter is also difficult to gauge, in part because
Sidney himself represents his argument as merely a one-sided continuation of a discussion in which he had already delivered 'the general sum'
of his 'travelling thoughts' (*LQ*,46.20). In the context of the controversy

as a whole, moreover, as the Oxford editors argue, Sidney's arguments, although powerful and straightforward, are neither unusual nor exceptionally inflammatory (*LQ*, 36–7). None the less, both the tone of the letter and its argumentative strategy betray something of the daringly open and aggressive stance that we have already observed in the Oxford affair. Sidney could have written a letter that gave some credit to opposing arguments and that highlighted rhetorically his confidence in the queen's judgment and his willingness to serve, whatever her decision. Instead, he developed only the negative side of the argument, subjected Anjou to direct *ad hominem* attacks, and failed to create a rhetorical distance between himself and his argument that would enable him to save face if he were unsuccessful. The persona of the letter, in short, reveals none of the rhetorical self-consciousness and sophistication that makes the persona of *A Defence of Poetry* so persuasive.

Although Sidney begins the letter with an extravagant and complimentary rhetorical flourish, he asserts almost immediately that he will unfold his argument in 'simple and direct terms' (46.14). The arguments that follow are indeed spare and straightforward, presented with virtually none of the deferential gestures or self-reflexive irony that one expects from a courtier's discourse. As Maureen Quilligan observes, the discourse becomes at times 'surprisingly blunt.'[14] Although it is difficult to demonstrate a rhetorical absence, a lack of deference, a glance at two other contemporary addresses to the queen on the same subject reveals the possibility of quite different personae. Sir Thomas Cecil's brief, which outlines methods of diverting the perils attendant upon the queen's decision to break off the marriage, a decision he acknowledges opposing, begins and ends with extraordinary gestures of service and loyalty. In his opening remarks to the queen, he asserted that he would 'spend his blood' not only in actions he himself supported 'but in any other thing' that she 'would have done'; in closing, he asked to be the first to 'spend his blood' to confront any peril she feared, 'without exception of persons, time, place or matter.'[15] Even Sir Thomas's father, Lord Burghley, whose position entitled him to considerably more authority before the queen, closed his lengthy memorandum in support of the marriage by requesting 'humbell pardone' for any errors that might have proceeded from his lack of judgment.[16] The rhetorical gestures of both father and son are those one expects to find in arguments before Elizabeth, but nothing like them is found in Sidney's elegantly written letter. In his relations with the queen, it seems, Sidney was unwilling or unable to engage in a rhetoric of deference.[17]

The portrait of Sidney not only conveys something of the aristocratic assertiveness that characterized Sidney's relations with the queen in *The Lady of May*, the Oxford affair, and the letter opposing the marriage to Anjou. More striking even than the heightened formality and elevation of the pose is its distinctive combination of civilian and military costume and gesture. Although it is easy to find analogues in other paintings to the pose of hand on sword, as we have seen, portraits that feature military apparel appear far less often, and invariably depict men celebrated for military experience and valour. Volume 2 of Strong's *Tudor and Jacobean Portraits*, for example, includes armed portraits of such notable military figures as the following: Sir Richard Bingham (Pl. 44), Sir Francis Drake (Pl. 128), Sir William Drury (Pl. 138), Sir Edward Hoby (Pl. 334), Sir Richard Grenville (Pl. 256), and Robert Devereux, earl of Essex (Pl. 229). The latter portrait shows Essex with the walls of Cadiz on fire behind him. Portraits that combine civilian and military dress are even more rare. In view of Sidney's lack of military experience, the military connotations of the portrait are particularly surprising.

As we know from his letters, after his return from his travels on the Continent Sidney yearned for an opportunity to serve in war. Since at least June 1574, when Languet approved of him having his first military experience under the 'skillful' General von Schwendi, a plan that never materialized, Sidney seems to have been on the alert for a campaign in which to initiate himself as a soldier. In a letter of 21 April 1576 he expressed the hope that he would be able to fight against the Turks, since, as he says, he would prefer 'to fight my first campaign in that kind of conflict, rather than involve myself in a civil war.'[18] From the summer of 1577 to the summer of 1578, the period in which Sidney's portrait was probably painted, his pursuit of a military appointment to the Netherlands was so vigorous that it provoked stern rebukes from his mentor Languet on three separate occasions. 'Most men of high birth are possessed with this madness,' wrote Languet on 2 May 1578, 'that they long after a reputation founded on bloodshed, and believe that there is no glory for them except that which is connected with the destruction of mankind.' Similar expostulations against the compulsion of aristocrats to prove themselves in war occur in Languet's letters of 15 February and 22 October 1578.[19] The aggressiveness Languet sensed in Sidney's desire for military adventure also appears obliquely, as we have seen, in his celebration of the reckless and virile hunter, Therion, in *The Lady of May*, a work that was written when the prospects for a military appointment in the Netherlands seemed good.

In view of Sidney's strong desire at the time for military service, it seems likely that the portrait alludes to his sense of his present predicament: he is a statesman ready for war yet still in civilian dress. If there is any coded comment directed at the queen in this painting, or at the nobles likely to frequent his sister's estate at Wilton, it probably lies in this unmistakable assertion of military readiness. As Duncan-Jones observes, 'the shadowy left hand' in the portrait, 'half closed around the sword hilt, points discreetly to a further ambition.'[20] The portrait may have enabled Sidney to play in art the double role he was denied at court, that of warrior-statesman.

Of all the contemporary portraits that provide a context for Sidney's, a painting of the earl of Leicester, executed sometime between 1575 and 1580, is probably the most relevant (Figure 2).[21] The pose in the two portraits is virtually identical. Like Sidney, Leicester is formally attired and stands turned slightly to his left, with his right hand on his waist and his left on the hilt of his sword; the chief difference between the two is that Leicester wears a hat and the great collar of the George of the Garter around his neck. In view of the close relationship between the two men at the time – Sidney was Leicester's heir and greatly under his influence and control – and the remarkable similarity in the poses, it seems plausible to conclude that Sidney's portrait might have been conceived in direct imitation of Leicester's. If one were to remove the gorget from Sidney's neck and add Leicester's moustache and beard to Sidney's face, his feathered cap to Sidney's head, and his Garter collar to Sidney's breast and shoulders, one would transform the figure of an aspiring statesman-warrior into one who had proved his worth already and had been appropriately honoured. Whereas Sidney's portrait suggests the role-playing of a young gentleman aspiring towards the positions of statesman and warrior, Leicester's suggests a convergence between role and reality: he has become what Sidney hopes to be. Perhaps Sidney's portrait is yet another instance of the emulative self-representation that was so much a part of his educational and social environment.

If Sidney's portrait possibly suggests a desire to emulate Leicester, and to be seen as doing so, it also carries a message that makes it far more idiosyncratic. In the Longleat version of the painting, the following couplet appears at the top right: 'Who gives himself may well his picture give / Else were it vain, since both short time do live.' Since it is likely that the Longleat version is the original, and that Sidney gave it to his sister, it is also likely that Sidney wrote the couplet; even if the Longleat version is a copy, moreover, Sidney may have added the couplet when presenting

Figure 2: Robert Dudley, Earl of Leicester, by an unknown artist.
By courtesy of the National Portrait Gallery, London.

the painting to his sister, as Duncan-Jones suggests.[22] As a personal expression, the sentiment is powerfully suggestive and potentially more revealing than anything else in the painting. The meaning of the lines is both unconventional and paradoxical. One would expect the verse to celebrate the long or perhaps even eternal life of the portrait in contrast to the short life of the sitter. Instead, both are given short lives, and the value of giving the self through art becomes therefore problematic in the extreme. This is an odd epitaph for the gift of a painting.

In the context of Sidney's immediate situation – his restlessness at court, his flirtations with poetry as a means of staving off idleness, his eagerness for military action – the epitaph might be explained as a slyly ironic signature, a way of underlining his impatience for action. If so, the gesture anticipates the one he would make in less than two years, when he dedicated the *Old Arcadia* to his sister while at the same time disparaging it as a work written for and in idle times. Both gestures suggest a deep ambivalence about the value of art as a substitute for action.

If we consider the couplet as part of the work, the portrait of Sidney adds an element that is lacking from his other courtly self-portrayals during this period, that of self-reflexive irony. Irony of this kind is so central to Sidney's later literary self-representations that it is striking to note its apparent absence in his relations with the queen at this stage in his career. The characteristic pose of the Elizabethan courtier, which coupled self-abasement with a desire for self-advancement, often called forth a sophisticated and playful tone of self-mockery. In his study of the convergences between courtly and poetic values in the sixteenth century, Daniel Javitch suggests that the rhetorical world implied by Castiglione's *Courtier* was more suitable to Elizabethan court life than that of Cicero's *De Oratore*, in which most of the courtiers had been trained. In Javitch's terms, ironically, Sidney's courtly rhetoric seems ineffectually Ciceronean – confrontational, earnest, aggressive, persuasive – whereas the rhetoric of his more purely literary works, including the self-representations, seems more in the vein of Castiglione: playful, ambivalent, ironic, ornamental, delightful.[23] Perhaps the ironic detachment that so vitalizes the literary works could only be achieved at the cost of withdrawal from court.

Considered as a whole, the 1577–8 portrait seems to employ formality and conventionality in a way that renders them personally expressive. Like the painting of Philoclea in the *Old Arcadia*, Sidney's portrait conveys not only a sense of character but an attitude towards his immediate situation. The self-image of the portrait is formal and restrained, yet it hints at the arrogance and aggressiveness that characterized his relations

with the queen. The gorget is around the neck; the hand is placed expect-
antly on the sword; and the couplet warns of the brevity of art and life,
implying the need for immediate action if anything is to be achieved at
all. Queen Elizabeth, whose power might have been suggested in any
number of ingratiating ways, is present in the painting only by implication, as the ultimate source of an impatience registered by the military
pose and ironic couplet. Taken in this way, the portrait can be said to
epitomize Sidney's restiveness in the role of courtier, and the couplet to
anticipate the ironical self-reflections that will follow in the *Old Arcadia*.

4

Philisides in Exile:
The *Old Arcadia*

In the autumn of 1579 Sidney withdrew from court. The immediate occasion for his withdrawal was tension in his relationship with the queen, resulting from his opposition to her proposed marriage with Anjou and his recalcitrance in the Oxford affair. In both cases he had challenged the royal prerogative – in the one by opposing a marriage that the queen had set her mind on, in the other by forgetting the behaviour appropriate to his place in the social hierarchy. Although not exactly banished from court, Sidney was in disfavour, and he himself had grown increasingly frustrated with his lack of success as a courtier. Since his return from the Continent in 1575, he had made little progress in the pursuit of his political ambitions. His absence from court lasted until the spring of 1581, when he announced his return with a characteristically aggressive expression of humility: his New Year's gift to the queen that year was a '"jewel of gold, being a whip, garnished with small diamonds in four rows and cords of small seed pearl."'[1] The gift provides an illuminating metaphor for the complex of emotions that underlies Sidney's presentation of himself as Philisides in the *Old Arcadia.*

Although ostensibly minor, the role of Philisides, the melancholy exile, represents in its own way a significant achievement. Through the invention of the role, I shall argue, Sidney was able to displace and to dramatize many of the inner tensions that characterized his immediate experience. Central to these concerns is his complex relationship with the queen, a relationship that is probed obliquely throughout the *Old Arcadia* in Philisides' melancholy obsession with the character of Mira. Of equal importance, however, is Sidney's ambivalent relationship to his newfound role as poet, an ambivalence that is most tellingly revealed in the contrast between the exhilarating energy of the work as a whole and the implied critique of poetry it represents, especially through the role of Philisides. In exile at Wilton, Sidney found in Sannazaro's *Arcadia* a version of pastoral exile that corresponded to his own predicament; in Sannazaro's personas, Sincero and Ergasto, Sidney found the prototypes for his own Philisides. In this act of poetic imitation, however, Sidney implies a critique of the traditional values of pastoral poetry and the traditional conceptions of the pastoral poet that Sannazaro celebrates. Philisides' melancholy paralysis is thus a playful mirror for Sidney's wittily ironic conception of his own condition.

During the roughly eighteen months of his combined banishment and exile, Sidney spent much of his time with his sister at Wilton and much of it writing the *Old Arcadia*. With this work, Sidney turned to a new kind of fiction-making and a new authorial role. The project was ambitious: an extended pastoral romance, imitating chiefly Sannazaro's *Arcadia* and Montemayor's *Diana*, but assimilating in complex ways a variety of classical and Continental models. Unlike *The Lady of May*, this fiction was not produced for a court occasion; nor did it have to meet the constricting rhetorical demands of court poetry addressed to the queen. As he indicates in the dedicatory letter to the work, Sidney wrote for his sister and their coterie.

Although his primary and immediate audience was limited, Sidney must have been conscious of a much broader potential audience, including both posterity and the queen; the sensitivities of the latter, in particular, must have been much on his mind. By choosing a role other than that of direct courtly persuasion, however, Sidney freed himself to engage in an act of the imagination that, in contrast to *The Lady of May* and letter of advice on the Anjou marriage, might be called disinterested. The creative energy apparent everywhere in the work testifies to a strong sense of release. The *Old Arcadia* can only be called disinterested, however, in an immediate political sense: Sidney did not address it to the queen and had nothing political to gain by it, either from her or from the statesmen around her. He had estranged himself from the role of courtier-poet. From a more personal perspective, however, the work is remarkably *self*-interested. It reflects not only many of Sidney's deep-seated preoccupations and implicit values, as one would expect, but it also reflects with an unusual immediacy concerns that grew directly out of his recent court experience. As a creative response to this experience, the *Old Arcadia* embodies the same wit, ironic self-disparagement, and sublimated aggression that were later to characterize Sidney's gift of a golden whip to the queen.

Although primarily a work about misadventures in love, the *Old Arcadia* places those misadventures in an intensely political context. At one time or another the protagonists all betray their political responsibilities for private passions. The plot is actually set in motion not by love but by Duke Basilius's foolish decision to abandon his court and responsibilities in order to avoid the prophecy that he believes threatens him and his family. All of the misadventures of the story, both political and domestic, are direct or indirect consequences of this decision. Although the representation is too oblique to be considered political allegory, Sidney's treatment of Basilius reflects unmistakably his frustration with the queen over the Anjou affair. In 1576, when Sidney had offended his friend and mentor, Hubert Languet, he expressed in a letter his desire for sufficient expertise in Latin to compose a tragical scene of self-justification (see above, 44–5). In 1579, having offended the queen, he composed in English a pastoral romance that displaced and extended imaginatively issues and emotions that had originated at court.

The *Old Arcadia* begins with Basilius, prompted by no more than a vague anxiety about his future security, consulting the oracle of Delphi and receiving an alarming prophecy, which cryptically discloses the action of the plot. He decides immediately to thwart the prophecy by retreating with his family from the court into the country. His mind already made up, he none the less consults 'for fashion's sake' (6.32) his best adviser, Philanax, a man who combines 'affection' and 'judgment' (5.31). Philanax regrets the initial decision to consult an oracle, argues against the remedy, and predictably fails to dissuade Basilius. In the summer and autumn of 1579, anxious about her future, Elizabeth made clear to the court her desire to marry Anjou. The opposition was fierce, both in the court and without, and the queen's mood dangerous; for writing against the marriage, in a work printed as *The Discovery of a Gaping Gulf*, John Stubbs had his right hand cut off. In this context, directed by his uncle and father, Sidney played the role of Philanax and addressed a private letter of advice to the queen.

Philanax's oration and Sidney's letter (*LQ*, 46–57) have much in common. Both argue that a peaceful reign of long standing should not be suddenly disrupted, since all change is potentially dangerous and more likely to bring harm than good. Philanax points out to Basilius the illogicality of his resigning his dukedom out of the fear of losing it, 'like one that should kill himself for fear of death' (7.32–3). Sidney argues that in marrying Anjou Elizabeth would inevitably be ruled by him and might even lose her kingdom. Much of his letter concerns the potentially disastrous political consequences of Anjou's rule. While Philanax envisages only the private, familial consequences of Basilius's decision, the plot of the *Old Arcadia* develops not only private but public consequences, and the latter play out in fantasy the disasters that Sidney foresaw in Elizabeth's marriage. Basilius's love for the amazon Cleophila arouses resentment in the people, especially since she is a foreigner who has gained excessive power, and the resentment explodes into a violent rebellion. By the end of the *Old Arcadia*, rebelliousness has spread to the nobles, who are themselves on the verge of civil war, and the threat of foreign invasion is overcome only by Euarchus's virtuous refusal to take advantage of the disorder in the dukedom.[2]

Although they reveal the intensity of Sidney's preoccupation with recent court experience, the echoes of the Anjou affair within the *Old Arcadia* also attest to his liberation from the constrictions of courtiership both as an individual and as a poet. The allusions are not of the kind that could have been presented in an entertainment for the queen. Given their obliqueness, however, and the intimacy of his audience, Sidney must have felt sufficiently safe to indulge himself. And so he did. The treatment of Basilius is harshly satirical throughout and culminates in the character's acknowledgment – to himself alone – that of all the misdeeds committed 'his own fault had been the greatest' (416.19–20). At the core of the *Old Arcadia*, then, is an act of imaginative displacement that enabled Sidney to achieve a vicarious revenge. The folly of the duke, in failing to heed the good advice of his counsellor, precipitates the kind of social and political disorder that Sidney himself had warned Elizabeth against in the letter about Anjou.

In part, this oblique fictionalizing of current court issues can be understood as a social game, in which Sidney can be seen titillating his courtly audience with glimpses of court affairs, disguising his commentary to exclude genuine outsiders, and complicating it sufficiently to escape censorship. Sidney's self-involvement in the *Old Arcadia*, however, seems at times much deeper and less conscious than one would expect of such a game, the emotional pressure behind the fiction more intense. Sidney himself seems to have sensed these underlying imaginative pressures, for in his letter to his sister he says that his head was so full of 'fancies' that it would have become a 'monster' if they had not been 'delivered' by his writing (3.19–20); in *A Defence of Poetry*, too, he refers to the writing process as one in which he was 'overmastered by some thoughts' and 'yielded an inky tribute unto them' (111.24–5). The urgency of the emotional involvement suggested by these comments tends to confirm the view that conflicts within Sidney surfaced to make the ending of the *Old Arcadia* unsettling and unresolved.[3]

The final moments of the *Old Arcadia* are problematic in a number of ways, but chiefly through their dissonance in tone and obscurity in moral judgment. Basilius's 'resurrection,' which restores harmony to Arcadia and might have been accompanied with a sense of joy and wonder, is remarkably understated, the marvel receiving less attention than the history of the potion that caused his apparent death. The duke's recognition of his own folly, moreover, as previously discussed, is treated with sardonic wit, as is his reconciliation with Gynecia, which depends upon discreet silences on both sides. The most important problem, however, lies in the treatment of the princes, whose amazing good fortunes are passed over in silence, receiving no comment either from them or from the narrator.

Throughout most of the narrative Sidney's presentation of the princes, although complex, is controlled. In large part this is achieved through the omniscient and intrusive narrator, whose attitude becomes increasingly judgmental as the narrative becomes more serious; in broad terms, the tone moves from sympathetic identification to sympathetic mockery to objective judgment. The presentation becomes seriously problematic only when the princes are imprisoned. From this point on all irony disappears and they are presented as epic heroes. The sentence that introduces the princes in their imprisonment sets the tone for the entire episode: 'In the mean time Pyrocles and Musidorus were recommended to so strong a guard as they might well see it was meant they should pay no less price than their lives for the getting out of that place, which they like men indeed (fortifying courage with the true rampire of patience) did so endure as they did rather appear governors of necessity than servants to fortune; the whole sum of their thoughts resting upon the safety of their ladies and their care one for the other, wherein (if at all) their hearts did seem to receive some softness' (370.21–9). In prison, the princes exemplify courage and patience towards their own suffering; they protect the women, even Gynecia; and they are moved to grief only when contemplating each other's plight.

The problem with this heroic fortitude is that it carries no recognition of the princes's complicity in their own undoing – not on the part of the princes, the narrator, or, apparently, the author himself. Reflecting upon Pyrocles' life and his own as he prepares to meet death, Musidorus asserts, 'We have lived, and have lived to be good to ourselves and others' (371.21–2). Musidorus has forgotten much about recent events, it seems, not the least of which is his narrow escape from an act of rape against

Pamela. In the same scene, discussing with Musidorus whether they will remember their friendship after death, Pyrocles argues affirmatively that they will unite their friendship and themselves 'in that high and heavenly love of the unquenchable light' (373.20–1). This 'high and heavenly love' is not what drove Pyrocles to disguise himself as a woman so that he could prove himself a man in the pursuit of Philoclea. Viewed in relation to their escapades, in short, the reactions of the two princes in book 5 seem more like heroic posturing than heroism, for they face their own and the princesses' deaths with no recognition of the moral complexity of their own positions. It is hard to escape the conclusion, so persuasively argued by McCoy and others, that Sidney's failure to hold his princes accountable has much to do with his own feelings of resentment against authority.

The implications of this failure of accountability, however, go beyond Sidney's resentments against political authority. Sidney's lapse at the end of the *Old Arcadia*, if we may call it that, calls in question his commitment to another kind of authority, that of poetry itself. A short time later, when he came to rationalize the value of poetry, Sidney celebrated above all its role as a moral teacher. In contrast to history, which was captive to a foolish world and therefore forced to show evil deeds being rewarded, poetry could show the workings of justice. This commitment to a doctrine of poetic justice is so central in Sidney's later thought, and in his practice in the revised *Arcadia*, that it seems odd for him to disregard it in the treatment of the princes. Yet the apparent hastiness with which the ending has been written suggests an almost equally odd indifference to the narrative outcome. Duncan-Jones has suggested that Sidney's 'many preoccupations during 1581' may have distracted him from his writing;[4] if so, his only hint of that fact is to be found in the narrator's concluding remarks about his 'dulled' pen and his unwillingness to continue the narrative (417.25). Whether caused by distraction or mere fatigue, the hasty ending of the *Old Arcadia* raises questions about the strength of Sidney's commitment to his work.

A revealing glimpse into Sidney's attitude towards the *Old Arcadia* is provided in his letter to his sister, which presumably accompanied his gift of the completed manuscript. The letter was printed in the 1590 and 1593 editions of the *New Arcadia*, and in all the later folios. Although it clearly belongs with the *Old Arcadia*, it does not appear in any of the manuscripts of that work. There is no evidence to suggest, therefore, that the letter circulated with the manuscript or that Sidney intended it as anything more than a personal and private communication. In its original context, then, the persona within the letter is an unusually intimate one, in which

Sidney represents himself as poet to his deepest sympathizer, his sister. As such, it offers us our most revealing glimpse of the private stance that Sidney took towards any of his literary works.[5]

Superficially, the letter resembles many of the dedicatory prefaces of the period. Sidney praises his sister and belittles his own efforts. The role of disparager of one's work is familiar and conventional, especially in an aristocratic and courtly context, with its demands of *sprezzatura*. The relative intimacy of the statement, however, suggests that the role was more than merely rhetorical. The language of self-mockery that Sidney uses, moreover, is idiosyncratic and highly volatile, suggestive of complex and divided emotions. The paradoxes and rapidly shifting metaphors, especially, suggest Sidney's unstable relation to his work and his strong sense of social displacement in his new authorial role. He begins by presenting the gift, oxymoronically, as 'this idle work of mine.' It is 'idle' because it is trivial, but also because it is a product of the author's own idleness. Its 'work,' the passage continues, is like that of the spider's web, elaborate but itself the result of domestic idleness and 'fitter to be swept away than worn to any other purpose.' He admits ownership – the idle work is 'mine' – but begrudgingly; he is 'loath' to be the father and would like to abandon it. He also sees himself as a bizarre mother, having delivered from his 'young head' what might otherwise have 'grown a monster.' And, finally, he becomes a kind of haberdasher, producing 'no better stuff' than 'glasses or feathers' (3).

In one sense this rhetorical exuberance seems playful and self-indulgent, especially since the self-mockery does not hide entirely a sly affection for the work it demeans (he hopes the work will be 'pardoned' and perchance even 'made much of' by his sister and her friends). The word-play might be explained away, then, as courtly *sprezzatura*. Self-mockery may be playful, however, and at the same time self-expressive.[6] The metaphors themselves suggest a strong sense of social displacement. Through them Sidney represents his identity in a variety of socially demeaning terms: of idleness, of reluctant paternity, of maternity, of giving birth to a deformed child, of making and selling ornaments. The emotional complexity of the whole is suggested by the final sentence, in which he mocks the work as 'no better stuff than, as in a haberdasher's shop, glasses or feathers,' yet then prays out of exceeding love for his sister that she 'may long live to be a principal ornament to the family of the Sidneys.' He produces ornaments that degrade the family through association with the haberdasher's shop; she, however, is herself an ornament to the family and therefore worthy of praise.

Although the persona's attitude towards his 'work' is expressed in volatile images of self-mockery, his attitude towards his sister is strongly and stably affectionate throughout. As Duncan-Jones has observed, both Philip and Mary were 'pregnant' at this time – he with the *Old Arcadia*, she with her first child.[7] Sidney's elaborate metaphors of paternity, maternity, and deformed births, therefore, may well derive from his concern for her condition and, ironically, for his own. If so, the comparison is very much in her favour. She was engaged in important woman's work, carrying on the family line; her 'idle times' were fully justifiable. He, in contrast, was idling away his time in a socially degrading activity and giving birth only to the deformities of a disordered mind.

Sidney's failure to achieve satisfactory closure to his narrative, then, may well express not only inner conflict surrounding his attitude towards authority and his role at court, as McCoy and others have argued, but, as part of the same syndrome, an underlying lack of commitment to his 'idle work' itself and the new authorial role it implied. Although one side of Sidney clearly revelled in his fiction, it is important not to misread his disclaimers of its worth as no more than the rhetorical gestures expected of a courtly author. The letter to his sister is echoed in a letter to his brother Robert, in which he refers to the *Old Arcadia* as his 'toyful book,' alludes sardonically to the political inaction at court, and strikes a theatrical pose of world-weariness: 'I write this to yow as one, that for my selfe have given over the delight in the world but wish to yow as much if not more then to my selfe.'[8] If in some sense the self-mockery is a social mask, it is a mask that Sidney chose to wear in private as well as in public, a mask that expressed his allegiance to the social role of public action for which he had been so carefully prepared.

The problem posed by the *Old Arcadia* was not only that it placed Sidney in the equivocal role of poet, but that his withdrawal from the world of the court took away what little justification there was for that role. As a courtier, Sidney had also played a writer's role, in devising *The Lady of May*, participating in court entertainments, and advising the queen. Although not the same as action, the use of words in that courtly context had its own kind of validity. With characteristic irony, Sidney implied as much when, in a letter reporting to Leicester about his sister's recovery from childbirth, he joked about a case of laryngitis that was keeping him from court. He was ' "so full of cold," ' he said, ' "as one cannot hear me speak: which is the cause keeps me yet from the court, since my only service is speech, and that is stopped." '[9] In this version of the courtier's role, speech is a poor substitute for action but better than silence. Courtly language of various kinds could be justified, as it was by Castiglione, as a means of ingratiating oneself with the prince in order to serve the state. Court poetry, then, could be an instrument of policy, in both a public and private sense. In withdrawing from court, Sidney may have freed himself from the constraints of a courtly role that had proved fruitless and demeaning, but he also lost any possible vocational justification for his poetry. It had now become merely a means of filling in idle hours and entertaining ladies. This is the trivial role to which Puttenham assigns poetry, when he associates it with 'idle Courtiers' who 'for their private recreation ... make now and then ditties of pleasure.'[10]

Sidney's emphasis upon his idleness is especially ironic in the context of the *Old Arcadia*, for the genre in which he chose to spend his idle time, that of pastoral romance, is itself associated with idleness. In courtly pastoral, as Louis Adrian Montrose has shown, the otium of the shepherd was peculiarly associated with the leisure of the gentlemen, one of the essential marks of which, in the words of Sir Thomas Smith, was the ability to ' "live idly and without manuall labour." '[11] Courtier-poets and shepherds, then, had one important thing in common: the time to write poetry. Sidney's resistance to poetry is in part a resistance to this gentlemanly idleness, not out of sympathy with real workers, real shepherds, but out of commitment to an aristocratic notion of service; with an almost Hotspurian energy, he seeks work – courtly work of the kind for which he was trained and that would make him an ornament to the Sidney family. Indulging in a characteristically introspective play of wit, Sidney translated his own unwelcome idleness into a fictional world entirely absorbed by idleness – a pastoral romance in which the courtly world is in retreat, in which shepherds while away the hours in song, and in which his own persona, Philisides, lives in unhappy exile.

In the role of Philisides, Sidney created a self-conscious and sophisticated way of placing himself in relation to his text. Self-representation is conventional in Renaissance pastoral, but the choice of a convention and the manner of developing it are none the less self-expressive. For a writer like Sidney, as we have seen in the letters to Languet, playing a conventional role was a means of exploring and defining the self. Sidney was attracted to pastoral self-representation, presumably, in part because the convention of the pastoral retreat enabled him to fictionalize his own immediate predicament. With its mixture of fiction and fact, engagement and detachment, self-mockery and self-assertion, the role of Philisides tells us much not only about Sidney at this crucial stage in his career but about the process of representing a self in a profoundly imitative culture.

The need to vent frustration in the form of personal fictions is one that
Sidney himself recognized, as we have seen, when he expressed the wish
to justify himself to Languet by means of a 'tragic scene'; for Sidney, the
fictionalizing of the self clearly met a deeply personal need. The gesture
was not simply personal, however, as we have seen in chapter 1, but cultural as well, a manifestation of the imitative process taught in the
schools, by which self-analysis and self-creation take place through role-
playing, through placing oneself imaginatively within the experience of a
fictitious other. In the culture of the court, as described by writers such as
Castiglione, this impulse could be turned to useful political ends – the
courtier shaping himself into a work of art in order to move the prince to
virtue. In exile at Wilton, Sidney was left with an imitative impulse no
longer grounded in service to the prince. He had attempted to play the
role of courtier in person and, on specific occasions, through courtly
spectacle and advice to the queen. Yet he had failed. The role of Philisides gave him an opportunity to explore that failure, and in so doing, to
turn it to rueful laughter for the entertainment of an appreciative inner
circle of family and friends.

The creation of a fictitious role involved Sidney in a very specific act of
literary imitation, for authorial personas appear in both of his major
sources, Montemayor's *Diana* and Sannazaro's *Arcadia*.[12] Comparison
with these sources, therefore, particularly with Sannazaro's *Arcadia*, provides an illuminating context for Sidney's self-representation. Although
Sidney's treatment of his persona is in many ways remarkably close to
Sannazaro's, it differs from that of both sources in one striking respect.
Both Sannazaro and Montemayor identify themselves with their narrators, who, as protagonists, stand at the very centre of their narratives. In
these works, the narrative as a whole becomes fictional autobiography,
the plot implicitly asserting the importance of the authorial self. In the
Old Arcadia, however, Sidney's narrator is carefully dissociated from the
author. Although the narrator is given a voice as commentator, he is
never identified and plays no role in the narrative. In what might have
seemed a stroke of wit to knowledgeable readers, Sidney placed his own
self-image off-centre, identifying himself with a figure so unimportant
that he is restricted almost entirely to occasional appearances in the
eclogues. If the creation of any self-representation necessarily involves an
act of self-assertion, the creation of Philisides might be said to unite self-
assertion with self-mockery. A similar combination of arrogance and
humility seems to underlie the gift of a whip to Queen Elizabeth.

Sidney's departure from the major sources takes on particular significance if we consider the treatment of persona in the source that most clearly determined his creation of Philisides, Sannazaro's *Arcadia*. Sannazaro not only assumes the role of Sincero, the narrator of his work, but that of another character within the work, the shepherd Ergasto. Both Sincero and Ergasto suffer from unrequited love and are provided with distinctive personal histories. In creating Philisides, Sidney fused both roles. From Ergasto, he took only the opening image, in which Ergasto lies in a state of melancholy under a tree; from the narrator, Sincero, he developed the important autobiographical episode in the eclogues to Book IV. What he omitted from both roles, however, is in some ways more revealing than what he borrowed.

Central to Sincero's role as narrator is his poetic self-consciousness. The *Arcadia* begins with a prologue that asserts the superiority of the world of nature to that of civilization and defends the author's choice of the pastoral mode: 'For surely it is a better thing to till a small field well, than to let the large piece wretchedly grow wild through ill government' (30). Implicit in this justification is the familiar Virgilian theme of progressing from pastoral to higher modes, a theme that recurs throughout the work in literary allusions and in the actions and comments of Sincero and other characters. In anticipation of one of Sincero's songs, for example, the shepherd Carino prophesies that it will be a prelude to future songs 'in loftier vein' that may lead to 'eternal fame' (74–5). The shepherd Ergasto, Sannazaro's other persona, voices a similar aspiration while mourning the death of his mother: he vows to immortalize her memory in poetry if it lies within his power (132–3). Through both of his self-representations, then, Sannazaro embodies his commitment to the role of poet and his aspirations towards a mode of expression higher than the pastoral. In doing so he gestures towards the Virgilian model that Spenser was to probe more fully in the 'October' eclogue of *The Shephearde's Calender*. In that work Piers resists Cuddie's efforts to persuade him to lift himself out of the dust and 'sing of bloody Mars, of wars, of giusts' (ll.38–9) because the heroes and patrons of the past are long dead and his own wings are not strong enough.[13]

Like Sannazaro and Spenser, Sidney alludes to the Virgilian model of the poet's career, but so briefly and dismissively that the allusion barely registers. He neither aspires towards the model nor attempts to deal with the problems it raises in a contemporary setting. Sidney's narrator makes only two pronouncements that bear upon his role as poet, and, significantly, they frame the narrative as a whole. In the first, the narrator introduces Pyrocles and Musidorus but asserts his inadequacy to relate their previous exploits: 'what valiant acts they did, passing in one year's space through the lesser Asia, Syria, and Egypt, how many ladies they defended from wrongs, and disinherited persons restored to their rights, it is a work for a higher style than mine' (11.3–6). In the second, which occurs in the final paragraph of the work, the narrator indicates his exhaustion with his story and leaves any continuation of it to 'some other spirit to exercise his pen in that wherewith mine is already dulled' (417.24–5).

In Sidney's *Arcadia*, unlike Sannazaro's, the pastoral mode is not defended in its own terms, as the tilling of a small field well; instead, it is merely dissociated from a work in a 'higher style,' presumbably epic, that is worthy of heroic exploits. The exhaustion with which the narrator concludes the narrative, moreover, closes off any further development, pastoral or epic, as a writer. Sannazaro's narrator chooses a humble style because it is appropriate to this stage in his development, and he defends the choice. Sidney's narrator, however, is silent on any rationale for his choice of style and merely asserts his incapacity for a higher one. Sannazaro's narrator looks forward to his development from a humble to a higher style; Sidney's, exhausted, leaves further adventures to 'some other spirit.' Sannazaro adopts the Virgilian model of the literary career; Spenser treats it as a serious but problematic goal; Sidney dismisses it altogether.

In view of Sidney's later revision of the *Old Arcadia*, in which he was to recount adventures of the kind he alludes to here, and in a 'higher style,' it is remarkable that he does not follow Sannazaro's lead and gesture towards his own poetic ambitions. From the vantage point of the *New Arcadia*, the *Old Arcadia* fulfils Sannazaro's own prescription: it is a work written in a humble style, appropriate to the beginning stage of Sidney's own development as a poet, and it paves the way for a more ambitious work in an epic mode. Such a development was clearly in Sidney's mind, since it is implicit in the narrator's comments about a 'higher style.' Paradoxically, however, he uses his narrator to foreclose rather than forecast later developments. He declines, in short, to present the act of writing as a present or even potential vocation. This is in sharp contrast to his use of persona later in *Astrophil and Stella*, where Astrophil, who is both author and character, spends much of his time exploring his role as a poet. Sidney's attempt to separate himself from his narrator in the *Old Arcadia* parallels the less explicit attempts to distance himself from his work apparent in its ending and in the dedicatory letter to his sister.

In restricting himself to a single persona, one excluded from the narrator's role, Sidney thus dissociates his own *Arcadia* from Sannazaro's and his authorial self from his fiction. Although he models the character of Philisides on Sannazaro's originals, moreover, he develops the self-representation in his own distinctive manner. He adds, for example, several features not present in Sannazaro's treatment of either Sincero or Ergasto: narrative clarity and continuity in the presentation of the character, a sense of mystery and suspense, and a consistent tone of playful mockery. Most significantly, by creating his own group of Arcadian shepherds in the eclogues and by adding the romance plot of Basilius and the princes, Sidney places his persona in a vastly enlarged fictional context, thus complicating considerably the representation of his own identity. To understand Philisides, one must see him in relation to the whole fictional world of which he is a part.

Philisides' most significant role in the *Old Arcadia* is as a singer of songs in the eclogues that divide each of the five books. In the first group of eclogues, he joins Geron in a quarrelsome debate; in the second, he sings a song to his echo; in the third, he sings the beast fable he learned on the banks of the Ister from Hubert Languet; in the fourth, he recounts the early years of his life, describes his dream-vision of the beginning of his love for Mira, and then presents the elegiacs he sent to her upon his decision to leave her forever. He appears or is alluded to briefly elsewhere in the work as well. In Book II, he matches Dorus's song of joyful love with his own song of grief, immediately after which, in his only display of action in the narrative, he 'valiantly' (126.16) seconds Dorus in battling the rebels. In Book III, the song that passes through Pyrocles' mind as he consummates his love with Philoclea is one composed by Philisides. In Book V, in the final paragraph of the work, Philisides is alluded to as one of the many characters who await the continuation of their stories by 'some other spirit' (417.24). The very insignificance of his brief entries into the romance plot adds to the irony with which the character is consistently portrayed.

As Sidney develops it, the process of self-representation necessarily involves an implied commentary on traditional fictional genres and roles.[14] To refuse the Virgilian model for his authorial persona, as we have seen, is to dissociate the self from one of the most potent and affirmative images created by the pastoral: the self as aspiring young poet. To represent the self as an exiled courtier playing the role of shepherd, as we shall see, is to challenge in a peculiarly immediate way the relevance of the pastoral to his own condition. Both Sidney and Philisides share the same predicament: they are courtiers in exile, attempting to come to terms with their condition by giving voice to their complaints. The question implied by that gesture of protest is whether the pastoral retreat provides answers to the existential pressures that make it necessary.

In his treatment of Philisides, Sidney not only subordinates his story to that of the main plot, restricting his role essentially to the ecologues; he also subjects the role to a radically different narrative development. As modes of fiction, the main plot and that of Philisides, if we can call it a plot, are mirror-images. In its outlines, the main plot is that of conventional tragicomedy, proceeding from error through resulting complications to ultimate resolution and renewal. As readers, we proceed from an initial action, Basilius's withdrawal from court, to its consequences, following a strict causal chain. Philisides' plot, in contrast, begins with a state of paralysis and, through the repeated expression of grief, gradually reveals its hidden cause. In this plot, instead of tracing an action to its conclusion, we trace a conclusion back to its original action; the narrative line is essentially lyrical, the unfolding of grief enabling the reader finally to penetrate its secret cause. In this sense the self-exploration that Sidney himself undertakes in the creation of his persona, the searching for the cause of his misery, is parallel to the exploration of the reader, who discovers at each stage in the ecologues more clues to the secret cause of Philisides' despair. Such a narrative method would have had obvious appeal for an intimate courtly audience, one aware of Philisides' identity and able to connect the persona to the person at each stage in the process.

Sidney's first and most compelling image of Philisides comes directly from Sannazaro, who opens his work with a description of himself as the melancholy Ergasto: 'Ergasto alone was lying, without saying or doing anything, at the foot of a tree forgetful of himself and of his flocks, not otherwise than if he had been a stock or stone, although in former days he was wont to be pleasant and gracious in greater degree than the other shepherds' (31). Sidney withholds the appearance of Philisides until the first ecologues, when he is singled out by the old shepherd Geron, who notices him lying 'upon the ground at the foot of a cypress tree, leaning upon his elbow, with so deep a melancholy that his senses carried to his mind no delight from any of their objects' (71.33–5).

Although Sidney took the image from Sannazaro, it clearly projects in the form of fantasy one role in which he presented himself at the time. In the previously cited letter to his brother, Robert, as we have seen, Sidney takes a similar rhetorical stance towards his own life. 'I write this to yow as one, that for my selfe have given over the delight in the world but wish to yow as much if not more then to my selfe.' A few sentences later he alludes to his 'toyful book,' the *Old Arcadia*, which he hopes to send by

February. The letter as a whole provides a useful gloss on the poetic debate between Philisides and Geron, for in writing to his brother Sidney is able to play both roles, that of elderly mentor giving advice on studies abroad and, momentarily, that of melancholiac, lamenting that life has passed him by. As he contemplated the foreign travels of his younger brother, Sidney must have been struck by the contrast between his own youthful promise at that stage in his life and his current situation. The hint of self-pity in the expression of melancholy suggests that Philisides' explosive attack upon Geron, which seems churlish in context, enabled Sidney to distance himself ironically from a deep-seated emotion. 'In these latter months of 1580,' observes Malcolm W. Wallace, 'Sidney's inaction and consequent gloom are reflected in all we hear of him.'[15]

Although Sidney takes his opening image of Philisides directly from Sannazaro's depiction of Ergasto, he replaces Ergasto's song, which identifies unrequited love as the source of his melancholy, with Sannazaro's eighth eclogue, a poetic argument between two shepherds, Eugenio and Clonico. Sidney's adaptation of Sannazaro's singing match, although very close to the original, highlights the nature of his identification with Philisides. Both singing matches feature attempts by sympathetic shepherds to persuade their companions to put aside a love that is destroying them. Both argue that women are not to be trusted (Sidney translates three lines to that effect directly from Sannazaro), that their love is self-destructive, and that activity will help rid them of passion. Sidney changes his model by intensifying the debate, by adding Philisides' intemperate attack on old men, and by amplifying the arguments against love.

Although conventional, Geron's arguments against love echo themes found in Languet's letters to Sidney during the years immediately preceding the *Old Arcadia*.[16] As we have seen in chapter 1, Languet's charges of idleness and inconstancy caused a crisis in his relationship with Sidney shortly after he assumed the role of courtier in 1575. Like Languet, Geron urges Philisides to strive for a 'constant temper,' a challenge that Philisides meets wittily by a *carpe diem* defence of inconstancy: 'Time shall in one my life and sorrows end, / And me perchance your constant temper lend' (72.22–3). Idleness too figures in Geron's arguments, and appears within a cluster of images that links Philisides' melancholy to Sidney's own ambivalence about his writing. Geron first dismisses passion as a 'toy,' the word that Sidney uses repeatedly of the *Old Arcadia* itself, and then within a few lines urges Philisides to 'let thy mind with better books be tamed.' He continues with a list of 'sports' that might prove diverting, a list that becomes increasingly associated with the arts of rule, concluding with, 'Cherish the hives of wisely painful bees; / Let special care upon thy flock be stayed; / Such active mind but seldom passion sees' (75.14–33). The need to keep a constant temper and, even while not actively employed at court, to maintain an active mind, devoted to preparation for eventual power, is a theme that runs throughout the correspondence with Languet.[17] Philisides' outburst against Geron – 'O gods, how long this old fool hath annoyed / My wearied ears!' (74.1–2) – may be the result of considerable frustration at the ineffectuality of such advice.

Philisides' stormy passion is presented ironically, however, suggesting that self-representation enabled Sidney to achieve a detachment that could escape him in daily life. As Rudenstine suggests, in the stand-off between Philisides and Geron both characters are 'judged, held in witty antithesis by Sidney's special handling of the pastoral-eclogue form.'[18] In view of Sidney's professed attraction to the idea of contemplative withdrawal, it is tempting to follow Rudenstine and read the argument between Geron and Philisides as the projection of an internalized debate between the private life of contemplative withdrawal and the public life of civic action. To extend the terms of the argument in this way, however, is to blur the focus on the central issue of love. To see the episode as a debate, moreover, is to distort its effect, for Philisides meets each of Geron's arguments with churlish disdain and finally breaks off by asserting that he has not even paid attention: 'Hath any man heard what this old man said? / Truly, not I who did my thoughts engage / Where all my pains one look of hers hath paid' (75.34–6). While Geron has been arguing, Philisides has been fixated on thoughts of his beloved. What one senses in the personal allusiveness of this passage is not so much an internal debate on Sidney's part but an ironic displacement of guilt for not living up to the social ideals that he himself had internalized.

One reason for the ineffectuality of Geron's advice lies in another of Sidney's additions to Sannazaro, one that, if taken seriously, would reduce Philisides' responsibility for his plight: his conviction of the hopelessness of his love. When Geron observes, quite reasonably, that Philisides' condition might change for the better – 'The stars thy state, fortune may change thy hap' – he is answered by a curiously hyperbolic assertion of the beloved's power:

> If fortune's lap became my dwelling place,
> And all the stars conspired to my good,
> Still were I one, this still should be my case,

Ruin's relic, care's web, and sorrow's food;
Since she, fair fierce, to such a state me calls,
Whose wit the stars, whose fortune fortune thralls.   (72.28–34)

Geron's answer to this is an antifeminist harangue, a few lines of which
are taken from Sannazaro. The harangue concludes with an imitation of
the following lines from Sidney's friend Edward Dyer: 'O frail unconstant
kind, and safe in trust to no man, / No women angels be, and lo, my mistress is a woman.'[19] Geron's version drops the contrast with angels but
adds an even more demeaning charge of natural servitude: 'A fickle sex,
and true in trust to no man; / A servant sex, soon proud if they be
coyed; / And to conclude, thy mistress is a woman' (73.28–30). Histor, up
to this point an auditor in the debate, identifies the lines as those once
used by the 'loveliest shepherd ... / That erst I knew' and excuses them as
lines uttered when the speaker was 'forced with rage' (73.31–4).

The hyperbolic assertion of the beloved's power, which places her in
control of both fortune and the stars; the jarringly reductive nature of
Geron's response, with its insistence that 'thy mistress is a woman'; and
the allusion to Dyer, one of Sidney's closest friends, all complicate the
picture of unrequited love that Sidney takes from Sannazaro's eighth
eclogue. Taken together, they provide the first hint that Philisides' desperate love might allude to Sidney's relationship with the queen. At the
beginning of the first eclogues, the narrator invites such suspicions of
courtly allegory by noting that the foreign participants are not all shepherds: Arcadia 'drew divers strangers, as well of great as of mean houses,
especially such whom inward melancholies made weary of the world's
eyes' (56.20–2). Even more provocatively, he notes that the eclogues
sometimes contain 'under hidden forms ... such matters as otherwise
[are] not fit for their delivery' (56.8–9), a conception of pastoral that Sidney develops further in *A Defence of Poetry*, where he defines the genre in
such a way that its subject-matter is essentially political and courtly. The
pastoral can show, he claims in the *Defence*, 'the misery of people under
hard lords or ravening soldiers,' and 'sometimes, under the pretty tales of
wolves and sheep, can include the whole considerations of wrong-doing
and patience' (94.36–95.5). Conventional throughout the Renaissance,
this view of pastoral as a mode of oblique social criticism is articulated by
Puttenham in *The Arte of English Poesie* and exploited by Spenser in *The
Shephearde's Calender*.[20]

The link between Philisides' 'fair fierce' and Elizabeth is strengthened
if one recalls that Sidney had in effect created the role of Philisides as

early as the Accession Day tournament of 1577, when he made his first appearance as a tilter at Whitehall. Echoes of this initiatory tournament appear in both the *Old* and *New Arcadia*. Although the details of the occasion are sketchy, the poems that Sidney composed for it suggest that he entered the tiltyard in the role of 'Philisides, the Shepherd good and true,' accompanied by rustical music and ploughmen, one of whom sang a song describing how Philisides had urged the husbandman Menalcha to join him to celebrate the 'chief of Cupides Sabaothe daies, / The Wake of those that honour Samos Ile.' This song was followed by another, in which the queen was praised as 'a roiall Saincte' of this 'Sabaothe day.'[21] In the former song Philisides is presented as in love with 'Mira' – he sings in 'praise of Mirrhaes hue' – whose name recurs as that of the mysterious beloved in the *Old Arcadia*. The allusion to England as 'Samos Ile' also reappears in the *Old Arcadia*, for Samothea is identified as Philisides' native land. In striking contrast to the *Old Arcadia*, however, the songs of this early Philisides are joyous, and the pose of shepherd conveys none of the melancholy that brings the later Philisides to despair.

The transition between the role of joyous shepherd played at the tilt in 1577 and that of melancholy shepherd in the *Old Arcadia* might be said to occur in *The Lady of May*, which Sidney composed for the queen's visit to Wanstead in May 1578. In this work, which features a competition between a shepherd and a forester, the shepherd, Dorcas, describes 'courtiers' he has seen, who 'under our field in bushes make their woeful complaints, some of the greatness of their mistress' estate, which dazzled their eyes and yet burned their hearts; some of the extremity of her beauty mixed with extreme cruelty; some of her too much wit, which made all their loving labours folly.' The object of this miserable passion, although expressed in even less hyperbolic imagery than that of Philisides, is unmistakably the queen. 'O how often,' Dorcas continues, 'have I heard one name sound in many mouths, making our vales witnesses of their doleful agonies! So that with long lost labour, finding their thoughts bare no other wool but despair, of young courtiers they grew old shepherds' (*LM*, 28.18–26). In *The Lady of May*, then, a work that leaves no doubt about the royal identity of the cruel beloved, Sidney anticipates the role he himself was to play in the *Old Arcadia*: that of a courtier in exile among shepherds, complaining in despair of the beauty, cruelty, wit, and power of the woman who has turned all his 'loving labours' to 'folly.'

The intrusion of Dyer's lines into Geron's verse in the *Old Arcadia* heightens the aura of political innuendo, for in the early 1570s Dyer himself had experienced the queen's displeasure for a prolonged period, and, as Ralph M. Sargent suggests, the poem in which the lines appear may well have been composed in response to that frustration. In a remarkable letter of 1572 to Christopher Hatton, advising him on how to play the role of courtier, Dyer had noted ruefully the paradox in her position as female monarch. 'First of all,' he advised Hatton, 'you must consider with whom you have to deale, and what wee be towards her, who though she does descend very much in her Sex as a woman, yet wee may not forgett her Place, and the nature of it as our Sovraigne.' The notion that 'thy mistress is a woman' could thus be used to debunk not only the conventional Petrarchan idealization of woman as goddess but the sovereignty of the queen. Dyer was on especially close terms with Sidney during the period in which he was composing the *Old Arcadia* and seems also to have withdrawn from court. Although the evidence is inconclusive, Sargent suggests that Dyer may even be represented in the *Old Arcadia* by the figure of Coredens.[22]

Identifying allusions of this kind in a work like the *Old Arcadia* is almost always problematic. If they were to be effective in literary terms and at the same time avoid the dangers of censorship, the allusions had to be oblique, to tantalize readers with a secret knowledge just beyond their grasp.[23] When the language of allegorical titillation is Petrarchan, moreover, as it almost invariably is when the queen is the presumed target, the possibilities of misinterpretation are magnified. In the context of Elizabeth's court, the very notion of 'courtship' was inevitably ambiguous, since the role of courtiers was to 'court' a virgin queen.[24] When an Elizabethan courtier describes a woman in Petrarchan terms as a queen or a goddess, then, it is sometimes difficult to know whether he is idealizing a woman or humanizing the queen. Although scholars generally agree that Philisides' complaints must allude to a particular woman, the identity of that woman remains in doubt. Three possibilities have emerged most often: Sidney's sister, Lady Mary; an unidentifiable court lady attending upon the queen; or the queen herself. As is already apparent, I am convinced by the arguments that identify Mira with the queen. On the negative side, I find the evidence linking Mira with an unidentified court lady or, especially, with Lady Mary, slim and unconvincing. On the positive, I am impressed by the connection between Mira and the queen in the poems of the 1577 tilt; by the correspondence between the role of Philisides and that of the courtier-shepherds in *The Lady of May*, who sound the 'one name' of the queen in their complaints; by the general conformity of Mira's attributes in the *Old Arcadia* with those of the queen; by the close parallels between Philisides' account of his relationship with Mira in the *Old Arcadia* and Sidney's relationship with the queen; and by the identification of Mira in the *New Arcadia* with Helen of Corinth, who represents one aspect of the queen.[25]

Philisides' role as forsaken lover is defined not merely in relation to the world outside the *Old Arcadia* but in relation to the world within. His plight is juxtaposed throughout with the developing events of the main plot. In Book I Philisides' frustrated passion runs comically parallel to that of the princes, with whom he is aligned indirectly throughout the work. All are strangers in Arcadia, and all experience what seems to be a desperate love. When Pyrocles first reveals his love to Musidorus, his friend responds in terms that resemble those of Geron: he belittles women, reminds him of his duty to himself, urges him to use reason against passion, gives advice on how to overcome love by turning the mind and body to other activities, and inveighs against solitariness and idleness, which have taken the place of 'the true exercise of virtue' (18.33–4). The chief difference between the princes and Philisides as lovers, and the source of continuing reciprocal ironies, is that, while Philisides is paralysed by his love, the princes commit themselves immediately to plans for sexual consummation. Pyrocles desires nothing 'more than fully to prove myself a man in this enterprise' (22.35–23.1). The difference is between equally comical forms of folly – the one desperately contemplative, the other hopefully active.

Philisides' hopelessness distinguishes him not only from the princes but from every other character in both the narrative and the eclogues. Although sometimes given to fits of despair, all of the characters of the main plot are actively engaged in the pursuit of their own ends, which are usually romantic. Even those not entangled in the main plot, such as Plangus or Strephon and Klaius, do not experience the depth of Philisides' despair. Plangus at least has a year in which to save Artaxia, and Strephon and Klaius live in the hope that Urania will return to them. In addition, Philisides is not only disconnected from the main plot but from plotting altogether. His is a life of stasis. His only deliberate action is mental action, the endless and obsessive reiteration of his hopelessness, and even that is only forthcoming when he is asked to contribute to the eclogues. As Philisides, in short, Sidney plays the role of a figure not only alienated from his own court, from which he is exiled, but from both the community of shepherds and the court of Basilius. In the midst of a world of complex passions and narrative intrigues, Philisides lives utterly estranged, venting his grief in essentially private, lyrical complaint.

Philisides' role in Book II mainly elaborates this melancholy solipsism, contrasting its static sense of futility with the increasingly hopeful prospects of the princes. In the narrative, he appears briefly in the company of Dorus, whose song celebrating the promise of Pamela's affection provokes a 'doleful' response that turns each of Dorus's lines against itself:

> *Dorus*: Feed on my sheep; my charge, my comfort, feed;
> With sun's approach your pasture fertile grows,
> O only sun that such a fruit can breed.
>
> ...
>
> *Philisides*: Leave off my sheep: it is no time to feed,
> My sun is gone, your pasture barren grows,
> O cruel sun, thy hate this harm doth breed.   (*OA*, 124.31–125.18)

While Dorus projects his feelings upon nature, Philisides projects his upon those of Dorus, his exact reversal of each of Dorus's images embodying wittily the churlish and obsessive quality of his self-absorption. His mind has become a mirror that reflects only its own melancholy image.

Before his song is completely finished, however, Philisides is pulled out of his paralysis by the 'horrible cries of the mad multitude' (125.31) bent on attacking the duke. Along with 'the other honest shepherds,' Philisides fights 'valiantly' (126.16–17) in seconding Dorus, but his actions are left unchronicled. This momentary interlude, the only time in the work when Philisides is moved to action, continues the comic parallelism between the persona and the princes. The princes play the role of heroes, saving the dukedom from the ravaging mob by a combination of physical and rhetorical prowess. Philisides is also valiant, his potential worth as a soldier made known, but his deeds are invisible and without consequence. The episode is one of playful self-mockery, with Philisides the pale shadow of the heroes, but it is also one of sly self-assertion, for it shows in Philisides the potential for heroic deeds. As we have seen earlier, Sidney's repeated attempts for military service may even have prompted the militaristic presentation of his image in the portrait of 1577/8. The most immediate autobiographical subtext for this self-mocking but ironically self-assertive treatment of Philisides is perhaps Sidney's futile quest for military service in the Netherlands during the spring of 1578.

Philisides resumes his passive melancholia in the eclogues to Book II, where he sings his second song. Ironically, this song, the most desperate in the work, is chosen by Philisides as an acceptable substitute for the story of his own fortunes, which Basilius has requested but which Philisides rejects because the time is 'far too joyful to suffer the rehearsal of his miseries' (159.31). The song deepens and extends the sense of solipsism expressed in the earlier reply to Dorus by implicating directly the world of nature. Here too the technique is that of mirroring, with each line of Philisides being answered by his own echo:

> *Philisides*: Echo, what do I get yielding my sprite to my griefs?
> *Echo*: Griefs.
> *Philisides*: What medicine may I find for a pain that draws me to death?
> *Echo*: Death.   (160.12–14)

As the above exchanges illustrate, the replies are never hopeful but merely serve to confirm the speaker's own despair, as if nature itself collaborated in his destruction. The verses end with Echo complicit in Philisides' damnation:

> *Philisides*: Tell yet again me the names of these fair formed to do ev'ls.
> *Echo*: Dev'ls.
> *Philisides*: Dev'ls? If in hell such dev'ls do abide, to the hells I do go.
> *Echo*: Go.   (162.25–8).

As in the earlier debate with Geron, Philisides faces his predicament with a hopeless and comical bravado, committing himself unflinchingly to perpetual despair.

Although there is nothing in either of Philisides' songs in Book II to suggest the identity of his love, the narrator's comment at the end of the Echo song tantalizes with possible political innuendo: 'Philisides was commended for the placing of his echo, but little did he regard their praises; who had set the foundation of his honour there where he was most despised' (162.29–163.1). The wording of the latter half of the sentence resonates with public, courtly overtones. In contrast, when Musidorus declares his love for Pamela, he says he has 'discovered the very foundation whereupon my life is built' (173.6–7). The difference between building one's life upon a foundation of love and setting the foundation of one's honour in a place suggests the difference between a private and public passion: the place for the foundation of honour is the court. As in Book I, the political innuendoes appear only fleetingly, but their recurrence accentuates the possibility of a political subtext to Philisides' despair.

Politics becomes unequivocally the major theme of Philisides' next eclogue, the Ister bank song in Book III, but only after a second, and even more unexpected, intervention by Philisides in the main plot. This occurs at the climax to Book III, the point at which Pyrocles, having seduced Cleophila, is poised to consummate his love. He has entered her chamber without her knowledge, has tried in vain to defend himself against her anger, has fainted with grief – ' "Oh, whom dost thou kill, Philoclea?" ' (235.14–15) – has been revived by her remorseful kisses and the sight of her beauty, has lifted her, without resistance, onto her bed, and then, 'having so free scope of his serviceable sight,' there comes into his mind 'a song the shepherd Philisides had in his hearing sung of the beauties of his unkind mistress, which in Pyrocles's judgment was fully accomplished in Philoclea' (238.1–4). At this point the narrator gives the audience the entire song, admitting only at the end the implausibility of the situation: 'But do not think, fair ladies, his thoughts had such leisure as to run over so long a ditty; the only general fancy of it came into his mind, fixed upon the sense of that sweet subject' (242.30–3). The narrator then draws the curtain on the lovers' fleeting pleasures, lest his pen 'might seem to grudge' at their 'due bliss' (243.4–5).

The major effect of this narrative tour de force is to titillate the reader, who is forced to read a song composed by Philisides while waiting eagerly for the consummation of the love between Pyrocles and Cleophila. The joke is given a further twist when the narrator admits that Pyrocles himself had not time enough to think through the song that we have had to read at length. Subtler and delayed ironies are produced when we consider that the author of the song was Philisides. Within the fiction, the invocation of Philisides at the moment of sexual consummation helps to intensify the expectancy of the audience, for his presence serves as a reminder of the rarity of such moments of bliss, a reminder the narrator himself provides at the end of the chapter when he alludes to the 'small respite' of the lovers' 'fiery agonies' (243.6). If it is possible to extend one's range of vision to contemplate Philisides' predicament at this erotic moment, the intrusion of his song, like his earlier entry into the battle against the rebels, produces a double effect. The open sensuality of the song further aligns Philisides with the princes, whose virility is not in question. The fact that Philisides produces songs, however, and the lovers actions, cuts the other way. Like his valiant actions against the rebels, Philisides' catalogue of his mistress's beauties seems important only as a sign of future promise.

The song itself is a highly successful version of the traditional blazon, or catalogue of the mistress's virtues. Philisides remains true to the main impulse of the genre by spending the vast majority of his words on the physical beauties, which he describes methodically, from front to back, from head to toe. The goodness of the beloved's soul, although conceptually more important than the beauty of her body – it is the 'fairer guest which dwells within' (242.23) – is rhetorically insignificant. If Philisides' responsiveness to physical beauty aligns him with Pyrocles, who enacts what both desire, his poetic practice aligns him with the narrator. The blazon, one might say, translates into lyric technique the titillation of the narrative. In the one, the audience, its appetite whetted by the description of the progress of Pyrocles and Philoclea towards their consummation, is fed only with Philisides' song and the narrator's closure of the curtains. In the other, the audience is taken on a journey from head to neck to breasts to ribs to navel to belly, only to be told that Cupid's 'chief resort' must be omitted, 'For such an use the world hath gotten, / The best things still must be forgotten' (240.26–8). The ultimate secret of courtly love, like that of courtly politics, can only be told in hints and insinuations.

The intrusion of Philisides' song into the narrative at this point thus blurs the boundaries between Pyrocles, Philisides, and the narrator, in all of whom Sidney has a close imaginative engagement. By identifying the song as Philisides', Sidney introduces an overtly erotic aspect to his persona, one that is not developed elsewhere in the work. He does so at considerable expense to psychological verisimilitude, for the high-spirited and celebratory tone of the blazon, which never even whispers of unrequited love, seems quite out of character with Philisides' present posture. In the *New Arcadia*, the song is reassigned to Pyrocles. As Ringler observes, Sidney clearly had great affection for this song; he revised it more than any other and alluded to it in Song V of *Astrophil and Stella* (*P*, 410n). Perhaps his obvious pleasure in the song, and his delight in the episode as a whole, led him to sacrifice the consistency of the fictional side of his persona for the immediate play of erotic wit – a wit that would only be intensified if the hidden subject were Elizabeth.

Fictional consistency resumes in the eclogues to Book III, when Philisides attends the wedding festivities of Lalus and Kala. The wedding of these two shepherds, a joyful celebration of innocent love, lies at the very centre of the narrative as a whole and comments ironically on the comical and dangerous passions in which the members of the court have become entangled. It is the one brief moment in the text when Sidney allows the notion of pastoral innocence and purity its full, if 'severely circumscribed,' effect.[26] When asked to contribute one of his 'country songs' to the festivities, Philisides, who has been 'revolving in his mind all the tempests of evil fortunes he had passed,' finds himself loath to sing his sorrows in a time of marriage but equally loath to 'betray (as it were) that passion to which he had given over himself.' As a compromise, 'a mean way betwixt both,' he sings a song 'he had learned before he had ever subjected his thoughts to acknowledge no master but a mistress' (254.13–20), a song he had learned from 'old Languet' (255.15). The song, which opens with a description of Philisides' hopeful youth, is a beast fable, an allegory of the beginning of monarchy. Just as the epithalamion celebrates the marriage of Lalus and Kala against a backdrop of disordered passions in the main plot, Philisides' song contrasts past innocence – his and the world's – with present affliction. The old rustic language of the song provides a stylistic counterpart to this sense of nostalgia.

Philisides' self-portrayal in 'Ister Bank' places his love melancholy in the context of the world he has lost. The allusion to 'old Languet,' moreover, underlines the autobiographical significance of the episode. Philisides sets the song at night on the bank of the Ister as he tends his 'little flock' (254.21). Fearing for their safety, he becomes conscious of the weight of his responsibility: 'Then found I which thing is a charge to bear' (255.10). To keep the flock from straying, he sings Languet's song to them. Languet, 'the shepherd best swift Ister knew,' drew him to a 'feeling taste' of God and to God's pleasure in a 'concord between our wit and will.' He liked Philisides, 'but pitied lustful youth,' and supported his 'slipp'ry years' with his own 'good strong staff' (255.16–30). Most significant, in view of Philisides' present plight, 'He still hoped well, because I loved truth.' Languet's affection for Philisides is so deep that when they are forced to part, he gives him over to 'worthy Coredens' with 'heart and eyes e'en sore' (256.1–3).

As Jean Robertson has noted, celebrations of former masters are common in pastoral verse (*OA*, 463n.). The celebration of Languet is no conventional compliment, however, but a powerful expression of lost identity. In a few lines, Sidney crystallizes the relationship reflected in the correspondence with Languet over many years. The song translates into pastoral terms the tenor of Languet's letters, which ceaselessly remind Sidney of his future political role, his responsibilities to the cause of Protestantism, the dangers of his youthful indiscretions – above all, of his great promise and the depth of Languet's love for him. Philisides' melancholy reminiscence thus carries into the world of the narrative, itself a world of lost innocence, Sidney's deeply personal sense of loss. The depth of feeling is conveyed by the rare absence of ironic self-mockery – the contrast between past hope and present despair is allowed to remain implicit – and the absence of any hint of mockery against old age and its tendency towards didacticism. And this despite the fact that, as presented, Languet's world-view differs little from that of the old shepherd, Geron, who earlier provoked Philisides into a rage. As we shall see in the eclogues to Book IV, Sidney's presentation of his persona keeps circling around emotions of loss and guilt.

The beast fable that Philisides sang to his sheep that night on the Ister tells of the end of political innocence. The fable begins at a time when humans do not exist and the beasts live in peace, governed by 'the beasts with courage clad,' who, 'like senators, a harmless empire had' (256.18–19). Either for envy or the mere desire for change, the beasts excluded from authority appeal to Jove for a king. Although he warns them against their request, Jove accedes and creates man, who receives his attributes from all of the beasts and who alone receives the gift of free speech. Man rules at first in the best interests of the beasts. Later, however, he begins to mine the earth and breed factions among the beasts to secure his power. He first helps the 'weaker sort,' thus alienating the 'nobler beasts,' whose aggressions he then punishes with death (258.15–21). Because they are not of 'great' but of 'gentle blood,' he chooses the horse and dog to rule over the weaker beasts, for which they are at first pleased. But then they themselves are tamed – the horse with 'fair bits,' the dog with a collar – and man turns to open tyranny, stripping the sheep of wool and the birds of feathers, and killing for 'glutton taste' and even for sport (258.22–259.9). The song concludes with a stanza of protest:

> But yet, O man, rage not beyond thy need;
> Deem it no gloire to swell in tyranny.
> Thou art of blood; joy not to make things bleed.
> Thou fearest death; think they are loath to die.
> A plaint of guiltless hurt doth pierce the sky.
>   And you, poor beasts, in patience bide your hell,
>   Or know your strengths, and then you shall do well.   (259.10–16)

Philisides' auditors react to the song with 'diverse judgements,' some of them, not surprisingly, wondering at the 'strangeness of the tale, and scanning what he should mean by it.' Geron, seeking revenge for earlier insults, condemns the song as inappropriate to a wedding and meaningless: 'this is the right conceit of young men who think then they speak wiseliest when they cannot understand themselves' (259.24–260.2).

Like Sidney's shepherds, modern scholars who have scanned the meaning of the tale have also arrived at diverse judgments. In Annabel Patterson's concise summary, the fable has been interpreted as 'an incitement to rebellion, in the line of Huguenot pamphlets like *Vindiciae contra Tyrannos*; as an expression of orthodox Tudor absolutism designed to ingratiate Sidney with the queen; as an assertion of the importance of a powerful aristocracy in maintaining the balance of power; and as a Calvinist allegory on the fall of man.'[27] To this we can add the recent arguments of Patterson herself, who sees the fable as being about political repression and censorship and the resulting need for equivocation in discourse; of Martin N. Raitiere, who uses the fable to dissociate Sidney from the anti-monarchist views expressed in the Huguenot pamphlets; of John A. Galm, who reads the fable as an allegory representing Sidney's opposition to the Anjou marriage; of Dennis Moore, who endorses Galm's interpretation but offers a more general political application; of Robert E. Stillman, who finds in the fable Sidney's support of a strong aristocracy; and, most recently, of Blair Worden, who sees it as an argument for the prevention of tyranny through the leadership of the nobles.[28]

The most persuasive interpretations of the fable are those that place it in the context of the anti-monarchist, or monarchomach, literature of late sixteenth-century France, to which Languet himself had probably contributed. In the view of William Ringler, for example, the fable aligns Sidney with the monarchomach position, specifically with the notions that the origin of legitimate political authority lies in the community and that the nobles are called upon to play an institutional role in protecting the people from tyranny (*P*, 412–13). From this vantage-point, the final lines of the song become Sidney's veiled invitation to his fellow aristocrats to reassert their lost authority: 'And you, poor beasts, in patience bide your hell, / Or know your strengths, and then you shall do well.' A phrase in Sidney's letter of 1580 to Edward Denny provides a convincing gloss on these lines, which imply the absurdity of living patiently in hell: 'For (alas) what is all knowledge? if in the end of this litle and weerisome pilgrimage, Hell become our scool*master*.'[29] The fable's conclusion seems equivocal enough to deflect censorship, general enough to avoid a specific doctrinal position, and aggressive enough to allow Sidney to express in fiction his belief in the latent power of a united aristocracy. As we shall see in later chapters, Sidney's increasing commitment to poetry throughout his career can be understood in part as an attempt to foster that power.

While Philisides' beast fable asserts in a veiled manner the power of the aristocracy, it also comments on and embodies, as Patterson has shown, the realities of censorship in an absolutist political system. In Sidney's case, the equivocation of meaning produced by such a system seems to have not only a political but a psychological significance. This becomes clear if we probe the implications of Sidney's self-representation as Philisides. It is important to remember that 'Ister Bank' is sung not by Sidney but by a persona, Philisides, who learned the song from Hubert Languet and who sings it only because it would be indecorous at a wedding to sing simply of his own present grief. Hence the song is not presented as Sidney's, or even as Philisides', but as Languet's. One can explain this complicated framing of the song, in part, as a self-protective mechanism, an insurance policy that could be used if the political attitudes of the song were challenged. But political protection is surely not the only reason for Sidney's obliqueness. The very remoteness of the song not only protects Sidney but tells against him, defusing any incipient threat that he may personally represent. Who is Philisides, after all, but a courtier who has lost his innocence and lives in a state of hopeless paralysis? No longer a promising youth, he is now in exile, given over to nostalgic reminiscences of past hopes and the singing of nostalgic songs that come from an earlier time of political activism and idealism. Languet's song may constitute a subtle call to political action among the nobility, but singing songs is not in itself a form of virtuous action. Absorbed in his own private suffering, Philisides sings only out of politeness and nostalgia, and, despite the potential relevance of the song to Basilius's misrule, no one present seems to understand or care about its meaning. At this stage in his career, Sidney may well have seen himself to be as irrelevant to Elizabeth's misguided government as Philisides is to that of Basilius.

The 'Ister Bank' song, in short, contains not only veiled political meanings but an implied critique of the ineffectuality of such discourse, at least as practiced by an exiled courtier like Philisides or Sidney. As such, it represents a critique of the pastoral form: not only because pastoral obliqueness runs 'the risk of going safe but unheard or misinterpreted,' as Patterson observes, but because, as represented by Philisides, the motive for pastoral expression is nostalgically escapist.[30] Within the fiction of the *Old Arcadia*, Philisides sings only out of social obligation, just as Sidney says he wrote only to please his sister, and his song represents an attempt to recover in fiction a lost time of innocence and political promise. Although 'Ister Bank' is a political song, the singing of it has no political consequences whatsoever – for Philisides, for his audience, or for the plot within which he exists. The framework for Philisides' song, then, not only protects Sidney from political repercussions but distances him ironically from any position of political influence or power. Languet's song contains a didactic political meaning; Philisides' singing of it expresses an ineffectual political nostalgia.

The autobiographical resonance that characterizes the 'Ister Bank' episode is accentuated in the eclogues to Book IV. Here too Philisides' subject is the loss of his own innocence in a context of political and historical decline. Prompted by the symmetry between his own melancholy condition and the state of the dukedom, which is in deep mourning for the supposed death of Basilius, Philisides at last agrees to 'impart some part of the sorrow his countenance so well witnessed unto them' (334.8–9). He begins by recounting his youth in Samothea, then describes the dream-vision in which he falls in love with Mira, and, finally, presents the 'elegiacs' he sent to her upon his departure. Although Philisides' grief may be emotionally appropriate to the present occasion, its obsessive inwardness marks his continued estrangement from the community around him. At the end of his elegiacs, Philisides 'would have gone on in telling the rest of his unhappy adventures,' but Dicus asks him to 'leave particular passions, and join in bewailing this general loss of that country which had been a nurse to strangers as well as a mother to Arcadians' (344.17–22). From the time of his argument with Geron, Philisides' relationship with the Arcadian shepherds is consistently strained. So deep is his impulse towards solipsism that he and the inhabitants of the pastoral world exist in a state of mutual incomprehension.

The prose passage in which Philisides recounts the story of his youth is written in direct imitation of Sannazaro, who includes in chapter 7 of his *Arcadia* an autobiographical account by his persona, Sincero. Asked to tell his story, Sincero tells of his noble birth in Naples; his reputation as a youth; his grandfather's possessions and their loss to the widow of King Ladisloo; his misfortunes; his falling in love at the age of eight; the unrequited nature of his love, which leads him to melancholy and contemplation of suicide; his abandonment of Naples; his unhappiness in Arcadia; and his constant remembrance of his beloved. At the conclusion of his autobiographical account, he prays for an end to his miseries (69–74). Despite the obvious differences in personal backgrounds, Sidney's version has much in common with that of Sannazaro. Both poets highlight their noble birth, their early reputation, their affection for their homeland, and their love melancholy. Both continue with songs that contain a dream-vision of the beloved. Taken as a whole, however, Sidney's changes to his original represent both a complication and a critique.

In the account of his past youth, Sidney, unlike Sannazaro, sets his persona in a remote and idealized homeland – Samothea, a mythic representation of ancient England.[31] The exiled Philisides' nostalgia is not directed to contemporary England, therefore, as is Sincero's towards contemporary Naples, but towards an ancient myth of England that provides an appropriate setting for his own youthful innocence. By changing the setting of Philisides' personal history, Sidney introduces an obliquely satirical perspective, for the Samothea he describes is contrasted with contemporary England. Samothea is 'a land which whilom stood / An honour to the world, while honour was their end, / And while their line of years they did in virtue spend' (336.15–17). In its decline from an original dedication to honour and virtue, the history of Samothea parallels Philisides' personal history; in both cases, past honour contrasts with present woe. Unlike Sannazaro, moreover, Sidney develops his personal history to accentuate the contrast between the promise of his youth and the despair of his present condition. Sincero can return from Arcadia to Naples, a place that he lavishes praise upon (118), but the innocent times of Philisides and Samothea are irrecoverable.

Philisides' account of his upbringing conforms so closely in its details to what we know of Sidney's as to blur the distinction between persona and author. What we are given is a selective account of Sidney's own youth. Although coloured by the fictional setting, the brief narrative (334.12–335.10) provides the closest glimpse we have in Sidney's writings of direct autobiography, a taking stock of past experience. The account he provides, ironically, although personal, seems filtered through a work like Elyot's *Boke of the Governour*, for the youth we see is virtually a textbook case, with accompanying rationale, of the Elizabethan conception of shaping a model ruler. Philisides' education begins as soon as his memory grows strong enough. Although the education emphasizes moral knowledge – 'what in truth and not in opinion is to be embraced' – it is sufficiently flexible to allow for other pursuits: 'Neither was I barred from seeking the natural knowledge of things so far as the narrow sight of man hath pierced into it.' Horsemanship and military exercises are provided 'because the mind's commandment is vain without the body be enabled to obey it,' and foreign travel is arranged to 'ripen' the judgment 'by the comparison of many things.' Implicit in the rationale for each of these activities are not only conventional assumptions about the education of a governor but a justification of those assumptions. Philisides presents not only a description but an implied defence of his own education.

Philisides not only endorses the rationale for his schooling but the remarkable control, both direct and indirect, exercised by his family. After he identifies the name of his country, Philisides' first gesture towards defining his identity is to place himself in the social hierarchy, in a position accorded by his parents: he is born of 'such parentage as neither left me so great that I was a mark for envy nor so base that I was subject to contempt.' If his social identity depends upon the blood of his parents, so does his upbringing, the nature of which is conventional and impersonal: he was brought up 'from my cradle age with such care as parents are wont to bestow upon their children whom they mean to make the maintainers of their name.' The goal, shared by other parents of the same social status, is perpetuation of the family name, not the development of the individual. True to this impulse, the family plays the active role in shaping the education; the young Philisides is passive recipient. When he reached an appropriate age, they 'offered' learning to him. His strength 'was exercised' with horsemanship. He 'was suffered' to spend some time in travel after he 'was thought able to be mine own master.' It is clear from this account that Sidney not only recognized the shaping power of his family but endorsed it. Philisides' depiction of his early training is that of a young man who has assimilated the conventional attitudes of his society, not subjected them to ironic appraisal or rebellion.

Parental control yields to personal responsibility at the moment of foreign travel, when the young Philisides is thought 'able to be mine own master.' Philisides notes with a hint of pride that this moment occurred for him earlier than for most, 'perchance by a sooner privilege than years commonly grant.' When he returns from his travels, he brings a promising reputation: he is 'thought of good hope (for the world rarely bestows a better title upon youth).' During this period, he himself assumes responsibility for his own life, which at first accords with the goals of his early education: 'I continued to use the benefits of a quiet mind; in truth (I call him to witness that knoweth hearts) even in the secret of my soul bent to honesty – thus far you see, as no pompous spectacle, so an untroubled tenor of a well guided life.' At this point, however, Philisides interrupts his narrative with an exclamation: 'But alas, what should I make pathetical exclamations to a most true event? So it happened that love (which what it is, your own feeling can best tell you) diverted this course of tranquillity.' Ironically, and paradoxically, this 'most true event' is presented in the form of a dream-vision, which ensures that its 'truth' remains mysterious and obscure.

The beginning of the dream-vision recapitulates in mythic terms the period in Sidney's life immediately after his return from the Continent.

Untroubled by thoughts of political ambition or other 'captiving snares'
(335.29), clear in conscience, 'in simple course, and unentangled mind'
(336.3), Philisides sleeps the sleep of the innocent. He dreams that he is
in the 'fairest wood' of Samothea, feeding his 'calmy thoughts' on
'nature's sweet repast': 'Her gifts my study was, her beauties were my
sport; / My work her works to know, her dwelling my resort' (336.14–21).
He occupies himself with the movements of the heavens, with the role of
destiny and fortune, and with the nature of the immortal soul, straining
with a mind then 'void of nearer cares, the depth of things to find'
(336.30). The description of studies in natural history probably alludes to
the time in 1577 when Sidney studied chemistry and natural history with
Dyer and Dee.[32] As Philisides strains in his innocence to understand the
'depth of things,' ironically, the moon breaks asunder with 'hugest noise'
to reveal Venus, Diana and a 'virgin pure' in a chariot guided by doves
and sparrows (336.30–337.10). Philisides is asked to choose between the
quarrelling goddesses, neither of whom is desirable; he rejects both for
their waiting woman, Mira, with whom he instantly falls in love: 'And Mira
I admired; her shape sank in my breast' (338.12). For this, he is punished
by both goddesses. Venus gives Mira a beauty that will forever kindle fire
in him, but Diana gives her chastity, which will keep him forever in 'ashes
of despair' (340.16).

As we have seen, this fictional displacement of what is presented as a
'true event' has given rise to various attempts at historical interpretation.
Mira's role as waiting woman to Venus and Diana might seem to support
the notion that she herself represents one of Elizabeth's ladies-in-waiting.
If so, however, Venus or Diana or both would represent the queen herself
in a crudely and dangerously satiric manner, without the safety of equivocation. Venus and Diana are indeed shadowy figures for the queen, but
the logic of the dream identifies Mira, not one of them, as the true ruler:
'To yonder nymph therefore (to Mira I did point) / The crown above you
both for ever I appoint' (340.7–8). Mira is given the rightful title to the
attributes of both goddesses, attributes that were conventionally celebrated in Elizabeth: beauty and chastity. The method is similar to that of
the shows put on for Elizabeth at Kenilworth in 1575 or to Peele's *Arraign-
ment of Paris*, in which, as Elkin Calhoun Wilson observes, 'Olympian
deities' were 'displaced by Elisa's majesty.'[33] The episode as a whole provides two versions of Elizabeth – a slyly satiric one in which she is identified with Venus and Diana, and an idealistic one, in which she is
identified with Mira. Sidney creates a similar duality in his representation
of queen Andromana and Helen of Corinth, as we will see, in the *New*

Arcadia, as does Spenser in developing the parallelism between Lucifera and Gloriana in Book I of *The Faerie Queene*. Grotesque mirroring of this kind seems a virtually censor-proof method of political equivocation.

If we take Philisides' dream-vision as a parable of Sidney's political failure to win Elizabeth, we can find within it a sly and sophisticated treatment of Elizabethan court politics. If Mira is Elizabeth, then she is by definition blameless: a beautiful young virgin, she inherits the crown from both goddesses and is given their beauty and chastity. She cannot be other than she is. The fault, then, seems to lie with Philisides, who swells with youthful vanity when he is asked to arbitrate the dispute between the goddesses: 'I that was first aghast, when first I saw their show, / Now bolder waxed, waxed proud that I such sway might bear; / For near acquaintance doth diminish reverent fear' (339.37–340.2). Although Philisides may be guilty of vanity, however, it is not vanity that occasions his downfall. From the moment he falls in love with Mira and is offered the position of arbiter, he cannot win. To choose one goddess is necessarily to offend the other. To choose Mira is necessarily to offend both. To refuse to choose is to betray his love for Mira. His predicament, then, is an inescapable consequence of his love.

The real culprits of the parable are neither Mira nor Philisides but the goddesses themselves, the presentation of whom is delightfully satiric and parodies the conventional idealization of Elizabeth and her relation to her court. Both goddesses are comical in appearance – Venus's dependence on cosmetics seems suspiciously like Elizabeth's, as Duncan-Jones notes[34] – and their dramatic entrance collapses quickly into bathos: 'When I such guests did see come out of such a house, / The mountains great with child I thought brought forth a mouse' (337.21–2). The goddesses seek an arbiter because their constant wrangling has driven away their worshippers, leaving them alone and aging in a declining world: 'Although we be divine, our grandsire Saturn is / With age's force decayed, yet once the heav'n was his' (339.1–2). The episode as a whole enables Sidney to travesty Elizabeth and her court in the figures of Venus and Diana, to celebrate Elizabeth as Mira, and to acknowledge his own youthful vanity in a way that both compliments the queen and implies her dependency on his choice. The mixture of flattery and satiric aggression might remind us once again of Sidney's gift of a whip.

If Sidney achieves a precarious balance in his presentation of the dream-vision, his account of the quarrel with Mira that drives Philisides into exile betrays the strain of deeper emotional involvement. Philisides describes his actions upon awakening from his dream in a manner that suggests Sidney's own relationship with Elizabeth. He mentions his per-suasion that 'in my nativity I was allotted unto her' (340.33–4), a belief that matches well with Sidney's early preparation for the queen's service. He also describes devoting himself exclusively to 'the pursuit of her favour' (341.2–3), a comment that probably alludes to Sidney's dependency on the queen as a courtier. He concludes with what seems to be a summary of Sidney's recent past, including his modest and occasional successes as a courtier, his increasing frustration with his role, the queen's displeasure with him in the Anjou and Oxford affairs, and his eventual decision to retire from the court: 'But having spent some part of my youth in follow-ing of her, sometimes with some measure of favour, sometimes with unkind interpretations of my most kind thoughts, in the end having attempted all means to establish my blissful estate, and having been not only refused all comfort but new quarrels picked against me, I did resolve by perpetual absence to choke mine own ill fortunes' (341.3–9).

By including within the dream-vision these political overtones, Sidney creates a fictional context for his self-representation that is at once true to his present predicament and implicitly critical of the relatively apolitical nature of his pastoral source. Traced to its origin in the dream-vision, Phi-lisides' melancholy is not only personal but political; his nostalgia is directed not only to his own hopeful youth but to the former innocence of Samothea. Sincero's home, Naples, is one in which Sannazaro has a rightful place, to be regained at the end of the pastoral retreat. Philisides' home is Samothea, an idealized version of an England that no longer exists and to which there is no possible return.

The verses that Philisides sends to Mira upon his departure move away from the world of myth. Instead, they record his emotions upon going into exile and include an account of the event that precipitated it. The narrative again conforms well with events in Sidney's own life, specifically his recent angering of the queen, either in the Anjou affair or, more likely, in the challenge to the earl of Oxford. The verses embody a com-plex and unsettled attitude towards that experience. The tone is in part resentful, with Philisides questioning Mira's desire for revenge:

> Must I be only the mark shall prove that virtue is angry?
>   shall prove that fierceness can with a white dove abide?
> Shall to the world appear that faith and love be rewarded
>   with mortal disdain, bent to unendly revenge?
> Unto revenge? O sweet, on a wretch wilt thou be revenged?
>   shall such high planets tend to the loss of a worm?   (342.17–22)

The accusations of vengefulness recall the actions of Venus and Diana in the dream-vision, and the final line even echoes Diana's protest that they, 'celestial pow'rs,' now serve 'worms' (338.28). Mira has at this point taken on some of the unattractive qualities of Venus and Diana.

Philisides goes on to admit his own fault for angering Mira, however, alluding perhaps to the Oxford affair, in which Sidney was moved to a rage by Oxford's demands for precedence on the tennis court and challenged him to a duel: 'Well, but faulty I was; reason to my passion yielded, / passion unto my rage, rage to a hasty revenge' (343.26–7). As in the dream-vision, however, and even more explicitly, the acknowledgment of fault is equivocal. Philisides first minimizes the blame: 'But what's this for a fault, for which such faith be abolished, / such faith, so stainless, inviolate, violent?' (343.28–30). He then reminds Mira of her past favour: 'Shall I not once object that you, you granted a favour / unto the man whom now such miseries you award?' (344.1–2). The verses conclude with his grief at what he had earlier described as exile – 'I did resolve by perpetual absence to choke mine own ill fortunes' (341.8–9) – but now calls his banishment: 'And banished do I live, nor now will seek a recov'ry, / since so she will, whose will is to me more than a law' (344.13–14). The shift from an image of voluntary exile to one of banishment completes the passage's emotional movement from guilt to resentment.

The mystery of Philisides' grief is thus eventually traced to its source, in the quarrel with Mira that led to his banishment. Once that fact is revealed, the figure of Philisides disappears from the narrative. Ironically, by consigning Philisides to endless grief Sidney avoids in his case the problems of closure that so unsettle the main plot. For Philisides' problem, there is no possible ending. By definition, his predicament is unresolvable, a true dilemma. He must love Mira, and Mira must be chaste, although in his resentful eyes she need not be cruel as well. The only resolution his role permits is that of continuing irresolution. In this sense, Sidney's existential and fictional roles converge: as exiles, both he and his persona are doomed to continue loving and to fail.

If Philisides were a purely fictional character, his fate would merely cast a small shadow on the happy outcome of the main plot, much as Shakespeare's comedies include a note of dissonance at their conclusion. As a self-representation, however, his impact is more significant, for his doom calls in question the validity of the entire narrative, implicitly mocking its optimistic evasiveness. Philisides tells his story, but the telling has absolutely no effect, either on him or on his audience; it is neither personally therapeutic nor socially instructive. Nor does Philisides learn anything from his sojourn in Arcadia. His estrangement is complete: banished from the presence of his beloved, he is exiled from his own society, alienated in Arcadia, and incapable of hope or change. He ends as he began, unreconciled to his suffering and in a state of melancholy paralysis.

By pursuing the logic of Philisides' destined love so remorselessly, Sidney implies another critique of his pastoral model. In the *Arcadia*, Sannazaro not only accepts the Virgilian notion of pastoral as a preparation for higher kinds of poetry, but, as Sukanta Chaudhuri observes, he gestures towards the cyclical and restorative vision of pastoral that was to dominate later Renaissance explorations of the form.[35] In Sannazaro's *Arcadia*, as we have seen, the persona-narrator, Sincero, retreats into the pastoral landscape, finds solace there, and eventually returns to Naples to pursue higher forms of poetry. Underlying all of the complexities of Sannazaro's treatment of the pastoral experience, therefore, is a simple and reassuring pattern. As Ralph Nash observes, the story is one of 'a young man's temporary withdrawal from his normal milieu, his ardent dedication to poetry, and his return to the world from which he had exiled himself' (24). For Sannazaro, the stories of his personas are metafictional versions of his evolution as a man and a poet. They imply a commitment to the pastoral as a regenerative mode of fiction and as a Virgilian training ground for higher kinds of poetry. Sidney, in contrast, counters this pastoral movement with his own version of desperate stasis: a condition in which there is no solace in the country, no regeneration, no transition to a higher style. For Philisides, there is no reassuring cycle of withdrawal and return but an endless line of exiled wandering and hopeless grief.

If we accept the idea that Philisides' story fictionalizes Sidney's relationship with the queen, we might say that Sidney politicizes the pastoral in a way that Sannazaro does not, by adopting the convention of using shepherd's songs to comment on courtly affairs. His treatment of this convention, however, is unusually complex. Other contemporary poets used the pastoral almost invariably to celebrate the queen. 'The "symbolic formation" of pastoral,' according to Louis Adrian Montrose, 'provided an ideal meeting ground for queen and subjects, a mediation of her greatness and their lowness; it fostered the illusion that she was approachable and knowable, lovable and loving, to lords and peasants, courtiers and citizens alike.'[36] Praise of this kind was never disinterested; it could be used to persuade, to cajole, and even to subtly criticize. Yet even if we acknowledge that self-assertion is often implicit in such poetry, Sidney's treatment of the convention seems unique. He presents no encomium or direct address to the monarch but the story of his relationship with her, a story in which both roles are developed and his is the more prominent of the two. The result, as we have seen, is a subtle and witty mixture of praise and blame, celebration and satire, self-reproach and self-justification that touches both parties and cannot be reduced to the simple goal of courtly manipulation. Unlike Spenser, whose non-aristocratic status and strong commitment to the role of poet gave him a stable vantage-point outside the court from which to celebrate 'Elisa, queen of shepheardes all,' Sidney could only write from within the court circle, even when in exile, and the complexity of his treatment of his relationship with the queen betrays that fact. Resistant to the role of poet and tied by vocation to the role of courtier, Sidney was not able to distance himself either psychologically or socially from any of his courtly subjects, including himself.

This degree of self-involvement, as we have seen already, leads Sidney to a portrayal of the convention of pastoral criticism as itself ineffectual. When Philisides sings the song that Languet taught him on Ister Bank, the futility of using the pastoral to 'glance' at greater matters becomes clear. The meaning of the song is itself cryptic, as any such 'glancing' must be, and none of the auditors understands it. Nor does it have any impact on the narrative, which itself depicts some of the dangers of misrule that the song is meant to address. The veiled exhortation to the nobles to assert themselves remains veiled. More importantly, the very impulse towards such singing is mocked, for Philisides is drawn to the song not because of any social activism but because it enables him to indulge his nostalgia for his friend Languet and for the promise of his lost youth. Political activism of this kind is difficult to distinguish from narcissism. In the role of Philisides, then, Sidney not only embodies a critique of the Virgilian model of the poetic career but of a standard social justification for pastoral, and one he himself accepts in *A Defence of Poetry*, where rhetorical demands insulate theory from the complexities of his own practice.

In representing himself as Philisides, then, Sidney engaged in a complex act of imitation. In part, the self-portrayal can be understood as a kind of autobiography, with the mixture of self-deprecation and self-justification that often characterizes the genre. Sidney includes in Philisides sometimes playful and sometimes serious allusions to his own hot temper, his eagerness for military experience, his amatory interests, his education, his friendship with Languet, and above all, his frustrating relationship with the queen, the hidden cause of his retreat at Wilton. By fictionalizing his self-portrait, however, and especially by placing himself in the role of a courtier turned shepherd, he achieved not only a measure of artistic detachment and of political security but a complex vantage-point from which to view the self. By juxtaposing Philisides with the princes, he could at once celebrate and mock his own potential for princely behaviour. More importantly, by imitating the pastoral model of Sannazaro he could experiment with a way of imagining exile, as a recreative state of withdrawal that was appropriate to an emerging poet and would lead to a return to society and a commitment to higher forms of poetry. Beyond Sannazaro, moreover, he could explore the conventional role of the pastoral poet as social critic.

The pastoral role of Philisides thus gave Sidney a set of literary conventions that enabled him to position himself imaginatively in relation to society and his social role. Through it he was able to test the validity of a conventional mode of poetic self-definition, one that must have seemed designed for the circumstances and setting of his own political retreat. By the end of his narrative, however, as we have seen, it becomes clear that the test is an artistic success only because it represents a personal failure. Pastoral retreat provides no resolution to Philisides' problems. With this result in mind, it is not surprising that after the *Old Arcadia* Sidney moved away from pastoral or that the Philisides of the *New Arcadia*, although also disguised as a shepherd, inhabits the world of the court. In an immediately personal and political way, Sidney had exhausted the genre. In the Philisides of the *Old Arcadia*, Sidney created a role that enabled him to project, with considerable energy and wit, his frustration with his role at court, his impatience with pastoral retreats, and his estrangement from his own creation.

To see the role of Philisides as instrumental in Sidney's progression beyond the pastoral is to imply that self-representation is also a kind of self-fashioning, that the process of playing a role produces a change in the self. As might be expected, convincing evidence for such a change is not available. In a broad sense the social impact of Sidney's self-representation as Philisides can be demonstrated – Sidney is referred to by that name from at least 1587 (*P*, 418) – but the personal, psychological impact, if any, remains hidden. As we have seen in chapter 1, however, the process of imitative self-representation was for Sidney and his humanistic culture not solely a matter of self-expression or social communication. Underlying the notion of imitation was the assumption that to make the self into a fictional character, as Sidney did, subjecting it to the discipline of a distinctive fictional world and a distinctive audience, could potentially transform identity. In terms of this process, any distinction we might be inclined to draw between making fiction and making reality is hard to sustain: the making of the fiction becomes the making of the self. Perhaps the most compelling evidence we have that Sidney's autobiographical recreations were truly re-creative in a psychological sense lies in his continuing preoccupation with the form. Every new role, as we shall see, comments not only on Sidney's own immediate experience but on the roles that have come before.

5

Astrophil and the
Comedy of Love

Astrophil and Stella repays attention of many kinds. The sequence offers a sustained and creative experiment in metrical and poetic forms, a sophisticated exploration of the wide-ranging emotions of love, witty meditations upon the nature of love poetry, an engaging and richly human pair of lovers, and a subtle narrative design. However one defines its success, the most striking and challenging feature of *Astrophil and Stella*, one that must be acknowledged in any account of the work, is its radically innovative treatment of persona. As S.K. Heninger, Jr, observes, in contrast to 'the usual circumstance of amorous lyrics, where the poet / lover reports the progress of his own affair,' Sidney 'calls into doubt the identity of the poet / lover so that a new relationship may evolve between poet and poem and reader.'[1] By creating a persona slyly named 'Astrophil,' by including biographical details that unmistakably identify the persona with himself, and by subjecting the persona to sustained irony, Sidney creates a poetic form in which both the speaker and authorial voice are radically ambiguous. By putting forward a dual self, by splitting the authorial voice from the persona, Sidney subjects not only his own identity but the conventional view of the Petrarchan poet to poetic interrogation; the self, as always in Sidney, is explored within the framework of a traditional literary genre, a distinctive poetic world.[2] As an exercise in self-representation, *Astrophil and Stella* is Sidney's most sophisticated achievement.

The poetic energy that drives this equivocal art, as I hope to show, springs from unresolved tensions in Sidney's conception of love and love poetry, as manifested in *A Defence of Poetry*. The tensions in question, I believe, were for Sidney incapable of resolution. The conflicts they embody, however, unlike those that compromise the representation of the earlier Philisides, are expressed in *Astrophil and Stella* with a high degree of disciplined aesthetic control. As Richard C. McCoy observes, the series is characterized by a 'clarity, humor, and assurance lacking in other works.'[3] The sophisticated poise that characterizes the tone of the sonnets, however, results not from the resolution of a personal dilemma but from its witty representation. In order to understand the nature and significance of this distinctive mode of self-representation, it will be necessary to trace the relationship of Astrophil to his prototype, Philisides; to examine Sidney's treatment of love and love poetry in the *Defence*; and to follow the development of Astrophil and, to a lesser extent, Stella throughout the series as a whole.

In many respects the character of Astrophil can be seen as an outgrowth of the persona Philisides in the *Old Arcadia*. As characters, they have much in common. Both are 'star-lovers,' whose evocative names link Philip Sidney to the infamous astronomer of the *Defence*, who, 'looking to the stars, might fall in a ditch' (82.29). Both begin as young men of good background and great civic promise. Both fall in love. Both fail to persuade their mistresses to reciprocate their love. Both are guilty of angering their mistresses. Both are ultimately banished and live in a state of despair. Although this is a conventionally Petrarchan story, Sidney's fascination with it suggests that it provided a psychologically meaningful symbol of his own experience of wasted promise, whether in the spheres of court affairs or romantic love.

Sidney's characterization of Astrophil thus represents a continuation of the autobiographical impulse manifested in Philisides. But it is also a sophisticated reworking and refinement. The method of representation in each case, for example, is remarkably different and reflects the external circumstances of Sidney's life during the periods of composition. Written when Sidney was in exile, the *Old Arcadia* shows Philisides himself in exile, his story reduced to narratives he tells to explain his present misery; as a character, he is static and irrelevant to the main plot of the narrative. Written when Sidney had returned to court, *Astrophil and Stella* shows Astrophil in the present tense, actively pursuing Stella while in the midst of courtly activities, the poems as a whole charting the course of his unsuccessful love. While Philisides is presented as a character without a plot, Astrophil is presented as both a character with and in a plot – a character whose poems are aimed at seduction and who himself undergoes change and development in the course of his unsuccessful love. The development of a clear, if sketchy, narrative line helps to distinguish *Astrophil and Stella* from other sonnet sequences in the period.

Both Philisides and Astrophil assume the roles of lovers, courtiers, and poets. As lovers, they seem to have much in common, yet the resemblances are only superficial. Philisides' 'love,' as we have seen, is a figure for Sidney's political courtship of Elizabeth, a convenient mask for his frustrations as a courtier. It is one of many sixteenth-century adaptations of Petrarchan language to the problematic nature of service at court. Astrophil's love, as he himself informs us in sonnet 28, is no allegory but a passion for a particular woman, the Stella who is later identified with Penelope Rich. Although it is possible to analyse the love affair in *Astrophil and Stella* as, in the words of Ann Rosalind Jones and Peter Stallybrass, 'a complex displacement of the ideological pressures of the court,' this is because the discourse of politics and Petrarchism were interchangeable in the court of Elizabeth, not because Astrophil's failure with Stella should be read as an allegory of his failure at court or because political failures are the 'real' source of the emotions behind the poems.[4] One of the chief differences between the love of Philisides and that of Astrophil lies in the virtual sexlessness of the former and the obsessive sexuality of the latter. Although sexual passion may have political implications, it is not always, even at the Elizabethan court, subordinate to the lust for political power.

Astrophil is a lover, then, and in a different sense from Philisides. He is also a courtier, and in a far more fully realized way than Philisides is a courtier in exile. Astrophil thinks about himself as a courtier, and his love affair takes place against a background of numerous details from the life of the Elizabethan court. Astrophil listens inattentively to boring courtiers discussing state affairs, he participates in tournaments, he rides on horseback to visit Stella, he insults her husband by name, he sees Stella sailing on the Thames – he leads a life, in short, that might well be based on events in Sidney's own life during 1581 and 1582. Although only a few of the details are factually verifiable, nothing in the sequence contradicts what we know of Sidney's or Lady Rich's lives at the time. Taken together, the experiential details of the series present a compelling, if highly selected, image of aristocratic existence at the Elizabethan court. No other sonnet sequence in the period achieves so richly textured a representation of social reality.

Astrophil is also more fully realized than Philisides as a poet. Both characters are lovers who turn to poetry for the sake of love, but only Astrophil is self-conscious about his role as author. Philisides emotes, whereas Astrophil both emotes and struggles with the language of emotion. Although not a poet by vocation, Astrophil deals often with the problems of writing love poetry, and in ways that correspond to pronouncements made by Sidney himself in *A Defence of Poetry*. Here too the persona is developed in such a way as to blur the boundaries between speaker and author, with some critics identifying Astrophil's views as Sidney's and some dissociating the two.[5] In the *Old Arcadia*, Sidney's critique of Sannazaro and the pastoral tradition is implicit in his framing of Philisides' poetic role, whereas in *Astrophil and Stella* Astrophil himself mocks those who imitate 'poore *Petrarch's* long deceased woes' (15.7). Sidney's critique of the Petrarchan tradition, as we shall see, is mediated through his critique of his own creation.

Not only are Astrophil's roles complex refinements of those of Philisides; the status of the persona as persona also takes on a new significance. Whereas Philisides is a minor character in a narrative that might continue without him, Astrophil is the 'author' of a poetic sequence in which his consciousness is the central subject. That consciousness, moreover, owes much of its dynamic energy to its complex and ambiguous relationship to the authorial voice behind it, the 'Sidney' who is the 'author' of Astrophil himself. In the *Old Arcadia*, as we have seen, self-representation serves a therapeutic function, sometimes at the expense of art; in *Astrophil and Stella*, therapy and art seem more fully integrated. In the sonnet sequence, moreover, the act of self-representation achieves a new significance, becoming a subject in its own right. No longer does self-representation function as in a *roman-à-clef*, with the reader speculating about the identity of such mysterious characters as Mira or Coredens, and about the real source of Philisides' malaise. In *Astrophil and Stella* the principals are unmistakably identified with Philip Sidney, Penelope Rich, and Lord Rich.[6] Identity is no longer at issue; meaning is. And the central meaning of the series lies not so much in the relationship between Sidney and Penelope Rich, or between Astrophil and Stella, whose presence is shadowy at best, as it does in the relationship between Sidney and Astrophil, poet and persona.

Despite the insistence of Sidney's autobiographical identification in *Astrophil and Stella*, we lack conclusive evidence for the most important biographical question raised by the sequence: what exactly was the relationship between Penelope Rich and Philip Sidney? We know a good deal about Lady Rich that is relevant to the sonnets: that her father, the earl of Essex, attempted to arrange a marriage between her and Sidney when she was thirteen and he twenty-two; that she came to court at the age of eighteen in 1581 and was married to Lord Rich; and that the marriage was unhappy. We also know that she bore Lord Rich four children; that in the winter of 1588–9 she became the mistress of Sir Charles Blount, with

whom she had four more children; that she participated actively in the
political intrigues of her brother, the earl of Essex; and that she was beautiful, courtly, and a sophisticated patron of letters. We know nothing outside the sonnet sequence, however, about the nature or extent of her
involvement with Philip Sidney or her feelings towards him.

The situation is similar for Sidney himself. There is no evidence that he
was ever interested in marrying Penelope; nor is there evidence to suggest that he saw much of her before or after she came to court in 1581,
although connections between the Sidney family probably created opportunities for a relationship of some kind immediately after her marriage.
Sidney returned from his 'exile' in the winter of 1581 and in the spring
participated in the tournament of the *Four Foster Children of Desire* and
other festivities held for the French commissioners who had come to
negotiate Elizabeth's proposed marriage with the duke of Anjou. The
duke himself arrived in London on 1 November 1581, Penelope's
wedding day. In the early spring of 1582 Sidney joined the train of courtiers escorting the duke to Antwerp. Sidney was much engaged in his
father's affairs later in that year and spent time with him on the borders
of Wales.

What we know about Sidney's life during the period in which he probably composed *Astrophil and Stella*, in short, tells us nothing directly about
his relationship with Stella. Certain indirect evidence, however, is suggestive. The contemporary identification of Stella with Penelope Rich,
Sidney's rueful comments on the experience of love in *A Defence of Poetry*,
and his alleged deathbed allusion to 'my Ladie Rich' as a 'Vanitie
wherein I had taken delight,' all point to the likelihood of an affair that
deeply engaged Sidney's imagination and emotions.[7] More generally, the
problem of sexual passion preoccupies Sidney throughout his literary
works – so much so that, as Katherine Duncan-Jones has observed, some
earlier critics and biographers found it embarrassing.[8] There is ample evidence to suggest, therefore, that the central problem of *Astrophil and
Stella*, the destructive nature of sexuality, was also a central problem for
Sidney himself, even if his precise relationship to Penelope Rich remains
an open question. The likelihood of deep emotional involvement in the
composition of the sonnets is increased, moreover, by their repeated
engagement with two other questions that preoccupied Sidney throughout his career – questions about the role of a courtier and about the
nature of poetry.

All three issues – love, political service, and poetry – also figure prominently in *A Defence of Poetry*, a work so uncertain in its date that it has been

plausibly assigned both to the winter of 1579–80 and the years 1582–3.[9] Since Sidney probably wrote most of the poems in *Astrophil and Stella* from late in 1581 to the summer of 1582 (*P*, 438–40), it is possible that parts of the two works overlapped. Both works are deeply intertwined conceptually, certainly, and I shall draw on the *Defence* repeatedly in this chapter to contextualize the treatment of Astrophil. The *Defence* also figures prominently in my interpretation of the role of Philisides in the *New Arcadia*. Any attempt to make a developmental argument on the basis of an exact date for the *Defence* would be artificial, however, not only because of the uncertain dates of the works but because of the compression of Sidney's career and the continuity of the major issues that concerned him.

Given the uncertainty surrounding Sidney's relationship with Lady Rich, it is not surprising that critics divide sharply on the question of his relationship to his self-representation, Astrophil. On one side are critics who tend to identify persona and author, reading the sonnets as Sidney's own meditations on love and poetry or as serving rhetorically his own seductive ends. On the other are critics who dissociate persona and author, interpreting Astrophil as a fictional character. Although there are exceptions, critics who take a biographical approach to the persona tend to read *Astrophil and Stella* as a collection of highly individualized and fragmentary lyrical utterances, whereas those who take a fictional approach tend to read the work as a unified narrative. The biographically oriented Richard A. Lanham, for example, sees the sonnets as individual efforts by Sidney to seduce Penelope Rich, each poem being 'conceived in the hope that it would be the last'; the fictionally oriented Alan Hager, in contrast, sees Astrophil as 'nothing more than a well-wrought Renaissance mask, a tool for showing us a simultaneously coherent and diseased imagination.'[10] It is possible, in short, to read *Astrophil and Stella* from diametrically opposed perspectives: either as a literal exercise in seduction by Sidney himself or as a fictitious narrative in which Sidney uses Astrophil to warn others against such acts.

An illuminating contrast to Sidney's equivocal use of persona can be found in Petrarch's *Rime*. The composition and arrangement of the *Rime* took place over Petrarch's lifetime, and the final one hundred poems were written after Laura's death. The speaker of the sonnets is identified with the author, and his perspective on Laura and on himself changes as the relationship evolves over time. A retrospective vision is thus central to the experience of the sequence. In *Astrophil and Stella*, in contrast, the speaker, Astrophil, exists in a restless, tormented present, and when the affair breaks off, his narrative simply ends. Astrophil is given no retrospective consciousness. The ironic perspective that such a consciousness affords is created instead by the implied author, whose narrative arrangement highlights ironies of which Astrophil is often unaware. In contrast to Petrarch, whose sequence elaborates a continuously evolving consciousness, identified with the author himself, Sidney creates what might be called a schizophrenic form: a sonnet sequence in which the speaker, although insistently identified with the author, is contained by a narrative design and an authorial voice that subject him to consistent irony; to complicate matters even further, at any moment in *Astrophil and Stella* the irony may dissipate and the authorial voice become sympathetically aligned with the speaker himself.

This paradoxical form could be explained biographically if we were to accept a speculative but none the less plausible scenario for Sidney's composition of the sequence. This scenario would also help to explain the contradictions in critical response to Astrophil as a persona. Suppose we assume that when Penelope Rich came to court Sidney became romantically involved with her, in a relationship that, whether merely flirtatious or adulterous, aroused powerful and conflicting emotions. To court Stella, seriously or playfully or both, Sidney wrote sonnets to her. As occasional poems, the sonnets lacked a narrative framework and a named persona; in the completed sequence, Astrophil is named only three times, in songs viii and ix, and, as Ringler makes clear, Sidney himself provided no title for the sequence (*P*, 548). The implied speaker would therefore be naturally identified with Sidney himself, in all the shifting postures and moods of love. A collection of sonnets composed in such a context would invite readings that identify the speaker with the author, that emphasize lyrical rather than narrative qualities, and that see its social function as seduction or seductive entertainment.

To pursue this scenario, suppose we imagine the affair at an end, and Sidney arranging the poems into an ordered sequence, in imitation of Petrarch and other European sonneteers; the two opening sonnets, clearly introductory and set in the past tense, invite such a perspective.[11] At this point, the collection would have taken on a different meaning for Sidney and a different social function. Both emotionally and rhetorically, he would have been in a position to detach himself, more or less, from the speaker of the sonnets, and to frame the narrative in ways that would highlight ironically the unsuccessful nature of the affair. Poems that began as bids to seduce a particular woman would at that point become, by virtue of a new narrative context, witnesses against themselves, telling a more general audience the story of their own failure. In such a situation, the speaker of the sonnets would no longer be Philip Sidney but a persona, Astrophil, controlled and disciplined by an omniscient author. A sequence composed in such a fashion would encourage interpretations that emphasize the dissociation of speaker and author, narrative continuity rather than lyrical discontinuity, and a moral or esthetic purpose aimed at a less restrictive audience than Penelope herself.

Although such a version of events can by no means be proved, it contradicts nothing in the factual record, as far as I am aware, and accords with what we know generally about the social function and circulation of sonnets at court. If it should be true, as I believe it is, then the sequence we have is a kind of palimpsest, with different readers responding to different layers in the process of composition. Sidney and his coterie audience would have presumably responded to the completed sequence with a double vision: behind the 'fictitious' persona, they would have seen the shadows of the original affair and the original speaker, the Astrophil who was at an earlier stage indistinguishable from Sidney himself. Such a vision of the series would help explain the discrepancy between Sidney's apparent embarrassment at the sonnets, expressed both in Moffet's account of his death and his own sensitivity to the moral ambiguity of love poetry in the *Defence*, and the moralistic critique of love that runs through the sequence as a whole. Given this continuing moral sensitivity to the problem of love, it is especially remarkable that Sidney allowed the ambiguity in persona – and hence, in moral perspective – to remain.

The psychology implied by this account of the composition of the sonnets provides one way of understanding the relationship between Sidney and his persona. Another is provided by Sidney's comments on love and love poetry in the *Defence*. Taken as a whole, I believe, these comments show that in writing *Astrophil and Stella* Sidney was not only working out the implications of his experience of love but was at the same time working out a novel conception of love poetry itself, one that owed much to his conception of comedy. *A Defence of Poetry* enables us to understand that for Sidney the experience of love represented both a personal and an aesthetic dilemma, one that he attempted to resolve through the medium of comic theory.

Love poetry is in many respects the central problem in Sidney's *Defence*. Sidney's avowed purpose in the work is to defend poetry against its accusers, and the most serious charge against it, he tells us, is that it 'abuseth men's wit, training it to wanton sinfulness and lustful love' (103.29–30). Sidney's response to the accusation is equivocal at best. He begins by ruefully admitting the problem: 'Alas, Love, I would thou couldst as well defend thyself as thou canst offend others. I would those on whom thou dost attend could either put thee away, or yield good reason why they keep thee' (103.35–104.2). He then goes on, disingenuously, to place the blame on 'man's wit' (104.13) rather than on poetry. The discomfort is both personal and poetic: poets cannot resist love, since they are human, and yet they cannot defend it by reason. Despite his Neoplatonic tendencies, Sidney does not attempt to justify love by celebrating its capacity for reason. Love is simply irresistible and irrational. The logic of Sidney's defence at this point thus requires him either to ban love from poetry altogether, a prospect that literary history renders doubtful, or to call for an equally unlikely restriction of love poetry to moralizing admonitions. He vindicates poetry in principle, as Alan Sinfield observes, only 'at the expense of most actual love poetry.'[12]

When Sidney discusses lyrical poetry concretely towards the end of the *Defence*, the same tension reappears. His first impulse in commenting on 'that lyrical kind of songs and sonnets' is to express the desire that such poems should be devoted to the praise of God, as he and his sister, Mary, were to do in the translations of the psalms (116.27–36). This is one answer to the problem of love poetry: to replace human love with divine. In the very next sentence, however, Sidney shifts to the subject of passionate love and complains at the lack of '*energia*' in the love poems of his contemporaries: 'many of such writings as come under the banner of unresistible love, if I were a mistress,' he observes, 'would never persuade me they were in love' (116.35–117.2). The contradiction is startling. In one sentence, poems of passionate love are implicitly rejected in favour of holy psalms; in the next, they are condemned for their inability to show passion convincingly. The tension could be resolved, at least hypothetically, by a moralistic argument about the dissuasive power of such exposure of the passions, the capacity of love poetry to offer admonitions against love. But this is clearly not Sidney's drift. Even if it were, moreover, it would resolve only one of the two problems acknowledged in the earlier passage. If the power of love is truly irresistible, then poetic admonitions are in vain. The convincing representation of passion, moreover, it could be argued, would only fuel the desire for that which cannot be resisted anyway. Any poem that touches the subject of love convincingly, in short, is subject to a dilemma.

'Dilemma' is probably the right word, for Sidney's difficulties with love, philosophically, aesthetically, and experientially, seem to have continued up to his death. An attempt at resolution occurs, however, in Sidney's discussion of comedy, in which he turns to an image of love, Hercules with a distaff, to illustrate his conception of the proper comic effect.[13] Sidney argues that many contemporaries misunderstand the nature of comedy, which depends not merely on laughter, as is commonly supposed, but also on delight. It is wrong too, he argues, to think of laughter as arising from delight. Although the effects of delight and laughter can be combined, they are not causally related; indeed, they are somewhat contradictory: 'in themselves they have, as it were, a kind of contrariety: for delight we scarcely do but in things that have a conveniency to ourselves or to the general nature; laughter almost ever cometh of things most disproportioned to ourselves and nature. Delight hath a joy in it, either permanent or present. Laughter hath only a scornful tickling' (115.16–21). As Geoffrey Shepherd has shown, Sidney's conception of laughter is conventional and owes much to commentators such as Trissino, who emphasized its dependency upon ugliness and deformity and the human pleasure in ridicule.[14] Such a notion of comedy lends itself to moralistic interpretations of laughter, as in traditional defences of satire, which justify ridicule in the name of social and personal reform. This notion of comedy can be used to justify moralistic interpretations of *Astrophil and Stella*, which treat the series as a negative exemplum.[15]

Sidney's notion of delight, however, and its conjunction with laughter, is rather more difficult to situate within his general conception of poetry. The discussion of comic delight is framed by Sidney's earlier invocation of the Horatian dictum that the purpose of poetry is to 'teach and delight' (80.2); delight and moral instruction are therefore intended to be complementary. The special function of delight, indeed, is its ability to 'move men to take that goodness in hand, which without delight they would fly as from a stranger' (81.11–12). In the context of comedy, however, the notion of delight becomes more complicated. As defined in the passage quoted above, delight results from a 'conveniency,' or conformity, with 'ourselves' or 'general nature.' A comic effect, then, must be somewhat paradoxical, involving on the one hand a detached feeling of superiority, a 'scornful tickling,' resulting from the perception of deformity, and on the other a sympathetic identification, resulting from a perception of the conformity of the imitation to our own nature or to general human nature. The latter effect, however, is highly problematic, for if carried too far the seductive power of delight may undermine the moral judgment supposedly provoked by the 'scornful tickling' of laughter. This is precisely the accusation brought against poetry by its enemies, who claim that 'with a siren's sweetness' poetry draws 'the mind to the serpent's tail of sinful fancies.' Sidney acknowledges, moreover, that Chaucer himself faulted comedy precisely for this abuse: '(and herein, especially, comedies give the largest field to ear, as Chaucer saith)' (101.31–4). As a form that includes both laughter and delight, comedy is therefore a highly volatile compound.

Sidney illustrates the mixture of delight and laughter in comedy by alluding to a figure that is especially significant for our purposes, that of Hercules in love: 'in Hercules, painted with his great beard and furious countenance, in a woman's attire, spinning at Omphale's commandment, it breedeth both delight and laughter: for the representing of so strange a power in love procureth delight, and the scornfulness of the action stirreth laughter' (115.36–116.2). The 'scornfulness of the action' in this example lies in the deformity attendant upon the contrast between Hercules' heroic masculinity and his 'effeminate' subordination to Omphale and love. The delight, in contrast, derives from 'the representing of so strange a power in love.' The ambiguity in this phrase captures two complementary sources for delight: on the one hand, our delight in what is represented, the 'strange' power of love, which conforms with our general nature; on the other, our delight in the 'representing' itself, the truthfulness and artistry of the painter's vision.

If the comedy of love depends upon delight and laughter, then, it evokes at least three rather separate responses, two of which seem to some extent incompatible. The first is fairly straightforward: we are moved to scornful laughter at the ridiculousness of the action, prompted therefore to avoid such folly ourselves. The second and third, however, are ambiguously intertwined. Why does the 'representing of so strange a power in love procureth delight'? Delight arises from 'things that have a conveniency to ourselves or to the general nature.' We delight, Sidney tells us, when we see a 'fair woman,' when we experience good luck, when our country or friends are happy. In the case of Hercules, it is difficult to apply these examples unless we find joy or beauty in the 'strange power' of love; if we do that, however, we are delighting in the very power that produces effeminate action, at which we laugh in scorn; the more we acknowledge the 'strange power' of love, the more we understand its irresistible nature, the less inclined we are to moralize. The experience is double and paradoxical: we are asked to delight in and laugh at essentially the same thing. But delight arises not merely from the conformity of the 'strange power of love to our general nature'; it arises from the 'representing of that power.' As Sidney makes clear elsewhere, delight is in large measure an aesthetic response: the poet comes to us, for example, 'with words set in delightful proportion' (92.7–8). Just as 'we are ravished with delight to see a fair woman' (115.22), we experience 'heart-ravishing knowledge' (76.25) through the beauty of poetry. In both cases, the word 'ravishing' suggests the equivocal power of the experience. Although Sidney's theory of comedy is ostensibly moralistic, the equivocations at the heart of it help to explain why *Astrophil and Stella* is not a moral tract, a 'demonstration' of Sidney's notion of comedy, but a comic representation of the equivocations themselves.[16]

As illustrated by the image of Hercules with a distaff, then, the comic effect includes scornful laughter at the follies of love, sympathetic delight at their universality, and aesthetic joy at their manner of representation. The distinctive energy of *Astrophil and Stella* as a mode of self-representation derives largely from its paradoxical and volatile combinations of all three responses. Its wonderful tonal variety, moreover, which ranges from lyrical pathos to boisterous comedy, results from the shifting emphases among these three perspectives.

Sidney's approach to the comedy of love, as we have seen in the example of Hercules, centres on comic effect and not on comic structure. Hence Sidney's views provide no guidance towards the form of *Astrophil and Stella* as a whole. The endless cycle of desire depicted in the final sonnet is certainly not comic in a structural sense, although its witty exploitation of Petrarchan clichés may create a rather bleak version of the comic effect Sidney describes in the *Defence*. In his preface to the 1591 edition of the sequence, Thomas Nashe captures something of its tonal complexity. Its 'chiefe Actor,' he says, is Melpomene, the muse of tragedy, and its argument follows accordingly: 'cruell chastitie, the Prologue hope, the Epilogue dispaire.' Nashe also calls the work, however, a 'Theater of pleasure' and a 'tragicommody of love ... performed by starlight.' And he presents the work to his readers by inviting them to offer their 'smiles on the Aulters of *Venus*.'[17] Tragedy, tragicomedy, comedy – the labels suggest the tonal variety of the sequence as a whole, not its structure. Perhaps the most accurate structural label, to borrow a trick from Polonius, is comical-ironical, since, as we shall see, the downfall of Astrophil is marked by a general shift in tone from sympathetic and often exuberant comedy to satiric irony. Even within this framework, however, the tone of individual sonnets varies greatly.

In exploring the shape of Astrophil's identity and the relationship between persona and authorial voice, I shall be emphasizing the narrative design of the sequence. In doing so, I shall necessarily cast in shadow many complex realizations of self that occur in individual sonnets and run the risk of seeming to confuse a lyrical with a narrative mode. The series as a whole, however, has a clear narrative design: it records the vicissitudes of a love affair that has a beginning, middle, and end, and centres on the consciousness of a character whose attitudes, opinions, and relationship to the authorial voice change over time. Although Sidney's dominant impulse is lyrical, his gestures towards a narrative line are more extensive than those of other English sonneteers in the period. The achievement of the sequence lies to a great extent in its depiction of the gradual evolution or, more precisely, dissolution of Astrophil's 'self,' and in its ordering of that process within a complex comic frame.

The sonnet that opens *Astrophil and Stella* serves as prologue to the series as a whole and a touchstone for its most distinctive comic effects. It may be useful, therefore, to consider these effects in some detail before embarking upon what must be a rather sketchy analysis of Astrophil's development. In sonnet 1, Astrophil presents himself as a young courtier untested in either poetry or love, whose desire to win his lady's favour through poetry leads him, first, to search for inventions in other poets and, then, having found that method useless, to follow his Muse, who tells him, '"looke in thy heart and write"' (1.14). Since the image of his love lies in his heart, the resolution of the poem provides a graceful compliment to Stella as well as an assertion of a commitment to poetic originality and truth. In this sonnet Astrophil speaks with a voice that is characteristic of the early sonnets in the series. Playful and self-mocking, passionate yet analytical, he struggles self-consciously, with a mixture of adolescent narcissism and frankness, to come to terms with his new experiences as lover and poet. It is an engaging and seductive voice, one that evokes sympathy for the difficulty of translating the experience of love into 'fit words' (1.5).

Even in this introductory poem, however, in which Sidney allows Astrophil his full youthful charm, a satiric undercurrent is apparent. Although Astrophil seems utterly frank, his language is subtly self-deceptive, ignoring questions that will emerge forcefully as the courtship develops. Astrophil claims to love 'in truth' (1.1), yet his first impulse is not to truth but to rhetoric: 'I sought fit words to paint the blackest face of woe' (1.5). Although the Muse's concluding exhortation, '"looke in thy heart and write"' (1.14) implies a union of truth and rhetoric, it remains an exhortation, and one that Astrophil is later unable to follow. Astrophil's purpose in writing, moreover, carries a further irony. His audience is Stella, and he writes so that in reading of his love she may progress from pleasure through knowledge and pity to grace. The description of the reading process is itself rather suspiciously methodical, almost calculating, but more significant is the ambiguity of the word 'grace' (1.4) with which the process culminates, for it enables Astrophil to focus on the problem of poetic invention rather than the potentially incriminating one of poetic purpose. As the series develops, it becomes clear very quickly that Astrophil's goal is physical seduction and that 'grace' is a euphemism for sexual favour. In a way that Astrophil does not intend, he does follow the exhortation of his Muse to look in his heart and write. The problem lies in what he and his readers find there. From the first, then, Astrophil's love is subjected to implicit moral judgment, a judgment that will become increasingly pronounced and satirical as the series proceeds.[18]

The 'delight' of the sonnet, however, to use Sidney's word, lies not in the 'scornful tickling' of moral judgment but in the imaginative energy of the representation. In this poem, as in many others in the series, the rendering of the situation is broadly comic, almost farcical. The farce, however, is coupled with refined wit, producing a comic blend that seems uniquely Sidneyan. The visual images with which Astrophil depicts his dilemma are as hyperbolically incongruous as that of Hercules with a distaff, the image that Sidney uses as a touchstone for the comedy of love in the *Defence*. The comic effect of each image, moreover, is multiplied by absurd visual puns. Astrophil turns the 'leaves' of other poets, hoping to shake some 'fruitfull showers' upon his 'sunne-burn'd braine' (1.7–8). He stumbles over 'others' feete' (1.11), although in a perfectly metrical line. He bites his 'trewand pen' and beats himself, helpless in the throes of childbirth – 'great with child to speake' (1.12–13). In the face of such verbal pyrotechnics, both the implicit moral judgment against Astrophil and the sympathy for his predicament tend to recede into the background. The ostensible theme of the poem, moreover, the rejection of a derivative Petrarchism in favour of the truth of the heart, is ultimately less central to the poem's effect than the exhilirating comic invention with which it is developed.

The distinctive pleasure that such poems provide derives essentially from the self-conscious wit of the act of representation itself – the 'representing of so strange a power in love.' The effect thus encompasses both poet and persona in a complex rendering of the comedy of love. By both identifying himself with and separating himself from Astrophil, Sidney is able to render the predicament of love with a combination of judgment, sympathy, and aesthetic delight. The method does not resolve the problem of achieving an appropriate attitude towards love or an appropriate poetics of love; instead, it allows for a complex representation of the problem itself, a comic poetics in which the poet himself is self-consciously implicated in all aspects of the problem. Astrophil's vanity as a poet is matched by Sidney's own obvious delight in his craft, and Astrophil's suspicious devotion to love by Sidney's own commitment to love poetry, the virtues of which even he could not articulate in the *Defence*.

Having apparently resolved the problem of poetic invention in sonnet 1 with the advice of his Muse, Astrophil adopts a rather self-congratulatory tone in several early sonnets that continue to explore the topic. All of these poems serve as compliments to Stella, who is the source of Astrophil's inventions, but they do so by asserting Astrophil's superiority to conventional poets. In sonnet 3, for example, Astrophil mocks poets who 'crie on the Sisters nine' (3.1); who ape Pindar, 'Enam'ling with pied flowers their thoughts of gold' (3.4); and who indulge in 'new found Tropes' (3.6) or 'strange similies' (3.7). He himself eschews such follies and merely copies what Nature writes in Stella. In sonnet 6, the targets are Petrarchan oxymorons ('faire stormes and freesing fires' [6.4]), the use of mythological and pastoral conventions, and emotional excess; in sonnet 15, the imitation of Petrarch and excessive alliteration. What distinguishes Astrophil from the conventional poets he sees around him is his devotion to Stella, which inspires in him, he claims, authentic and original emotion and language.

Although Astrophil's stylistic judgments correspond closely to those Sidney himself expresses in the *Defence*, it is none the less important to perceive the ironies that surround them. For one thing, as critics who identify Sidney with Astrophil are forced to concede, Astrophil is guilty of the very faults he finds in others; he himself admits as much in sonnet 55, where he vows no longer to invoke the Muses or to 'sugar' (55.10) his speech but merely to cry 'incessantly' (55.11) Stella's name. Irony is also present in the fact that Astrophil's poetic efforts meet with no success. 'Come let me write,' he announces to himself in sonnet 34, and the answer is '"And to what end?"' (34.1). Various reasons, none satisfactory, are proposed: to 'ease / A burthned hart' (34.1–2); to please readers with his pain; to win fame for the rarity of his disease; to relieve himself by venting his grief. The only motive that convinces, very tentatively put forward, is that some readers may find in his poems '*Stella's* great powrs, that so confuse my mind' (34.14). The form of this poem itself imitates Astrophil's mental disorientation, showing that Stella's great power destroys rather than inspires poetic invention. As in most of the self-reflexive poems of the sequence, the final effect creates a division between speaker and author: the former, befuddled by Stella, produces a poem of stumbling ineptitude; the latter, ironically detached but sympathetically inclined, creates a *tour de force* that reproduces a poetic failure. Astrophil's poem creates laughter, the author's poem, comic delight.

The ironies of Astrophil's failure as a poet increase as the series proceeds, and he seems conscious of them, but they are themselves contained within an overarching framework of which he seems only dimly aware. If Astrophil's stylistic preferences find echoes in the *Defence*, his conception of poetic purpose does not – or does so only in contradiction. Astrophil's purpose in writing is to seduce. The central argument of the *Defence*, however, is that poetry is a better teacher than history or philosophy because it moves readers to virtuous action. In the *Defence*, moreover, Sidney develops a psychology of reading similar to that which Astrophil envisages in sonnet 1: lured by the pleasure they find in poetry, readers are both morally instructed and moved to imitate the virtues they find there. This psychology places a heavy moral burden on the poet, and one of the curious evasions of the *Defence* is precisely the question as to whether that burden is justified; Sidney is at pains to deny poets any divine inspiration, yet he provides no other basis for believing that a skilful poet could not as easily move readers to vice as to virtue. His treatment of love poets, as we have seen, suggests consciousness of a continuing dilemma.

If Sidney evades the question of the moral capacity of the poet in *A Defence of Poetry*, he places it at the ironic centre of *Astrophil and Stella*. And he does so at Astrophil's expense. Although Astrophil is quite self-conscious about his poetic style and, as we shall see, about his lack of virtue in loving, he consistently evades the one question that might make him stop writing altogether. Only once, in sonnet 77, when he tries to convince himself that he might rest content with the knowledge of Stella's many virtues and beauties alone, does he seem self-conscious about the conflict between his desire and his role as poet. 'Yet ah,' he confesses in the final line, 'my Mayd'n Muse doth blush to tell the best' (77.14). Nowhere else does he acknowledge the moral problem of using poetry for seduction. One of the ironies in the poems on writing poetry is that, while Astrophil claims to be above artificial poetic conventions, his purpose as a poet, the motive of seduction, is entirely conventional in both social and literary terms.

In the *Defence*, as we have seen, Sidney acknowledges the moral problem of love poetry, rather reluctantly, and in terms that reflect upon Astrophil's evasiveness. The sonnets thus expose Astrophil as poet to the moral critique that Sidney himself skirts in the *Defence*. Given the proximity of the two works, it is likely that Sidney's ironic treatment of Astrophil represents an attempt to come to terms with a problem, both romantic and poetic, that called into question the 'unelected' poetic vocation to which he was increasingly drawn.[19] Perhaps falling in love with Penelope Rich forced a confrontation with the naïve optimism of the *Defence;* or perhaps the wide gap between persona and authorial voice in *Astrophil and Stella* permitted a candour inhibited in the *Defence* by the rhetorical demands of the occasion.

The engagingly naïve and self-congratulatory quality of the early sonnets on poetry carries over into another group of poems that develop Astrophil's attitudes as a courtier. In these poems too the experience of love causes Astrophil to see himself as a figure set apart from the world around him; he thus becomes a critic of conventional court behaviour as well as conventional court poetry. His world centres not on the queen, whom he never mentions, but on Stella, who displaces her as a courtier's object of idolatry. In sonnet 9, for example, Stella's face becomes 'Queene *Vertue's* court' (9.1), and all of its features the parts of an awesome palace. Occurring as it does in a vividly realized court setting, Astrophil's silent erasure of the queen from his poems becomes a figure for his political estrangement – a sign of his commitment to the private world of love.

In this erasure Astrophil resembles his author, whose failure to celebrate Elizabeth in the language of Petrarchan idolatry, either in these or in other poems, must have had political connotations. As we have seen, some critics read *Astrophil and Stella* as a displacement of Sidney's political frustrations, with the relationship between ineffectual lover and cruel mistress becoming a figure for Sidney's relationship with the queen. As a document of court life, however, *Astrophil and Stella* is equally political as a sonnet sequence devoted exclusively to private love. In the courtly context, the erasure of the queen from such a sequence may well have had a startling effect.

Astrophil's fixation on Stella distracts him from court affairs, and a number of early sonnets register his mockery of courtiers who are immersed in them. In sonnet 23 he scorns the 'curious wits' of the court, who, seeing 'dull pensiveness' (23.1) in Astrophil's eyes, interpret it in their own lights as arising from scholarly pursuits, or service to 'the Prince' (23.7) or 'ambition's rage' (23.9), no one guessing the truth that all his thoughts are devoted to Stella. Sonnet 27 pursues a similar line of thought, with rumour-mongers attributing Astrophil's 'darke abstracted guise' (27.1) to 'that poison foule of bubling pride' (27.6), whereas his

highest ambition is actually Stella's grace. In sonnet 30 Astrophil lists the
questions that 'busie wits' (30.12) frame to him about British and Continental political affairs and turns his indifference to them into a compliment for Stella: 'I, cumbred with good maners, answer do, / But know
not how, for still I thinke of you' (30.13–14). Sonnet 51 mocks a courtly
politician for subjecting Astrophil to 'all the grave conceits your braine
doth breed' (51.6), while his heart 'confers with *Stella's* beames' (51.12).
All of these poems end in compliments to Stella, for Astrophil's indifference to courtly affairs arises from his fixation on her; they also reveal a
satirical Astrophil, however, who mockingly dissociates himself from the
world of political intrigue and gossip that constitutes the Elizabethan
court.

  Although it is difficult to resist Astrophil's delight in his superiority to
the 'busie wits' who surround him, these satirical poems, like those he
directs against conventional poets, rebound against him in subtle ways.
The 'curious wits' of sonnet 23, for example, speculate that Astrophil's distraction might arise from the unworthy motive of ambition, but they also
speculate that he might be busy with his studies or with redressing 'state
errours' (23.8). Sonnet 30 raises issues that were of immediate concern to
Sidney and other courtiers in the summer of 1582, such as the status of the
Turkish threat against Spain and the effect of recent military defeats on
William of Orange's rule of Holland; it includes, moreover, a reference to
the fate of his own father's work in Ulster. Within Astrophil's mockery of
court politics, then, one finds occasional undercurrents of unconscious
irony. The very affairs other courtiers believe engage his mind are affairs
he should have been engaged in, for they represent the political commitments that have been abandoned out of love for Stella. As a satiric
observer of his treatment at the hands of politic courtiers, moreover,
Astrophil himself inevitably becomes tainted by their persistent quest for
hidden meanings; as Jones and Stallybrass observe, Astrophil's mockery of
the public world implicates him in 'their ways of seeing.'[20] The court
world Astrophil depicts is a world of obsessive spying and gossiping, and
he himself spends a good deal of time watching others watch him. In this
way his satiric impulse becomes a form of comic narcissism.

  The adolescent vanity implicit in this preoccupation with observing
and being observed is captured wittily in sonnet 41, Astrophil's comically
naïve account of his victory in a tournament. The theme of the sonnet is
looking at Astrophil. He obtains the prize, he says at the opening, both by
the judgment of the 'English eyes' and the French (41.3–4). He then
records the various ways in which observers have misinterpreted his suc-

cess: horsemen attribute his victory to his 'skill in horsemanship'; town folks, to his strength; a 'daintier judge,' to his skill at feinting; 'luckie wits,' to 'chaunce'; his family, to heredity (41.5–11). All, however, 'shoote awrie,' for the 'true cause' of his victory is that '*Stella* lookt on, and from her heavenly face / Sent forth the beames, which made so faire my race' (41.12–14). Although this poem continues Astrophil's critique of the court world for its prying eyes and self-reflexive speculations, it turns that critique against Astrophil himself, whose gentle mockery so obviously fuels his own desire for applause. Although the poem ostensibly redirects that applause to Stella, it does so by making her, like everyone else, an audience for Astrophil.

In the early part of the series, Astrophil's naïve self-indulgences as lover and poet remain engaging, partly because of his passionate energy and wit, partly because of his attempt to transcend convention. Sidney's technical bravura and occasionally outrageous comic effects, moreover, complicate the picture of Astrophil by inviting us to keep one eye on the poet himself. Early in the series, too, Astrophil occasionally confronts the moral problems that flow from his increasing awareness of the sexual nature of his passion. The grounds of his resistance to this love, the teachings of school and church, are entirely conventional but none the less compelling for that: he never undermines them as irrelevant to his situation but merely discovers, time and again, that they cannot destroy or redirect his passion. Virtue, he knows, opposes 'vaine love' (4.3), but he consigns its restraints to 'Churches or schooles' (4.6). Religion tells him that we are all pilgrims on earth, but his love remains earthly (5). Reason argues against 'love and sence' (10.9) but becomes itself corrupted by love of Stella: 'Reason thou kneel'dst, and offeredst straight to prove / By reason good, good reason her to love' (10.13–14). The social and moral values that underlie such resistances to love are those that were inculcated in Sidney by his family, his mentors, and his humanistic education. They are the same values invoked in the uncomfortable discussion of love poetry in the *Defence* and by Philisides in the *Old Arcadia* when he contemplates his youth.

Astrophil's feelings of guilt at the loss of these values are also reminiscent of Philisides'. Sonnet 18, for example, one of the most subtly ironical in the series, develops these feelings with the kind of autobiographical resonance that Philisides' narrative of his history provides in the *Old Arcadia*. In this poem Astrophil is called to audit by Reason and forced to admit that he is bankrupt of 'all those goods, which heav'n to me hath lent' (18.4). He cannot pay the debt he owes to Nature and, even worse, can provide no excuse, for he has 'most idly spent' (18.8) his wealth. The sestet brings the poem to a hyperbolically self-destructive conclusion:

> My youth doth waste, my knowledge brings forth toyes,
> My wit doth strive those passions to defend,
> Which for reward spoile it with vaine annoyes.
> I see my course to lose my selfe doth bend:
>   I see and yet no greater sorow take,
>   Then that I lose no more for *Stella's* sake.   (18.9–14)

The voice here is much like that of Philisides, yet it touches deeper emotions of loss and self-reproach. Astrophil has no Mira to blame for an argument, or a Diana or Venus to blame for his fate. He portrays his debt as one to his own nature, moreover, not merely to his family or society. His poetic self-consciousness, too, in the admission that 'my knowledge brings forth toyes,' adds a self-reflexive quality to the guilt that is expressed in the *Old Arcadia* not by Philisides but by Sidney himself in his prefatory letter to his sister. The bankruptcy culminates, finally, in a loss that strikes at the moral centre of the sequence – the loss of self.

The cumulative moral pressure of the poem gives to the final couplet an intensity that is rare in the series. Astrophil concludes his audit not only with a clear-headed acceptance of the inevitable loss of self but with grief that the loss could not be greater. The totality of the commitment to love verges on heroic self-sacrifice, an acceptance of a world well lost. The climactic expression of this self-sacrifice, however, 'Then that I lose no more for Stella's sake,' exposes a flaw in Astrophil's apparent heroism. He is ready to lose his self, he says, 'for Stella's sake.' The phrase is nicely ambiguous. It could mean, sympathetically interpreted, that he will sacrifice himself so that Stella will gain by it. Stella shows no signs, however, of any lack that could be remedied by Astrophil's sexual passion. The phrase could also mean, more plausibly and more cynically, that he is ready to lose his self in order to possess Stella. Either interpretation ends remorselessly in Astrophil's lust. What seems to be a self-sacrificial commitment to a tragic love proves finally a species of self-deception. By evading in the final line the nature of his commitment to Stella, Astrophil discloses the hypocrisy underlying his pretensions of self-sacrifice.

Not all of Astrophil's early struggles with sexuality end in self-deception or hypocrisy; the majority end in impasses, with Astrophil admitting the competing and irreconcilable claims of both sexual passion and virtue, as in sonnet 5, where he accepts both the truth of Christianity and the truth

of his love for Stella. Since Astrophil cannot marry Stella or deny his passion, the only escape available to him is the kind of sublimation provided
by Neoplatonism, as developed by Cardinal Bembo in the *Courtier*, whereby
the identification of beauty with virtue may convert sexual love into spiritual. Many of the early sonnets treat the conflict between sense and spirit
in Neoplatonic terms, but the possibility of such a love is developed most
fully in sonnet 25, which begins with the recollection of Socrates' statement 'That Vertue, if it once met with our eyes, / Strange flames of *Love* it
in our soules would raise' (25.4). Virtue herself has taken Stella's shape,
'that she / To mortall eyes might sweetly shine in her,' and through that
shape Astrophil experiences the truth of the Neoplatonic doctrine: 'It is
most true, for since I her did see, / Vertue's great beautie in that face I
prove, / And find th'effect, for I do burne in love' (25.10–14). Here the
irony belongs to Astrophil, since he recognizes in the paradox of his experience the futility of the Neoplatonic dream. He burns in love, that he
knows, but with the flames of sensuality, not with the purifying flames of a
love of virtue. Like Reason's efforts to persuade him through argument,
Virtue's attempt to convert him through the love of beauty ends not only
in a failure of spirituality but in an increase in sexual passion.

The inadequacy of Neoplatonism recurs frequently throughout the
series and is deeply linked to Astrophil's failure as a poet. If the source of
Astrophil's poetry is Stella's image, and if that image is identified with virtue and beauty, then not only Astrophil's love but his poetry should be
virtuous. Stella's face, not the lines of other poets, becomes the text he
imitates: 'in *Stella's* face I reed, / What Love and Beautie be, then all my
deed / But Copying is, what in her Nature writes' (3.12–14). Yet this, the
perfect literary text, fails in its effect: Astrophil is not persuaded by
Stella's beauty to a virtuous love or to virtuous poetry. Instead, he grows
increasingly restive with virtue and impatient to seduce. If Stella's perfect
text has a damaging effect on Astrophil, his own imperfect text, inspired
ironically by the image that lies in his heart, has no effect on Stella: she
never yields to his passion.

Through the language of Neoplatonism, Astrophil's love for Stella thus
becomes a parody of the reading process as described by Sidney in *A
Defence of Poetry*.[21] In that work, the doctrine underlying sonnet 25 is
framed more tentatively: '*if* [my italics] the saying of Plato and Tully bee
true, that who could see virtue, would be wonderfully ravished with the
love of her beauty ...' (98). Despite the tentativeness, the notion is treated
seriously and becomes the basis for a moral psychology of reading that is
challenged not only by Astrophil's purpose in writing, as we have seen

earlier, but by his experience as a lover. He copies Stella's image but in poems that aim at her seduction. The ineffectuality of Stella's 'text' belies the optimism of the *Defence* about the capacity of poetry as a moral force. Stella is, after all, a perfect poem: she is beautiful, speaks beautifully, and promotes virtue; yet she is utterly ineffectual, and in ways that challenge Sidney's attraction towards Neoplatonic conceptions of both love and poetry.

This challenge to the underlying assumptions of the *Defence* is mounted most explicitly in sonnet 71, where Astrophil, having by now become fully committed to seductive conquest, expresses some lingering regrets. In this sonnet, Stella becomes herself a book:

> Who will in fairest booke of Nature know,
> How Vertue may best lodg'd in beautie be,
> Let him but learne of *Love* to reade in thee,
> *Stella*, those faire lines, which true goodnesse show. (71.1–4)

In Stella's text readers find the overthrow of all vices, not by 'rude force but sweetest soveraigntie / Of reason' (71.6–7). Not content to be 'Perfection's heire' herself, she strives 'all minds that way to move, / Who marke in thee what is in thee most faire' (71.10–12). Astrophil, however, remains an unconverted reader, drawn by her 'faire lines' not towards virtue but towards his own desire: 'So while thy beautie drawes the heart to love, / As fast thy Vertue bends that love to good: / "But ah," Desire still cries, "give me some food"' (71.12–14). As a lover and poet, then, Astrophil becomes entangled in a psychology of reading and writing that mocks the one put forward in the *Defence.* Stella is a perfect poem, yet her text produces in Astrophil obsessive sexual passion that itself generates texts of seduction. This is hardly the imitative effect that Sidney envisages in the *Defence* when he imagines the poetic creation of one heroic image of Cyrus bringing more Cyruses into the world (79.10–16). The comic anticlimax with which the poem ends jolts us not only with the 'strange power' of love but with the self-conscious wit of the author, whose elaborately ironical design evokes comic delight.

The flaws in Astrophil's poetics of seduction are perhaps most wittily exposed in sonnet 45, which captures his increasing cynicism as courtier, lover, and poet. Lamenting that his woeful expressions produce no effect on Stella, and observing that she is so moved by listening to a tragic fable of love that tears come to her eyes, Astrophil concludes that fictions 'breed' more 'grace' (45.10) than his own ruin. He therefore urges Stella to imagine him a tragic text: 'Then thinke my deare, that you in me do reed / Of Lover's ruine some sad Tragedie: / I am not I, pitie the tale of me' (45.12–14). The sonnet elaborates playfully the point that Sidney himself makes about poetry in the *Defence* – that fictions move more powerfully than facts. Astrophil departs from the *Defence*, however, in attempting to use that knowledge for the purpose of seduction.

The poem's effect hinges on the final phrase, 'the tale of me,' which not only converts Astrophil himself into a tragic poem but identifies both with his sexual desire: his 'tale' is his 'tail.'[22] Here and throughout the series, Sidney's comic imagination combines farce and pointed wit. Astrophil's desire reduces both himself and his fiction to the story of his 'tail.' Even more ironical, given the contrast between truth and fiction ostensibly at the centre of the poem, is the way in which Astrophil's final plea to fictionalize himself is redundant. Although Astrophil asks to be read as a fiction only at the end of the sonnet, the 'verie face of wo' that he wears in the opening line as a sign of the truth of his love is itself 'painted' in his 'beclowded stormie face' (45.1–2). The allusion to painting recalls sonnet 1, in which Astrophil had sought 'to paint the blackest face of woe' in order to win Stella's 'grace' (1.4–5). In both places the image of the painted face links Astrophil's love to corrupt art and the artificial world of the court. Astrophil reproaches Stella in sonnet 45, moreover, not for failing to pity him in his woe but for failing to pity his 'disgrace'; what galls him is his public humiliation. A poem that seems based upon a distinction between Astrophil's true love and fables of love thus ends by reducing Astrophil's love, in person or in print, to a fiction, and his fiction to a 'tail.' It seems no coincidence that in *A Defence of Poetry* Sidney uses the same pun to characterize one of the arguments aimed at 'poor poets': that poetry 'is the nurse of abuse, infecting us with many pestilent desires; with a siren's sweetness drawing the mind to the serpent's tail of sinful fancies' (101.30–3).[23] The phrase echoes not only the pun on 'tail' but the notion of Stella's beauty 'drawing' the poet to love.

In the early stages of the sonnet sequence, one senses several possible lines that Sidney could follow in his treatment of Astrophil's love. Astrophil's early responsiveness to moral pressure, as we have seen, could develop into serious moral and spiritual self-exploration in the manner of Petrarch, say, or Shakespeare. Or the problem of sexuality could be resolved by a Neoplatonic escape from the burdens of sensuality, as described by Bembo in the *Courtier*, or by a Christian repudiation of sinful love, as embodied in Sidney's poem, 'Leave me ô Love, which reachest but to dust.' Or Astrophil could be ennobled by an unfulfilled love, as happens to Strephon and Klaius in the *New Arcadia* (5). Instead, Sidney chooses a very simple, even simplistic, method of development. Stella remains for Astrophil the epitome of virtue, and he devotes himself with increasing cynicism to his lust and to attempts at seduction. The early moral energy in poems such as sonnet 18 is dissipated as the series proceeds. Although it never quite disappears, the inner drama of self-exploration gives way increasingly to an external drama of seduction and courtly intrigue. The diminishing sympathy for Astrophil that accompanies this development results in increasingly stark contrasts between comic delight and satiric laughter.

Although moral qualms linger in Astrophil as late as sonnets 71 and 72, the early struggle between virtue and love reaches a definitive end in sonnet 52. The sonnet presents a lawsuit between Virtue and Love, each of whom claims ownership of Stella. Since Virtue does not contest Love's ownership of Stella's external beauty and Love does not contest Virtue's ownership of her soul, the question becomes, which is the true, the essential Stella? Astrophil identifies himself with Love and urges Love to conclude the suit by settling for Stella's body: 'Well *Love*, since this demurre our sute doth stay, / Let *Vertue* have that *Stella's* selfe; yet thus, / That *Vertue* but that body graunt to us' (52.13–14).

Although sonnet 52 is not a very complicated poem in thought or emotion, its language does have important implications. The most obvious point is that Astrophil is willing to abandon the soul for the body. This is his most cynical and open commitment yet to lust. The tone accentuates the cynicism, for the language is that of the law courts, where bargains are struck by self-interested parties not interested in justice. That Astrophil can imagine dividing Stella's soul from her body, moreover, shows how far he has moved from thoughts of Neoplatonism, which sees love as a means of spiritual ascent. Most striking is the explicit identification of Stella's soul with her 'selfe.' Astrophil accepts a dichotomy between spirit and flesh, admits that Stella is essentially spirit, and yet is willing to abandon spirit for the body. He has thus moved from the position of consciously throwing away his own self – 'I see my course to lose my selfe doth bend' (18.12) – to consciously throwing away Stella's. At this point Astrophil's veils of idealization and self-deception are completely withdrawn and Stella becomes nothing but the body he desires. Such cynicism is the logical result of Astrophil's reduction of himself to a tail in sonnet 45. The wit of the poem lies in its melodramatic portrayal of Astrophil as a conniving lawyer, desperate to strike any deal that feeds his lust: 'Well *Love*, since this demurre our sute doth stay ...'

The culmination of this cynical commitment to seduction occurs in sonnet 69, which forms part of a cluster of poems – sonnets 68 to 72 – that mark a crucial stage in the development of the narrative. At this point Stella has finally declared her love for Astrophil, but only on the condition that he reciprocate it virtuously. The sonnet begins with Astrophil's raptures, charming in their exuberant spontaneity, but ends with a cynical indifference to Stella's condition that encompasses his several roles, as poet, lover, and courtier. 'O joy,' he begins, 'too high for my low stile to show' (69.1). The word 'stile,' which seems at first restricted to its literary meaning, becomes increasingly ambiguous, for the ensuing lines create a context that is clearly social and political, making his 'stile' a question of status: Astrophil sees his 'blisse' as 'fit for a nobler state than me' (69.2). The courtly context is elaborated further as Astrophil invites his friend to share in his joy, for this is a friend who penetrated Astrophil's courtly disguises, who 'saw through all maskes my wo' (69.5). As the poem develops, it becomes increasingly political, with an apparently spontaneous expression of joy at Stella's love being gradually converted into a cynical exuberance at new-found dominance. As Jones and Stallybrass note, in this poem Astrophil's language 'founds love in power.'[24]

The machiavellian language of the sestet, which begins with an announcement of Stella's compact, brings this metamorphosis to an exhilarating comic close:

> For *Stella* hath with words where faith doth shine,
> Of her high heart giv'n me the monarchie:
> I, I, ô I may say, that she is mine.
> And though she give but thus conditionly
> This realme of blisse, while vertuous course I take,
> No kings be crown'd, but they some covenants make.   (69.9–14)

Astrophil's aspiration for a high 'stile' thus centres on Stella's words of 'faith,' which give him the monarchy of her heart. With machiavellian cunning, however, Astrophil is prepared to violate the truth of words, making a covenant which he intends to break. Having thereby achieved his 'realme of blisse,' he will have achieved the high 'stile' appropriate for the greatness of his joy. The machiavellianism is thus at once poetic, political, and sexual.

The brilliantly comic and exuberant egotism of this sonnet conveys several of its most pointed ironies. Ten of the fourteen lines contain explicit self-references – to 'my low stile,' 'my wo,' 'my miserie,' 'my spring,' and the like – and the climactic expression of joy is an ecstatic celebration of the power of self: 'I, I, ô I may say, that she is mine.' This is a high style indeed, an ironic reversal of the self-sacrifice that Astrophil commits himself to in sonnet 18, where he finds in the prospect of the loss of self only sorrow that he can 'lose no more for *Stella's* sake' (18.14). Astrophil's exuberant address to his friend increases this irony, for the friend is presumably the one addressed earlier in sonnet 21, where he warns Astrophil against destroying the promise of his youth. This is the friend who Astrophil now assumes will share in the joy of his conquest: 'Come, come, and let me powre my selfe on thee' (69.6). The invitation is particularly ironic, for Astrophil does pour himself out in this sonnet, emptying out any spiritual pretensions that might yet qualify the remorseless simplicity of his sexual drive. His commitment to the machiavellian pursuit of sexual power aligns him with the courtly world of political intrigue that he had earlier scorned. As is often the case in the series, however, even at its most moralistic, the exuberance and self-conscious wit of the authorial voice, inviting our delight in the sheer joy of the comic representation, tends to complicate moral judgment.

The second song, which follows shortly after sonnet 69, carries forward its cynical tone and translates Astrophil's machiavellian intentions into comic action. The song dramatizes Astrophil's reactions to catching Stella asleep. As Astrophil surveys Stella's body, he becomes increasingly aroused, each stanza playing upon her vulnerability and his opportunity to take his revenge for her cruelty to him. In stanza four, he decides to attack: 'Now will I invade the fort; / Cowards *Love* with losse rewardeth' (ii.15–16). He immediately checks himself, however, not with any moral qualms, but with fear of her 'just and high disdaine' (ii.18): '*Love* feares nothing else but anger' (ii.20). So he contents himself with stealing a kiss, rationalizing, as in sonnet 69, that greater success will follow: 'Who will read must first learne spelling' (ii.24). Astrophil's anticipation of triumph is short-lived, however, for Stella awakens in anger, and he flees full of self-reproach for his cowardice: 'Foole, more foole, for no more taking' (ii.28).

As in sonnet 69, the metaphoric structure of the second song implicates each of Astrophil's social roles in his folly. The commitment to political power embodied in sonnet 69 is reflected in the military language of the song, by which Cupid is 'disarmed' (ii.8), Stella's guarding hand 'grants a free resort' (ii.14), and the act of love becomes an act of 'taking' (ii.28), an invasion of a 'fort' (ii.15). The metaphoric identification of spelling with kissing, and reading with the act of love, carries forward the debasement of language that in sonnet 69 leads to breaking one's word in order to achieve a high 'stile.' It alludes as well to sonnet 71, in which Stella becomes the 'fairest booke of Nature' (71.1) and reading her a way to move towards her perfection. In sonnet 71 Astrophil acknowledges the failure of the Neoplatonic progression with some regret: '"But ah," Desire still cries, "give me some food"' (71.14); in the second song, however, reading itself is identified with sexual consummation, and he reproaches himself for 'no more taking.'

Astrophil's theft of a kiss in the second song is exposed to another, subtler kind of irony, created by the backdrop of the event itself. In the second half of the sequence the poems become increasingly dramatic, an effect heightened by the clustering of songs in this section, and as a result the social environment of the lovers becomes increasingly prominent, casting its own indirect commentary on the nature of the relationship. In the second song, one cannot escape the melodrama of the moment: Stella alone, defenceless and asleep; Astrophil surveying her body, part by part, deciding to attack, then faltering, but finally stealing a kiss; Stella awakening angrily; Astrophil comically fleeing, cursing himself for how little he has taken. As in other poems that cluster in this part of the sequence, the perspective from which we view Astrophil becomes dualistic. The middle term in Sidney's conception of the comedy of love, sympathy for the irresistible passion of the lover, has relatively little impact: Astrophil in this episode is more caricature than character. The impact of the song thus depends upon a dynamic tension between moral judgment on the one hand and aesthetic delight on the other. The moral implications of the event are serious, and probed ironically in its language, but the playfully melodramatic representation of the episode subordinates moralistic laughter to comic delight. The dominant effect owes more to our appreciation of Sidney's self-conscious artifice than to our amusement at Astrophil's folly.

The comic melodrama continues in the fourth song, in which Astrophil's efforts at seduction are rebuffed at the end of each stanza by Stella's '"No, no, no, no, my Deare, let be."' Again the setting and characters are stereotypical. The lovers are alone at night; Stella's husband, allegorized as 'Jealousie it selfe' (iv.10), and even her mother are fast asleep. Astrophil whispers his words of persuasion, urging the rightness of the place and time. As his arguments develop, however, their conventionality becomes increasingly pronounced, until it becomes clear that the song itself is a debased imitation of the *carpe diem* motif. Astrophil, who began the sequence asserting his originality, turns at this moment to an ancient refrain. In doing so, to make matters worse, he trivializes it, departing from his Horatian and Catullan originals. In the ode by Horace, I.xi, Leu-

conoë is urged not to cast her eyes upon the future but to 'reap the harvest of to-day' because life is short. In Catullus's 'Let us live, my Lesbia,' a
more direct source, Lesbia is urged to love because, unlike the sun, which
sets to rise again, lovers sleep in death eternally. Astrophil's appeal is of a
different kind. He imagines the household sleepers themselves, including, presumably, Stella's husband, urging the lovers to 'take time while
you may' (iv.28) not because life is short but because the opportunities to
make love are rare: 'Niggard Time threats, if we misse / This large offer
of our blisse, / Long stay ere he graunt the same' (iv.31–3). For Horace
and Catullus the urgency of the *carpe diem* appeal derives from the omni-
present threat of death; for Astrophil, it derives from the practical difficulty of future assignations. In his version, a domesticated, niggardly time
threatens not the awesome finality of death but inconvenience. Sidney's
mockery of Astrophil by situating his appeal within the *carpe diem* tradition anticipates Ben Jonson's even more ludicrous assignment of his own
carpe diem poem to the old and lustful Volpone.

The song ends with a bit of buffoonery that is also far removed from the
spirit of the Horatian or Catullan *carpe diem*. Astrophil strives with Stella
physically and even compares himself grotesquely to Mars – 'Leave to *Mars*
the force of hands' (iv.45). When she swears to hate him if he does not
desist, he abandons his pursuit and curses his destiny: 'Cursed be my des-
tines all, / That brought me so high to fall: / Soone with my death I will
please thee' (iv.51–3). Although Stella's concluding refrain – '"No, no, no,
no, my Deare, let be"' – suggests a sympathetic resistance to the thought of
his death, her refusal to yield has brought Astrophil to the point of bathos.
His attempt at seduction having failed, the hero, another Mars, is left cursing his destiny while he looks fearlessly towards death and while his erect
penis, 'brought so high,' collapses.[25] Astrophil's lust reduces him to a ster-
eotype, transforming his quest for heroic individuality, as lover, courtier,
and poet, into a comical and conventional pursuit of sex.

In the eighth song, Astrophil renews his efforts at seduction. In this
song, however, the event is not dramatized, as in the fourth song, but
recounted as narrative with dialogue. Astrophil and Stella thus become
actors within a story told by the author. The setting has changed from a
bedroom at night to a 'grove most rich of shade' (viii.1), the pun on
'rich' implying that the property belongs to Stella's husband. The mood
too has changed; Stella is shown suffering under the 'foule yoke' (viii.10)
of her marriage, and the lovers are meeting for 'mutuall comfort' (viii.6).
Despite these changes, Astrophil's responses remain essentially those of
the fourth song. Attempting to persuade Stella to make love, he soon
relapses into the familiar *carpe diem* appeal:

'Never season was more fit,
Never roome more apt for it;
Smiling ayre allowes my reason,
These birds sing: "Now use the season."'   (viii.53–6)

As in the fourth song, Astrophil trivializes the *carpe diem* motif, substituting for its urgent invocation of the prospect of death a naturalistic appeal to the rightness of the time and place. Having exhausted this appeal, he again tries his hands but is again repulsed, this time more delicately: 'But her hands his hands repelling, / Gave repulse all grace excelling' (viii.67–8). This time, instead of promising to hate him if he continues, Stella denies his physical desire but admits her own love for him. In five stanzas Stella finally comes alive as a person, expressing the depth of her feeling for Astrophil and reaffirming in a terse and emotional couplet her earlier commitment to a virtuous love: 'If thou love, my love content thee, / For all love, all faith is meant thee' (viii.91–2). The lines challenge Astrophil once more to the pursuit of virtue.

Stella's lines take on considerable power because they mark the culmination of her gradual and indirect emergence as a human being. For the most part, as Gary Waller observes, Stella, 'like other Petrarchan mistresses,' is silenced by a patriarchal discourse, 'acknowledged only as she is manipulated by or impinges on her lover's consciousness.'[26] At this point in the series, however, as Nona Fienberg suggests, the remote and idealized female object of desire characteristic of Petrarchan sonneteers takes on 'some autonomy of voice and character.' But even this gesture is severely compromised. When Stella refuses Astrophil, her apparent autonomy is immediately undermined: first, as Fienberg recognizes, because she does not declare her independence but 'her dependence on another man, her husband,'[27] but more importantly, because she herself lapses, with delicate tenderness and refinement, into mere conventionality:

'Trust me while I thee deny,
In my selfe the smart I try,
Tyran honour doth thus use thee,
Stella's selfe might not refuse thee.

Therefore, Deere, this no more move,
Least, though I leave not thy love,

> Which too deep in me is framed,
> I should blush when thou art named.'   (viii.93–100)

This is for Stella a defining moment, and the self it reveals is subtly at odds with the image projected by Astrophil up to this point. One might be tempted to say, as does Thomas P. Roche, Jr, that Stella remains triumphantly committed to honour and that her apparent resentment of its tyranny is merely a gracious concession to Astrophil's feelings.[28] In the total context, however, her conception of honour is inescapably ironic. Stella blames the 'Tyran honour' for her refusal, not her 'selfe.' Implicit in this statement is not an opposition between honour and desire but between contrasting notions of virtue – one external and conventional, the other internal and defiantly unconventional. The 'Tyran honour' is presented as an external force, reputation, that constrains behaviour by means of public humiliation: 'I should blush when thou art named.' Stella's 'selfe,' however, has been earlier identified with essential inner virtue. In sonnet 52, it is said to be immune to love, and, in Astrophil's imagined lawsuit between Virtue and Love, represents her soul:

> And therefore, though her beautie and her grace
> Be *Love's* indeed, in *Stella's* selfe he may
> By no pretence claime any maner place.
> Well *Love*, since this demurre our sute doth stay,
> Let *Vertue* have that *Stella's* selfe; yet thus,
> That *Vertue* but that body graunt to us.   (52.9–14)[29]

In rejecting Astrophil, then, Stella acts for reasons that run counter to her representation throughout the series: she, like Astrophil and the busy courtiers around him, is now captive to a world of external appearances, motivated more by the threat of social humiliation than the loss of intrinsic honour. Finally allowed a human voice, Stella proves all too human, the willing victim of the social conventions under which she chafes. She neither challenges those conventions nor seriously defends them.

Stella's rejection of Astrophil in this song leaves both Astrophil and the author stunned:

> Therewithall away she went,
> Leaving him so passion rent,
> With what she had done and spoken,
> That therewith my song is broken.   (viii.101–4)

The importance of this moment is accentuated by the fact that for the only time in the sequence the author asserts himself directly, prompted by his identification with Astrophil's suffering and by his sorrow at the whole situation.[30]

Included in that situation, although unremarked by Astrophil, are the implications of what Stella has 'done and spoken.' For Astrophil, Stella's rejection marks the end of his hopes of conquest. For the author behind Astrophil, however, it marks the end of the Petrarchan mode of idealization. The stereotypical emblem of perfect virtue, once given voice, becomes the stereotypical court lady, trapped in an unhappy marriage but worried about social disgrace. This is the person whose 'selfe,' in what now seems a mere fantasy of Astrophil's, was described as 'not content to be Perfection's heire' but as striving 'all minds that way to move' (71.9–10). In Shakespeare's sonnets, the debunking of Petrarchan idealization in the figure of the dark lady creates a compelling moral tension between virtue and vice, love and lust; in Sidney's, the debunking is finally accomplished without moral debate or struggle, merely by allowing the Petrarchan symbol to speak for herself. When Stella speaks, she does not strive to move Astrophil to virtue but to avoid a blush. As we shall see, Stella's blush is recalled later as an important symbol of her submission to social convention.

Stella's voice is also heard in the eleventh song, with no less reductive effect. In this song Astrophil complains beneath her window at night, demonstrating his obsessive loyalty even as she trivializes their love by expressing surprise that his feelings have not yet changed. Absence, time, the sight of 'new beauties' (xi.21), she assures him, will soon bring his love to an end. She breaks off the conversation, moreover, when she thinks someone might be overhearing them and orders him away: ' "Well, be gone, be gone I say, / Lest that *Argus* eyes perceive you"' (xi.41–2). The episode not only humiliates Astrophil – as he says, he is forced to run away from 'lowts' (xi.45) – but portrays Stella's love as a courtly game. For her, it seems, the affair has run its course, and she cannot quite understand that Astrophil will not be satisfied by the passage of time or thoughts of new conquests. Her fear of discovery, moreover, further accentuates the triviality of her notion of honour, placing the scene in a familiar setting of domestic intrigue. As Neil L. Rudenstine observes, Stella 'has retreated to the safer world of courtly values and the noncommittal dalliance of the game.'[31]

If Stella's love is trivialized by her passive acceptance of the social code of honour, Astrophil's is trivialized by his obsessive and comical lust, which reaches an ironic climax in the tenth song. Banished from Stella, Astrophil gives himself over to melancholy imaginings. He wonders when he will see her again and whether when he does he will discover that she has forgotten him. The prospect of discovering himself remembered and not 'debard from beautie's treasure' (x.9) brings him such joy that he imagines the scene, sending 'Thought' to 'take up the place' (x.13–14) for him. Because Thought is unseen, he can fulfil all of Astrophil's sexual fantasies. He begins by kissing Stella's lips, and then, assuming Astrophil's 'most Princely power' (x.31), overcomes her 'weake defences' (x.36) and devours, with 'greedy licorous sences, / Beauty, musicke, sweetnesse, love' (x.33–4). The final step is sexual consummation, accompanied with 'dalyings,' 'dovelike murmurings,' 'glad moning,' exchanging of eyes and hearts, and 'joying till joy make us languish' (x.37–42). This sexual fantasy having reached its climax, Astrophil calls a halt to such imaginings, for they are only destroying him: 'My life melts with too much thinking' (x.45). In an unconscious multiple pun, he orders Thought to 'thinke no more but die in me' (x.46) until he shall be revived by drinking nectar at Stella's lips. The 'dying' that takes place in Astrophil's thought is as close as he gets to the 'death' that he promises Stella when she rejects him in the fourth song.

The sly sexual wit of this song makes it one of the most broadly comical poems in the series. The richest source of comedy lies not so much in the language of the song, however, as in its structural position. This moment is the unexpected consummation of all of Astrophil's efforts at seduction. It is a moment of extraordinary poetic justice, with narcissistic lust reaching its logical conclusion in solitary fantasies of sexual conquest. Astrophil's roving 'thought' becomes in effect a perfect poem, achieving its seductive ends directly, unmediated by untrustworthy words. Astrophil's fantasy of consummation thus fulfils at the same time his sexual, political, and poetic desires; it carries with it, however, a radical loss of self, a solitary, even solipsistic 'death.' In the comical nightmare of Astrophil's imaginative climax, Sidney confronts the possibility of a complete dissolution of the self.

From this point on the sonnet sequence becomes an extended anticlimax. Astrophil continues in a state of unhappy banishment, living amid a variety of unhappy distractions. Stella becomes ill. He sings once under her window but must slink away when she fears discovery by her husband. He endures sleepless nights. He misses an opportunity to see her. He becomes increasingly the courtly Petrarchan lover, living a private life of despair in the midst of typical courtly distractions. As the love affair gradually dwindles away, the liveliness and individuality of both characters diminish, and they become gradually absorbed into the world of social convention that they have been unable to escape through love.

Characteristic of this tendency towards social absorption is sonnet 103, which reinvokes the image of Stella's blush. Watching Stella from a window as she sits with other court ladies in a boat on the Thames, Astrophil observes the wind blow her locks, dishevelling her hair. Discomfited, she blushes, at which he exclaims that her 'faire disgrace' (103.13) deserves a place higher than honour itself. Considered by itself, the poem's hyperbolic celebration of a trivial event conveys a certain charm, but the major source of wit lies in the poem's allusion to the eighth song, which it parodies. Astrophil's imagination makes of sonnet 103 too an attempted seduction. Ravished by her beauties, the 'wanton winds' become Stella's lovers, twining themselves in 'her golden haire' (103.6–7). Forced by Nature to fly, they depart with a 'puffing kisse' (103.11) that displays her locks. Stella blushes at what Astrophil calls this 'faire disgrace' (103.13), which he then interprets as the highest honour. Ostensibly a courtly compliment from Astrophil to Stella, the poem delicately mocks both parties: Stella for responding to dishevelled hair as if it were a serious moral blemish, Astrophil for finding the 'disgrace' so 'faire' that it triumphs over honour itself. The sonnet thus reinforces the comic effect of the eighth song by reducing to travesty the kind of situation that Stella invoked in rejecting Astrophil, an occasion when her fears of 'Tyran honour' would make her blush. The confusion between spiritual and social values implied by Sidney's witty juxtapositions looks forward to Pope's *Rape of the Lock*, in which Ariel fears that Belinda may 'stain her honour or her new brocade.'

The final two poems of the sequence bring the relationship and the narrative to an ironic close. In sonnet 107, Astrophil asks Stella to release him for some service at court, a request that reverses the superior indifference to court activities he has manifested throughout the series. Since she is 'Princess' (107.1) over all his powers, he must first get her permission to depart. He therefore asks that she release his panting heart; that she give to his thoughts her 'Lieftenancy / To this great cause, which needs both use and art' (107.7–8); and that she dismiss his wit until it has achieved 'what [her] owne will attends' (107.11). Lest she baulk at his request, he closes by reminding her that the shame of a servant often redounds upon the master: 'O let not fooles in me thy workes reprove, / And scorning say, "See what it is to love"' (107.13–14).

The nature and tone of Astrophil's request imply a considerably diminished commitment to Stella. Astrophil asks only for temporary release, granted, but to ask for release of any kind would have been unthinkable at earlier stages in the series. Although earlier poems treat Stella as Astrophil's queen, she has been so in quite a different sense; standing at the centre of Astrophil's universe, she rendered more limited notions of political rule trivial and absurd, unworthy of his attention. Her face was 'Queene *Vertue's* court' (9.1), not Queen Elizabeth's court. In sonnet 107, however, Stella is reduced in imaginative stature; she is a mere 'Princess' of Astrophil's powers, and only asked to act 'as a Queene' (107.9). She is treated, moreover, as a courtier might have treated Elizabeth herself. Astrophil wants to participate in a 'great cause,' and he uses all his rhetorical wiles to achieve that end, including the continuing threat of public shame at the hands of the busy wits at court. Since sonnet 104 makes it clear that Stella is now publicly identified as Astrophil's love, as we have seen, this threat now conveys real meaning. Despite his rage and frustration at the probing eyes of the courtiers in that sonnet, Astrophil is now willing to use their gossiping as a means of persuasion. He pleads for his release, in short, as desperately as he earlier pleaded for his passion.

The climax of the poem lies in the final couplet: 'O let not fooles in me thy workes reprove, / And scorning say, "See what it is to love."' More telling, finally, than the threat of shame is Astrophil's assumption that he is a creation of Stella, one of her 'workes,' and that his actions will reflect upon their love. Implicit in this pose is a path that Astrophil's love might have taken but did not – the Neoplatonic path that could reconcile the ideals of spiritual love and service at court. The courtier should become a better courtier for loving his lady. This is the kind of love that Astrophil pretends to as he attempts to answer the warning of his friend in sonnet 14:

> If that be sinne which doth the maners frame,
> Well staid with truth in word and faith of deed,
> Readie of wit and fearing nought but shame:
> If that be sinne which in fixt hearts doth breed
> A loathing of all loose unchastitie,
> Then Love is sinne, and let me sinfull be.   (14.9–14)

This early and naïvely hypocritical claim serves as an ironic shadow to sonnet 107, a reminder of the conventional ideal of courtly service through love. This ideal was also invoked in sonnet 72, in Stella's offer of a virtuous love:

> Service and Honor, wonder with delight,
> Feare to offend, will worthie to appeare,
> Care shining in mine eyes, faith in my sprite,
> These things are left me by my only Deare.   (72.9–12)

The sonnet closes, however, with the inevitable return of Desire, who, unsatisfied with these offerings, 'wouldst have all' (72.13). By the time that Astrophil requests a return to service at court, the ideal of service has been emptied of meaning.

The final poem of *Astrophil and Stella*, sonnet 108, brings both the love affair and the sonnet sequence to an anticlimactic end. In sonnet 1, Astrophil announced the truth of his love and his desire to convey that truth through poetry, thus winning Stella's grace. Looking first at other poets for sources of invention, he discovered that he must look instead into his own heart. In sonnet 108, Astrophil once more looks into his heart, but what he finds there, although he does not appreciate the irony, is the conventional image of the Petrarchan lover, caught in an endless cycle of joy and despair. The series that began with mockery of the derivative effort of other poets ends with a sonnet so derivative that its conventionality draws comment from the Oxford editor, William Ringler (*P*, 490). The sonnet traces the cycle of Astrophil's emotions in the fires of his heart. When sorrow melts down his lead, a joy shines from Stella, his 'only light' (108.4). The joy breeds delight, but as his young soul flutters upward to Stella, 'rude dispaire' clips his wings and 'wraps' him in 'his night' (108.7–8). Sorrow brings delight, then, and delight, sorrow. The final lines of the poem, which bring the series to an end, provide no escape from this futile cycle but merely suggest Astrophil's rueful acknowledgment of its mystery: 'So strangely (alas) thy works in me prevaile, / That in my woes for thee thou art my joy, / And in my joyes for thee my only annoy' (108.12–14). The series began with a naïvely self-deceptive faith in the inner truth and persuasiveness of the heart; it ends with the heart a 'darke fornace' (108.3) and the lover solipsistically imprisoned in an endless cycle of Petrarchan clichés.

Astrophil's final predicament embodies the dilemma of love in terms that recall Sidney's own words in the *Defence*. Astrophil's rueful comment, 'So strangely (alas) thy works in me prevaile,' echoes Sidney's 'so strange a power in love' (116.2), the phrase by which he characterizes the image of Hercules with a distaff. Astrophil's endless cycle of hope and despair, moreover, enacts the frustration behind the wish in the *Defence* that those on whom Love attends 'could either put thee away, or yield good reason why they keep thee' (104.1–2). By the end of the sequence Astrophil has lost not only the commitment to passion that rendered the court world trivial and irrelevant but the expansion of consciousness that led him to analyse his experience and the conscience that provoked him to thoughts of self-reproach. He does not break off his love. He does not sublimate it into something higher. He does not experience moral recognition or even moral anguish. He merely summarizes his present predicament with the same Petrarchan clichés he had earlier treated with scorn. As Richard C. McCoy observes, the 'final note' of the sequence 'is one of complete submission to romantic convention.'[32]

Although the final poem of *Astrophil and Stella* internalizes Astrophil's grief, the final stages of the love affair, as we have seen, provide a strong social dimension to the comic misfortunes of love. As the affair comes to an end, Astrophil and Stella become in some sense ironic emblems of an Elizabethan court that ultimately absorbs them both. Unlike Petrarch, say, or Shakespeare, Sidney is finally less concerned with the inward moral and spiritual experience of love than with its social implications. At each stage in the progress of their love the behaviour of Astrophil and Stella is profoundly influenced by their social roles. Although he aspires to transcend the world of the court through the experience of love, Astrophil becomes at the end a rueful emblem of its trivializing power. The final shape of the narrative is crushingly conventional: a young and promising courtier falls in love with a married lady at court; he woos her aggressively, neglecting his responsibilities; she resists, fearful of endangering her reputation through adultery; banished from her presence, he returns to court affairs but still suffering the pangs of unrequited love. If such a rendering of the story seems reductive, Sidney himself invites the reduction by highlighting its ironic design.

What saves the sequence from simple moralism, however, is the exhilarating play of wit that evokes what Sidney calls comic delight. If the series were merely satiric, as some critics suggest it is, it would be difficult to explain not only the responses of critics who identify Astrophil with Sidney himself but Sidney's own rueful ambivalence towards love poetry, as expressed in the *Defence*. Sidney's wit, as we have seen, is itself an equivocal force. The delight that it evokes depends in part upon sympathy, the recognition that Astrophil's plight represents something true in human nature and irresistible, and in part upon aesthetic pleasure, evoked by the self-conscious wit of the authorial voice. Both pleasures are in their own way potentially subversive of moral judgment. And both complicate Sidney's practice of comedy to such an extent that it cannot be confined within the boundaries of his own theoretical aspirations in the *Defence*. The 'mixture' of laughter with 'delightful teaching' called for in the *Defence* is thus highly volatile and difficult to control in practice. The representation of comic ambivalence, moreover, is an achievement that Sidney's theory of poetry, dependent upon unequivocal moral effects, could not admit.

In representing himself as Astrophil, as we have seen, Sidney was not merely coping with the experiential reality of love but situating that love self-consciously within the Petrarchan tradition. The importance of Petrarch's own poetry to *Astrophil and Stella* is difficult to define with any precision. Whereas Philisides' role in the *Old Arcadia* contains exact imitations of Sannazaro, involving Sidney in a sustained act of imitation, Astrophil's contains only insignificant traces of Petrarch.[33] When Astrophil refers directly to '*Petrarch's* long deceased woes' (15.7), the allusion makes clear that his satiric target is not Petrarch himself but his poor imitators, one of whom, ironically, he will himself become. By the time of *Astrophil and Stella*, the Petrarchan tradition, developed on the Continent rather than in England, had absorbed so many different poetic tendencies, from serious Neoplatonism to witty anti-Petrarchism, that it is difficult to generalize about its nature. The Petrarchism that captured Sidney's imagination, and with which Astrophil struggles, is that most closely identified with Petrarch himself and with the Neoplatonic development of Petrarchism closely associated with Cardinal Bembo.

Astrophil's attitude to Petrarchism, as we have seen, can be distinguished from that of the authorial voice, whose ironic framework contains and transcends it. For Astrophil, Petrarchism is primarily a question of style. What he inveighs against is the lifeless conventionality of much love poetry, its failure to be grounded in truth to the beloved and truth to the lover's experience. Stripped of its naïvely self-congratulatory air, Astrophil's struggle to find a language that both reflects individual truth and moves his reader echoes Sidney's own concerns, as voiced in *A Defence of Poetry*. Both Astrophil and Sidney, one might say, are engaged in a reaction against poetic artificiality and a quest for what in the *Defence* is called 'forcibleness or *energia*' (117.8–9).

Astrophil, however, succumbs to the very conventionality he opposes, and in this sense is dissociated from the authorial voice; Astrophil's quest for originality, as Maria Teresa Micaela Prendergast observes, is revealed as a 'solipsistic and finally absurd fantasy of poetical empowerment.'[34] Sidney's poetry in *Astrophil and Stella*, as Robert L. Montgomery argues, 'encloses and presents dramatically, but is neither identical with nor determined by the poetics of Astrophil.'[35] Astrophil's poetic failure is stylistic because he himself falls victim to Petrarchan clichés, but it is also, and more importantly, moral. For Astrophil, the pursuit of style is only important as a means of seducing Stella. If he were to succeed stylistically, he would still fail poetically, since he would have diverted his technical mastery to unworthy ends. If Sidney used Astrophil to work out poetically some of his ideas about the deadening effect of imitation and the need for a certain kind of poetic energy, as he seems to have done, he also used him to explore the moral limitations of poetry devoted to love.

The moral failure of Astrophil implies a critique of the Neoplatonic idealism that, largely through the influence of Cardinal Bembo, had become intertwined with the Petrarchan tradition.[36] Sidney's remorseless reduction of love to lust throughout the sequence challenges the tendency within Petrarchism to idealize the experience of love through Christian or Neoplatonic modes of sublimation. Even more striking, perhaps, is the comical and satirical tone of the sequence, which at moments reduces Astrophil's love to the level of bathos. A cynical attitude towards love was cultivated among the French sonneteers, as Anne Ferry observes, but only as 'playful anti-Petrarchan gestures' that were themselves 'established conventions.'[37] Sidney, one might say, took what in other sonnet sequences is usually a momentary pose and made it the ground for his series as a whole.

The subversion of Stella as Petrarchan ideal perhaps constitutes Sidney's most subtle and serious challenge to Petrarchan idealization. For the bulk of the sequence, Stella exists as a Neoplatonic Petrarchan ideal, a remote and stylized symbol of an active and proselytizing virtue. In her case the stereotyping that underlies this symbol is virtually invisible for most of the sequence because there is no vantage-point outside Astrophil's language from which to see Stella herself. Once Stella is given voice, however, and her virtue is grounded in the reality of a blush, the centre of Petrarchan idealization no longer holds, and Astrophil's earlier image of Stella is revealed as superficial and naïve.

Another subversion of Petrarchism occurs in the reduction of what in Petrarch and other sonneteers is a serious, lyrical, and meditative form to a pervasively comical mixture of social drama and narrative.[38] The sharpening of the narrative line makes action more prominent than thought, highlighting the ethical and social aspects of love rather than the metaphysical or contemplative. By the end of Sidney's sequence, both Astrophil and Stella have been reduced to figures in a conventional court romance. The final result of Sidney's narrative is to define their love as more social than individual, more conventional than original. The tendency towards meditative 'individualism' so pronounced in the development of the sonnet from the time of Petrarch gradually gives way in *Astrophil and Stella* to conventional modes of thought and action. In this regard the setting of the sequence is more reminiscent of the court in Shakespeare's *Love's Labour's Lost*, where sonnets become narcissistic court games, than of the inward space of Petrarch's memories of Laura.

Astrophil's love, then, is a labour lost. Yet Astrophil is and is not Sidney, and in this ambiguity lies Sidney's most complicated response to Petrarchism. On the one hand, as we have seen, Sidney's innovative distinction between persona and authorial voice may be taken as a critique of the representation of self traditional in Petrarchan sonnet sequences. If one locates Sidney exclusively in the authorial voice .of *Astrophil and Stella*, the critique of Astrophil as Petrarchan lover seems relatively straightforward. The authorial voice, poised and in control, frames Astrophil's story, subjects it to satiric judgment, and energizes it with comic delight. From this vantage-point the series becomes a disaster for Astrophil but a success for the author, Sidney himself emerging from the affair unscathed and triumphant. The exploration of the self thus involves a breaking free of the constraints of genre.

Yet the split between the authorial voice and the persona, as we have seen, is not absolute. At some level Astrophil and the authorial voice are one. The comic ambiguity that remains seems a perfect embodiment of the rueful ambivalence that is expressed towards both love and love poetry in the *Defence*. Sidney captures this ambivalence by writing love poetry that represents the process of representation – that represents the self representing the self as lover. The result is a series of boxes within boxes, a series that asserts paradoxically the involvement of the authorial voice in the very process it comically frames. The role of the comic poet of love becomes in its own way as paradoxical and as subject to the force of love as that of Astrophil himself. This depiction of comic ambivalence marks a kind of aesthetic achievement and a view of the poetic self that neither conventional Petrarchan poetry nor Sidney's own definition of the poet's role could accommodate.

Hence the rueful ambivalence at the centre of Sidney's attitude towards love poetry has a subversive effect not only upon many of the conventional attitudes of Petrarchism but upon the Neoplatonic and moralizing tendencies within his own poetic theory. As a book of love, Stella does not incite her reader to virtue. As a love poet, Astrophil also fails, devoting himself not to spiritual ideals but to seduction. The comic framework that contains both characters, moreover, does not provide a stable perspective on their love, or at least a perspective that flows logically from the poetic theory of the *Defence*. This complication, as we have seen, is the result of poetic choice – of Sidney's innovative decision not only to divide the poet of the sequence from the authorial voice but to identify both speakers with himself. The complexity of perspective that results subverts the idealizing tendencies of *A Defence of Poetry* but gives to *Astrophil and Stella* its most distinctive source of poetic energy.

In their repetition of themes that centre upon the social role of the poet and poetry, both *Astrophil and Stella* and *A Defence of Poetry* suggest the intensity of Sidney's preoccupation with his own social role at this point in his career and, especially, with the way in which that role was becoming increasingly entangled in poetry. In representing himself as Astrophil, Sidney assumed the posture of the very kind of poet that critics of poetry, such as Stephen Gosson, found reprehensible. The contrast between *Astrophil and Stella* and the idealizing theory of the *Defence*, as Paul Allen Miller observes, suggests that 'internalized conflict,' more than any 'external cause,' may have 'led Sidney to believe that poetry needed "defence."'[39] Even apart from the conflict between poetic idealization and passionate experience, the subject of poetry was fraught with inner tension, deriving from Sidney's prior and ultimate commitment to a political vocation at court. When he turned to defending poetry against what was as much an internal as an external attack, Sidney chose a new persona – not that of lover, courtier, and poet, but that of warrior-poet, leader of a revived aristocracy and a militant nation.

6

The Poet as Warrior:

A Defence of Poetry

Like other great works of Renaissance intellectual history – Bacon's
Advancement of Learning, for example, or Machiavelli's *Prince* – Sidney's
Defence of Poetry continues to live not so much through the validity of its
arguments as through the vitality of its prose. Emerson's comment on
Montaigne's *Essaies*, 'cut these words, and they would bleed,' captures
what we often feel in the presence of such language, that the energy from
which it flows is as much imaginative as intellectual and drawn from deep
within the whole person. To understand and appreciate this kind of imaginative energy, one must go beyond the traditional questions of philo-
sophical and rhetorical method and explore the biographical and social
context within which the work was conceived. Such an approach seems
particularly important for an essay in the genre of the *Defence*, for, as Margaret W. Ferguson has shown, a poet's apology for poetry is necessarily a
self-interested expression of 'personal desires.'[1]

From the perspective of self-interest, the paradox of the *Defence* is that
Sidney's 'personal desires' did not centre on poetry. By birth, class, training, and election, as we have seen, his real vocation was to serve the state.
Only when he was denied such service, kept from 'fitte imployments' by
the 'unnoble constitution of our tyme,'[2] as he put it to his friend Edward
Denny, did he turn seriously to poetry. The vocation of poet was not a live
option for men of Sidney's training and status. Poetry was suspect not
only because it was a contemplative rather than an active pursuit but
because, even among modes of contemplation, it was inferior. At school it
was relegated to the lower forms; its competitors in the *Defence*, history
and philosophy, were reserved for more mature minds. When Sidney's
mentor, Hubert Languet, advised him on the discipline that would be
central to his future career as a statesman, he turned not to poetry but,

after Holy Scripture, to moral philosophy and history: '... I consider noth-ing more beneficial to you than that branch of moral philosophy which teaches what is right and wrong. As for reading history, there is no reason for me to try to convince you, since you lean toward that study of your own accord, and you have already made great progress in it.'[3] Through-out the extensive correspondence with Languet, which ranges over the whole of Sidney's educational program, not once does either correspon-dent mention the value of poetry. Nor does Sidney assign poetry any role when advising his brother, Robert, or his friend Edward Denny on their education.[4]

For men of Sidney's status, poetry was at best a courtly game – to be pursued with great energy and passion, perhaps, like other games, but not to be confused with the serious business of life. As such, it was inti-mately tied to the life of the court. In Castiglione's *Courtier*, letters them-selves are defended only with difficulty against the value of arms, and Castiglione recommends poetry only for entertaining the ladies.[5] Sidney's own dedication of the *Old Arcadia* to his sister follows suit by specifying a female audience. Both Languet and Sidney found Elizabeth's court dan-gerously 'effeminate,' moreover, and one of Sidney's arguments in the *Defence* is that poetry is not itself an art 'of effeminateness, but of notable stirring of courage' (109.29). Although Sidney uses the word 'man' in the familiar generic sense to refer to the poet throughout the *Defence*, its actual meaning is more restrictive. To assign value to poetry requires an assertion of its masculinity.[6]

Although we tend to associate Queen Elizabeth with the proliferation of poetry in late sixteenth-century England, during Sidney's time her encouragement of court poetry was minimal, except in so far as it was integrated into court pageantry through such occasions as progresses, and devoted mainly to celebrations of herself. As Steven W. May has shown, the pattern of court poetry established by poets such as Wyatt and Surrey under Henry VIII had been broken under Edward and Mary, to the extent that May is able to identify only eight poems in English by courtiers in Elizabeth's reign before 1571.[7] Only gradually did the court environment become receptive to poetry, and Elizabeth herself, despite her own occasional verses, does not seem to have provided very strong encouragement. Certainly Sidney does not recognize her in the *Defence* as a poet or a supporter of poetry, a striking omission in view of his desire to elevate the role of poet. Her example would have lent support to his claim that 'kings' had heretofore not only supported poets but had been poets themselves (110.11–14). In *The Arte of English Poesie*, George Puttenham astutely celebrates poetry through repeated allusions to the queen, whose noble muse, not surprisingly, 'easily surmounteth all the rest that have written before her time or since.'[8] In A Defence of Poetry, as in Astrophil and Stella, the felt absence of the queen and the disparagement of the 'time' in general imply Sidney's restiveness in the role of courtier and his disaffection from the values of the court.

We do not know exactly when Sidney wrote the Defence, and the evidence that exists is very inconclusive. In an earlier version of this chapter, I expressed agreement with the Oxford editors of the work, who suggested as most likely 1579–80, a period coinciding with the final stages of the Old Arcadia (DP, 59–63). Since that time, however, one of the Oxford editors, Katherine Duncan-Jones, has apparently revised her opinion to 1582–3, chiefly on the ground of the close relationship between the Defence and Astrophil and Stella. She also cites the negotiations for Sidney's marriage to Frances Walsingham as providing an occasion in which Sidney might have felt called upon to defend his increasingly serious commitment to poetry.[9] My approach to the Defence does not depend upon an exact date, for the central problem Sidney confronts, defining poetry as a worthy aristocratic commitment, was one that preoccupied him throughout his writing career. The underlying drives I find in the work, moreover, remain constant in Sidney's life from his arrival at court in 1576 to his death at Arnheim in 1586.

Duncan-Jones's suggestion that Sidney's most immediate audience might have been Sir Francis Walsingham is very plausible. The match with Frances Walsingham meant a great deal to Sidney and his family, and her father was not known for his interest in the arts. A serious-minded puritan and statesman, more likely to be drawn to the heavily moralistic and utilitarian conception of service outlined by Elyot in the Governor than the aesthetic and Italianate conception provided by Castiglione in the Courtier, he may well have looked askance at the poetic interests of his potential son-in-law. Even if he did not write with Walsingham specifically in mind, Sidney's arguments are surely directed at men of his type, serious Protestant humanists whose vocation was service to the state.[10] The rhetoric of the Defence derives much of its ironic energy from the fact that Sidney himself was such a man.

Throughout the roughly ten years of his maturity, Sidney sought to fulfil his political vocation. Although he seems to have been open to almost any kind of responsible appointment, his most consistent goal, it seems fair to say, was that of military action. Since at least June 1574, when Languet approved of him having his first military experience under the 'skilful' General von Schwendi, a plan that never materialized, Sidney seems to have been on the alert for a campaign in which to initiate himself as a soldier. In a letter of 21 April 1576 he expressed the hope that he would be able to fight against the Turks, since, as he says, he would prefer 'to fight my first campaign in that kind of conflict, rather than involve myself in a civil war.'[11] The initiatory importance of this kind of action is shown in Sidney's concern that his brother too seek out foreign wars; in 1580 Robert, then travelling on the Continent, informed their father of Philip's advice 'that if there were *any good warrs*, I should go to them.'[12]

During 1578, Sidney's pursuit of a military appointment to the Netherlands was so vigorous, apparently, that it provoked stern rebukes from his mentor, Languet, on three separate occasions. 'Most men of high birth are possessed with this madness,' wrote Languet on 2 May 1578, 'that they long after a reputation founded on bloodshed, and believe that there is no glory for them except that which is connected with the destruction of mankind.' On 22 October 1578 Languet became even more personal: 'You and your fellows, I mean men of noble birth, consider that nothing brings you more honour than wholesale slaughter.' In the light of Greville's description of Sidney's impetuosity at the battle of Zutphen, in 1586, Languet's warning of 15 February 1578 seems prophetic: 'I would not even if I could, weaken or blunt the edge of your spirit, still I must advise you now and then to reflect that young men who rush into danger incautiously almost always meet an inglorious end, and deprive themselves of the power of serving their country; for a man who falls at an early age cannot have done much for his country.'[13] The same kind of impetuosity that led to Sidney's death at Zutphen, at least in Fulke Greville's account, can be seen throughout Sidney's career – in his verbal attack upon Edward Molyneux, for example, his challenge to the earl of Oxford on the tennis court, or his abortive attempt to join Drake's adventure against Spain.

Although Sidney was in part an adventurer, ready to seize almost any project when his idleness at court became too frustrating, he sustained throughout his maturity a single, clear goal – to participate as warrior or statesman in aggressive action against Spanish power on the Continent. Sidney's frustrations at court derived not only from his own inability to act but from the idleness and 'effeminacy' of the court itself and from what he felt to be the wavering and pacifist policies of the queen. Sidney's hopes for his own career were intimately involved in the broader policies of the militant Protestants, men like Walsingham and Leicester, who throughout the period attempted to persuade Elizabeth to support the rebels in the Netherlands and to take an aggressive stand against the power of Spain in Europe and America. In his biographical account of Sidney, Fulke Greville provides a lengthy account of his grand schemes to suppress Spanish power; although Greville tends to conflate his own designs with Sidney's, his description suggests none the less how deeply both men were committed to this cause.[14]

In warning Sidney against his passion for war, Languet linked him repeatedly to other 'men of high birth.' For most young Elizabethan aristocrats, war was still a rite of initiation, a test both of their masculinity and their worthiness to high rank. Although Sidney could justify his desire for war in terms of broad political policy, it seems clear that less rational motives were also at work. The desire for an aggressive national foreign policy was inevitably bound up with his personal desire to prove his membership in an aristocracy that still imaginatively defined itself as a warrior class. It was also bound up with his masculine opposition to the 'effeminate' policies of a female ruler and the 'effeminate' behaviour of her court. Since both his father and grandfather had proved themselves as soldiers early in their careers, moreover, family loyalties were also involved. One might add, too, Sidney's personal aggressiveness, which he seems to have had in common with other young men of his generation. The desire for war, then, was for Sidney not only an expression of a reasoned political policy but of his deepest social values and psychological needs.

Elizabeth, however, had proved unwilling to accommodate those needs, and Sidney's failure to achieve any serious role at court had led him into an increasingly serious commitment to poetry. To accept fully the role of poet, however, would require from Sidney a considerable reorientation of values. It would mean transforming a delightful avocation, one that, like all worthwhile games, called forth an intense but carefully circumscribed commitment, into a real vocation. For a man of Sidney's training and rank, this would be a revolutionary act. The most dangerous opponents of poetry were for Sidney not rabid puritans like Stephen Gosson, who had recently attacked poetry in print, but the humanists and statesmen whose values had shaped his own identity, men like Sir Francis Walsingham, Hubert Languet, or his own father. When Sidney set out to define his role as a poet, he had, at least hypothetically, two choices. One was to abandon altogether his quest for public service and devote himself to his avocation. In the seventeenth century, when the role of virtuoso became an acceptable cultural model among the English aristocracy, he might have done so; in his own time, however, a culturally acceptable life of retreat from direct public service did not exist.[15] To withdraw from the active life of the court would betray the 'self' to which his mentor, Languet, had repeatedly urged him to remain true. The second and only viable choice was to redefine poetry in such a way as to make it serve this very 'self.' The central argument of the *Defence* thus hinges on the poet's capacity to serve the state by inciting 'men' (especially in the gendered sense) to 'virtuous action.' The surface argument of the work, however, is in some ways less revealing of Sidney's imaginative effort or his rhetorical success than less direct but more personally expressive tricks of style. It is the persona behind the argument that proves most subtly persuasive, making poetry itself a kind of heroic action and the poet himself an epic hero.

Sidney selected a form for his argument that highlighted the importance of his persona – that of the classical oration. English prose provided no precedent for a work of this kind, and the Italian theorists he seems to have drawn upon provided other kinds of models. In view of his ambivalence towards his own role as poet, it is somewhat surprising that he did not choose the popular dialogue form, which More had earlier exploited to reflect his own complex stance towards his *Utopia*, a work that Sidney praises in the *Defence*. Unlike More, who creates ironical perspectives through the opposition of the voices of More and Hythlodaeus, Sidney contains both the sceptical and positive sides of his vision within a single voice, that of his own persona. Like Sidney's other self-representations, the persona in the *Defence* mixes feelings of self-justification with self-mockery. Although this persona lacks the independent fictional identity of a Philisides or Astrophil and is therefore not distinguishable from an authorial voice, it is none the less a self-representation, not a 'self': a voice adopted for the argument and audience of the moment.

In placing an ambivalent speaker at the centre of a traditional oration, Sidney extends the exploration of self into that of the rhetorical form within which the self takes meaning. As Margaret W. Ferguson observes, the defence of poetry is a typical Renaissance mixed genre, combining elements of epideictic with elements of forensic and deliberative oratory.[16] The implied rhetorical ends, therefore, include praise, judgment of innocence or guilt, and persuasion about public goals. Each of these motives may be found in Sidney's *Defence*. Each, however, is compromised by the representation of the self that stands at the very centre of the work: the poet whose very identity is the subject under consideration. The orator in this case praises himself, defends himself, and persuades the public of his importance to the general welfare. It is characteristic of

Sidney that he sought to represent the self as poet within a form that tightened the contradictions in his own attitude towards poetry, forcing the self-representation into paradox. The incongruities that surface between the speaker and the expectations aroused by the generic frame call into question both the stability of the self and the stability of the rhetorical model within which the self is inscribed.

One of the familiar symptoms of a Sidneyan persona, a sense of nostalgia for past promise, appears in the justly famous opening of the *Defence*, Sidney's allusion to his youthful training as a horseman: 'When the right virtuous Edward Wotton and I were at the Emperor's court together, we gave ourselves to learn horsemanship of John Pietro Pugliano' (73.1–3). The sustained analogy that follows, between Pugliano's self-interested praise of horsemanship and Sidney's self-interested praise of poetry, is a brilliant rhetorical device, as has often been observed, establishing Sidney's aristocratic persona and disarming criticism by acknowledging at the outset the extent to which all efforts at defending one's vocation are tainted by 'self-love' (73.24). Written in a relaxed and playful style, circulated among an intimate circle of family and friends, the *Defence* aims to persuade the aristocratic elite to which Sidney himself belonged and whose scepticism about poetry he partly shared. To see the opening merely from a rhetorical perspective, however, is to miss the expressive power of the witty but compulsive gesture towards a lost youth, when training in horsemanship carried with it a true sense of vocation.

As we have seen in the autobiographical allusions of the *Old Arcadia* and *Astrophil and Stella*, this nostalgia for a vanished time of 'great expectations' is characteristic of Sidney's earlier personas. The desire to defend the self against the charge of betraying youthful 'great expectations' might be considered the core emotion of all of Sidney's self-representations, and ironic self-mockery the most successful literary stratagem. Attacked in a letter by Languet for betraying their friendship, the adolescent Sidney deflects his obvious anger by expressing the wish for enough knowledge of Latin to create a tragic scene. Philisides, the persona of the *Old Arcadia*, laments his lost youth and innocence while venting his anger against the cruel Mira, whose injustice against him has caused his exile. Astrophil, too, plagued by guilt at his betrayal of his youthful promise, attempts to defend himself by a series of unsuccessful stratagems, many involving self-deceptions, until he finally yields himself to lust. In representing himself as a poet who has been 'provoked' (73.30) to defend poetry, Sidney selected a persona and literary form that met long-standing psychological needs.

Sidney's nostalgia for his youthful training in horsemanship is particularly important in the *Defence*, for skill as a horseman was an essential feature of aristocratic manhood for both Sidney and his audience. In his letter advising his brother, Robert, on his education, written on 18 October 1580, Sidney himself echoed Pugliano's insistence in the *Defence* that one 'enrich' practice of the skill with 'the contemplations therein' (73.6–7); Robert, Sidney says, must join the thorough 'contemplation' of horsemanship 'with the exercise.'[17] In the autobiographical passage of the *Old Arcadia*, Philisides recalls his youth as a time when, instead of being dissipated in a hopeless love, his 'strength was exercised with horsemanship, weapons, and suchlike other qualities as, besides the practice, carried in themselves some serviceable use' (354.25–7). *Astrophil and Stella* features several sonnets (41, 43, 49) in which Astrophil describes himself as a horseman. Sidney's allusions to this role seem more playful in the *Defence* than in *Astrophil and Stella* or the *Old Arcadia*, where the nostalgia mingles with the melancholy of a hopeless love, but common to each is an ironic contrast between youthful promise and present waste. Deprived of 'some serviceable use,' Sidney's skills as a horseman had no meaning.

As Sidney's career as a courtier developed, ironically, his skills as a horseman became widely known and admired, not through activity in war, but through his participation in tournaments, such as those held annually on 17 November to celebrate the Accession Day of the queen or the one held in the spring of 1581 to honour the French embassy negotiating the proposed marriage with the duke d'Anjou. The importance of these tournaments to Sidney's evolving sense of his identity is very great, as we shall see in chapter 7 when we consider the Philisides of the New Arcadia. To a certain extent, they represent a courtly equivalent to the conception of poetry put forward in the *Defence*. In Sidney's imagination both tournaments and poetry came to represent an opportunity to translate military aggression into symbolic display.

Having been trained as a horseman, Sidney tells us, he has 'slipped into the title of a poet,' the 'unelected vocation' that he has now been 'provoked' to defend (73.29–31). The word 'title' conveys perhaps a double irony – alluding not only to the lack of status of poets among the aristocracy but to Sidney's own hope to inherit the title of his uncle, the earl of Leicester, a hope that was dashed in 1580 or 1581 when Leicester produced an heir. Sidney commemorated this event publicly by appearing at a tournament with the word 'speravi' ('I hoped') slashed through.[18] His preoccupation with the language of titles throughout the *Defence* suggests an intimate connection between his lack of status as a poet and his aspirations toward high rank. As we shall see later, Sidney gives poetry 'a most just title' to be prince over other skills that lead to virtuous action (83.8–9), and he dissociates himself and his peers from any desire to be 'accounted knights of the same order' as those writers so vulgar as to print their work (111.16). He also laments that before he ever 'durst aspire unto the dignity,' he has been demeaned by admission into a guild, 'the company of the paper-blurrers' (111.17–18).

This extreme sensitivity to the question of titles also characterizes another defence written by Sidney, that in which he attempted to counter the diatribe written against Leicester by the anonymous author of *Leicester's Commonwealth*. Although a brief and relatively unsuccessful work, the *Defence of the Earl of Leicester* provides an instructive parallel to *A Defence of Poetry*. Sidney defended poetry as someone who had 'slipped' into the title of a poet. Upon the death of Leicester's young son on 19 July 1584, Sidney had once again slipped into the title of heir to the great earl. In both cases the defence of another subject or person is to a great extent a self-defence, and in both cases the self-interest is apparent. As Duncan-Jones indicates, Sidney's most sustained, though hardly most relevant, argument on behalf of Leicester concerns the legitimacy of his title, an issue that Sidney admits is of paramount interest to himself: 'I do acknowledge, I say, that my chiefest honour is to be a Dudley, and truly am glad to have cause to set forth the nobility of that blood whereof I am descended' (*DL*, 134.17–19).[19]

The lack of any hint of self-mockery in the establishment of Leicester's, or Sidney's, title in the *Defence of Leicester* contrasts remarkably with the pervasive self-mockery of Sidney's establishment of his 'title' as poet in *A Defence of Poetry*. The contrast in personas, and the resulting contrast in the quality of writing, are highlighted in the absurd gesture with which Sidney ends the *Defence of Leicester*, a challenge to a duel. 'But to thee I say,' he addresses his unknown opponent, 'thou therein liest in thy throat, which I will be ready to justify upon thee in any place of Europe where thou wilt assign me a free place of coming, as within three months after the publishing hereof I may understand thy mind' (140.24–8). Sidney was never able to test the mettle of his anonymous enemy, for the *Defence of Leicester* was never printed. The work enables us to understand, however, the emotional energy underlying Sidney's preoccupation with titles in *A Defence of Poetry* and to appreciate the difference in literary power and complexity between two Sidneyan personas – one defending his poetry, the other the purity of his blood. The latter exhibits in extreme form the same lack of obliqueness that characterizes Sidney's courtly rhetoric in the letter advising the queen against marriage with Anjou.

Sidney's characterization of poetry as his 'unelected vocation' (*DP*, 73.31) conveys even deeper ironies than his accepting the 'title' of poet. The strong religious connotations of the word 'vocation' in the period, as we have seen in chapter 1, give the concept great ironic weight. Shakespeare depends upon such resonance in *1 Henry IV* when Falstaff claims, ''Tis no sin for a man to labour in his vocation.' As a young child, Sidney was elected, or chosen, by God and his family to serve the state. This was his peculiar vocation, but also one common to his class. In his letter to his brother, Robert, advising him on foreign travel, Sidney had urged him 'to furnish your selfe with the knowledge of such thinges, as maie be serviceable to your Countriee, and fitt for your calling.'[20] For Sidney to endorse poetry as his 'calling' or 'vocation' would be as unlikely as for Prince Hal to accept thievery as Falstaff's. In the *Old Arcadia*, Musidorus's comical disgrace as a lover is highlighted by his request to Basilius that he be allowed to 'practise' his 'chosen vocation' by serving the clown Dametas as a shepherd (54.9); his actual calling, as he reveals later in song, is the no less compromised 'love's most high vocation' (138.3). Sidney's use of the word 'vocation' to describe his activity as poet is equally suspect: he had neither elected the service nor been elected to it.

A single sentence in an early letter from Languet (28 January 1574) illustrates vividly the gap between Sidney's early expectations and his present predicament. Reminding Sidney that his 'position in life' will not let him 'grow grey in the study of letters,' Languet urges him to imitate Aeneas: 'Keep in mind that the words of the poet apply to you: "Remember to rule the nations with your sway."'[21] The passage that Languet quotes occurs at the point when Anchises, whom Aeneas is visiting in the underworld, urges his son to remember his duty to lead Rome towards her imperial destiny. Sidney, likewise, was to lead England towards its destiny, to rally the Protestant cause on the Continent. At the time of writing the *Defence*, Sidney may well have seen himself as growing grey in the study of letters, since he had 'slipped' from his heroic and 'elected' vocation into that of poet. Instead of imitating Aeneas, he was reduced to celebrating him while defending poetry, and in terms, ironically, that recall Languet's earlier exhortation: 'Only let Aeneas be worn in the tablet of your memory, how he governeth himself in the ruin of his country ...' (*DP*, 98.16–17).

The deeply self-expressive quality of Sidney's rhetorical stance in the *Defence* is suggested further by the way in which the same self-mocking phrases haunt both his private and his public writings about poetry. The self-references in the *Defence*, for example, echo those of the dedicatory letter of the *Old Arcadia*. In the *Defence*, his vocation is the product of his 'not old years' and 'idlest times' (73.28–9); in the letter, his narrative comes from a 'young head' and is an 'idle work' to be read at 'idle times' (3.2,18,27) In the *Defence*, he hopes that he will be 'pardoned' for following in the footsteps of his master, Pugliano (73.33); in the dedication, he hopes that his story will be 'pardoned' (3.13) for the sake of its father. Towards the end of the *Defence*, confessing his lack of discipline as a poet, he says that he wrote only because he was 'overmastered by some thoughts' and 'yielded an inky tribute unto them' (111.24–5). In the dedication he confesses to handling his work 'trifingly,' adding that it came from a head 'not so well stayed as I would it were' and 'having many fancies begotten in it' that demanded release (3.18–20) A reference to the *Defence* as an 'ink-wasting toy' (121.1) echoes an apparent allusion to the *Old Arcadia* as his 'toyfull booke' in a letter to his brother; this is the same letter in which he advises Robert to study both the theory and practice of horsemanship.[22]

This dense network of cross-references, which includes the *Defence*, the dedication and autobiographical portrait of the *Old Arcadia*, and the personal correspondence, lends some support to the date of 1579–80 as the period of composition of the *Defence*. More important than the question of date, however, is the consistency of the persona. The self-representation in the *Defence*, it seems, is not merely a mask donned for a specific literary occasion but a pose that Sidney adopted consistently in public and in private – so consistently, indeed, that, in the absence of evidence to the contrary, we must take it as not only socially but psychologically expressive. Sidney's self-mockery about his role as poet is effective rhetorically because it projects psychological needs that Sidney shared with his aristocratic audience. Throughout the *Defence* Sidney's most powerful appeal lies not in the arguments he marshals, many of which are treated briefly or offhandedly, but in his ability to personify poetry for an audience of humanist aristocrats. As A.C. Hamilton has observed, 'the *Defence* is deeply and powerfully persuasive throughout, not because its argument immediately convinces us, but because Sidney convinces us that we should believe *him*.'[23] Sidney's peers could believe *him*, paradoxically, because he only partly believed himself.

To focus only on the inner scepticism of the *Defence*, however, is to ignore the other side of Sidney's persona, which is equally persuasive and voices his powerful aspirations. Sidney sought to vindicate the role of poet. To do so, he chose not to repudiate his former commitment, his devotion to active service, but to convince his audience, and himself, that this commitment could be achieved through poetry. All 'earthly learning,' Sidney argues, has one end: 'virtuous action' (83.7); in leading men to this end, poetry is superior to all other forms of learning, even to history and philosophy. This argument, the core of the *Defence*, has been amply explicated by critics. What has generally passed unnoticed, however, is the extent to which the argument is driven by deep and perhaps not fully conscious designs. In his choice of examples and, above all, in his choice of metaphors, Sidney attempts to fuse through his persona the antithetical symbols of the contemplative and active lives, the poet and the horseman, transforming the marginal and 'effeminate' figure of the poet into the leader of a militant aristocracy.[24]

Sidney's opening allusion to horsemanship, the proper training for a warrior-prince, does not stand alone. Throughout the *Defence* his most consistent metaphors for the poet's role are those of war. To mark the climactic points in his argument, for example, he transforms a scholarly debate into a military engagement. When he first announces the poor reputation of poetry, he says its critics provoke 'great danger of civil war among the Muses' (74.6). After he evaluates the competing claims of poetry, history, and philosophy, he concludes by placing 'the laurel crown upon the poets as victorious' (90.36–7). Before turning to his refutation, he adds that 'the laurel crown appointed for triumphant captains doth worthily (of all other learnings) honour the poet's triumph' (99.20–2). Summarizing the refutation, he urges the planting of more laurels in England, to 'engarland the poets' heads,' and reminds his audience that the honour of being 'laureate' belongs only to poets and 'triumphant captains' (109.32–4). Whereas for Petrarch the ceremony of being crowned poet laureate on the steps of the Capitol represented an attempt to restore the ancient Roman tradition of honouring poets, for Sidney the laureate crown represents an attempt to capture for poetry the ancient heroic connotations of military triumph.[25] In *A Defence of Poetry*, the crowning of the poet is a metaphor for military victory.

Sidney's tendency to militarize his argument, evident in the repeated allusions to the conqueror's laurel crown, appears as well in the crucial passage that defines the goal of 'all earthly learning.' Beginning with the comical image of the astronomer, who, while looking at the stars, falls into a ditch, Sidney goes on to distinguish between the 'serving sciences,' such as astronomy or mathematics, and the 'mistress-knowledge,' ethics and politics, which alone leads to virtuous action. The 'serving sciences,' he says, are 'all directed to the highest end of the mistress-knowledge, by the Greeks called ἀρχιτεκτονική, which stands (as I think) in the knowledge of a man's self, in the ethic and politic consideration, with the end of well-doing and not of well-knowing only – even as the saddler's next end is to make a good saddle, but his further end to serve a nobler faculty, which is horsemanship, so the horseman's to soldiery, and the soldier not only to have the skill, but to perform the practice of a soldier. So that, the ending end of all earthly learning being virtuous action, those skills that most serve to bring forth that have a most just title to be princes over all the rest' (82.28–83.9). The allusion to horsemanship derives from Sidney's source, Aristotle's *Ethics*. Sidney's adaptation of the passage illustrates the subtle way in which his militant, aristocratic values shape his argument.

In the *Ethics* the reference is brief and simply illustrative: 'But in those cases where some arts combine (as, for instance, under horsemanship is comprised the art of making bridles and all other horse furniture; and this and the whole art of war is comprised in generalship; and in the same manner, other arts combine together).'[26] Sidney not only extends the reference but implies a complete hierarchy of skills, ascending from saddler, to horseman, to soldier, to soldier with theory, to soldier with theory and practice, to prince. In the *Defence*, moreover, the image of the horseman is part of the sustained metaphoric pattern of war. Sidney thus uses Aristotle's neutral illustration to insinuate into his definition of the goal of all learning the image of the warrior-prince. The image, moreover, reverses the implications of Sidney's introductory self-mockery about slipping into 'the title of a poet' (73.29–30), for this title is now 'a most just title to be princes over all the rest.'

The image of the warrior-prince recurs throughout the *Defence*, sometimes with a rather unexpected emphasis. In his treatment of the lyric, for example, Sidney devotes only a single clause to poems in praise of God, more than thirty lines to poems in praise of warriors, and no word at all to other representatives of the genre. His theme in this section is the lyric's incitement to heroic action. He tells how 'the old song of Percy and Douglas' moves his heart more than a trumpet. He recalls hearing at Hungarian feasts songs 'of their ancestors' valour, which that right soldierlike nation think one of the chiefest kindlers of brave courage.' He notes that the 'incomparable Lacedemonians did not only carry that kind of music ever with them to the field, but even at home, as such songs were made, so were they all content to be singers of them.' This kind of poetry, he concludes, is 'most capable and most fit to awake the thoughts from the sleep of idleness to embrace honourable enterprises' (97.5–33). In this passage it is difficult to distinguish poets from warriors, for singing leads to war and war to singing; both are part of an unending cycle of heroic verse and action.

Sidney's discussion of the lyric slides easily into his discussion of another genre that celebrates warrior-princes, the epic. Although he aims to defend all poetry, at nearly every turn in his argument Sidney draws his illustrations from the heroic. When he needs examples of the ideal types provided by poetry, he mentions Theagenes, Orlando, Cyrus, and Aeneas (79.2–4). When he seeks to prove that poets need not write in verse, he cites Xenophon and Heliodorus (81.28, 31). When he argues for the poet's capacity to depict perfect models of human behaviour, he invokes Cyrus, Aeneas, and Ulysses (88.26). When he seeks to show that a feigned example is as instructive as a true one, he turns to Xenophon (89.24). When he desires to illustrate the capacity of poetry to entice men into virtue with pleasant tales, he mentions Achilles, Cyrus, and Aeneas (92.20). Although these repeated gestures towards the heroic can be explained in part rhetorically, as a choice of the noblest ground from which to defend a position, they spring from deeper and more intensely personal motives. At the time of writing the *Defence* Sidney was at least contemplating, and perhaps engaged in, his transformation of the *Old Arcadia* into a work fully epic in scope. The repeated allusions to the *Aeneid,* moreover, and particularly to the less familiar *Cyropaedia* by Xenophon, seem to express some of the same nostalgia found in his allusions to youthful training in horsemanship; both texts were included in the curriculum of Shrewsbury School, and their heroes would have been treated as models for emulation.[27] In his early correspondence with Languet, as we have seen, Sidney was urged to emulate Aeneas.

Sidney's deep attraction to epic is betrayed not only by his constant references to it but by the power of his descriptions. Consider, for example, the imaginative excitement captured in the following passage, with its rapidly changing metaphors, its breathless shifts in syntax, and its climactic conclusion: 'There rests the Heroical – whose very name (I think) should daunt all backbiters: for by what conceit can a tongue be directed to speak evil of that which draweth with him no less champions than Achilles, Cyrus, Aeneas, Turnus, Tydeus, and Rinaldo? – who doth not only teach and move to a truth, but teacheth and moveth to the most high and excellent truth; who maketh magnanimity and justice shine through all misty fearfulness and foggy desires; who, if the saying of Plato and Tully be true, that who could see virtue would be wonderfully ravished with the love of her beauty – this man sets her out to make her more lovely in her holiday apparel, to the eye of any that will deign not to disdain until they understand' (97.34–98.9). Although Sidney defends such genres as comedy and tragedy on equally moralistic grounds, as repositories of negative examples, he does so without the vigour and bravado so evident in this passage. What most stirs his imagination is poetry that is inspirational as well as instructive, poetry that, by exalting the role of warrior-prince as leader of a great nation, feeds his own aspirations and those of the militant aristocracy to which he belonged.

The image of heroic poetry 'ravishing' its readers with 'love of beauty' suggests the paradoxical way in which Sidney attempts to transform poetry's greatest liability, its dangerous appeal to the senses and emotions, into its greatest strength. Instead of denying this appeal, Sidney tends to accentuate it metaphorically. Because of man's 'infected will' (79.26), he must be enticed into virtuous action. Hence poetry is a 'sweet food' (80.24), a 'food for the tenderest stomachs' (87.25), a 'heart-ravishing knowledge' (76.25), a 'medicine of cherries' (93.13), a 'charming sweetness' (74.26) that 'entices' (92.2) one into goodness. The logic of Sidney's argument on this point is extremely vulnerable. He places a great burden on the poetic power and moral integrity of the poet, who must seduce but only to the right end, and on the moral capacity of readers, who, despite an 'infected will,' must respond only to the right kind of enticement. As we have seen in chapter 5, Astrophil and Stella might be taken as an oblique but self-conscious demonstration of the failure of the argument made here, from the closely related vantage-point of Neoplatonic love. Astrophil is seduced by the book of Stella's body, but not towards virtuous action. In the Defence, the Neoplatonic argument persuades emotionally, if at all, through the power of metaphor.

Something of this metaphoric sleight of hand can be seen in the passage previously quoted, in which epic 'ravishes' readers with images of heroic virtue but at the same time 'daunts' them with its very name and its awesome 'champions.' In that passage syntactical ambiguity creates an implicit identification of heroic poetry, heroic poet, and epic hero. In the opening line, it is 'the Heroical,' the genre itself, 'whose very name' proves daunting. A momentary ambiguity a few lines following, however, makes it uncertain whether it is the genre or the epic champions 'who doth not only teach but move to a truth.' And finally, with 'this man sets her out,' the genre becomes personified in the poet. Throughout the Defence, as we have already seen in the case of the lyric, Sidney tends to identify the poet with the heroes he celebrates and to combine images of seduction and aggression, of 'ravishing' and 'daunting,' performing a kind of alchemy by which poetry's 'sweet food' is transformed into a sword of valour.

Sidney's defence against the common charge that poetry incites lustfulness provides another example of this kind of metamorphosis. He first concedes that, 'being abused,' poetry, 'by the reason of his sweet charming force ... can do more hurt than any army of words' (104.25–6). Imagery of sweetness and song – 'sweet charming force' – modulates immediately into imagery of war: 'any other army of words.' Sidney continues by arguing that all skills – physic, law, theology – are subject to the same abuse. Because poetry is capable of the greatest harm, he concludes, it is also capable of the greatest good: 'Truly, a needle cannot do much hurt, and as truly (with leave of ladies be it spoken) it cannot do much good: with a sword thou mayst kill thy father, and with a sword thou mayst defend thy prince and country' (105.1–4). In the course of the argument Sidney thus transforms the sweet seductiveness of poetry, that which links it to 'ladies' – to love, food, medicines, sewing – into the virile power of the sword. The poet, no longer enticer, becomes the epic hero, his poem the sword with which he defends his prince and country.

As the image of the epic hero brandishing his sword in defence of his prince and country implies, Sidney sees the poet as an inspirer not merely of individuals but of whole nations. His final section of the *Defence* thus centres on the status of poetry in contemporary England. The detractors of poetry argue that it feminizes nations. 'They allege herewith,' says Sidney, 'that before poets began to be in price our nation had set their hearts' delight upon action, and not imagination: rather doing things worthy to be written, than writing things fit to be done' (105.7–10). Countering this argument with the observation that the greatest military heroes of Greek and Roman history were inspired by poets, Sidney concludes that poetry is not an art of 'effeminateness, but of notable stirring of courage' (109.29).

Not only does Sidney argue against the view that poetry causes a nation to decline from action into contemplation, or from masculine courage into effeminate cowardice, he also turns the conventional argument on its head. In his analysis of contemporary England, he sees poetry's low estimation not as a cause but as a symptom of the country's military weakness. Because it goes hand in hand with martial prowess, he argues, poetry is the potential cure for effeminacy: 'that poesy, thus embraced in all other places, should only find in our time a hard welcome in England, I think the very earth lamenteth it, and therefore decketh our soil with fewer laurels than it was accustomed. For heretofore poets have in England also flourished, and, which is to be noted, even in those times when the trumpet of Mars did sound loudest. And now that an overfaint quietness should seem to strew the house for poets, they are almost in as good reputation as the mountebanks at Venice' (110.25–33). The wry resentment at England's 'overfaint quietness' recalls a letter Sidney wrote to Languet from court, in which he admits, with similar irony, that 'by reason of indolent ease' his mind is beginning 'to lose its strength, and relax without any reluctance'; what is the good of knowledge, he asks, 'unless room be afforded for putting it into practice, so that public advantage may be the result, which in a corrupt age we cannot hope for?'[28] Both the letter and the passage in the *Defence*, with its lament for the passing of England's heroic traditions, crystallize Sidney's frustration at his own inaction, at the 'effeminacy' of the court, and at what he considered Elizabeth's weak and vacillating policies.

The poor reputation of poetry in contemporary England, Sidney continues, testifies paradoxically to its great worth: 'Truly even that, as of the one side it giveth great praise to poesy, which like Venus (but to better purpose) had rather be troubled in the net with Mars than enjoy the homely quiet of Vulcan: so serves it for a piece of a reason why they are less grateful to idle England, which now can scarce endure the pain of a pen' (110.33–111.2). Poetry, like Venus, prefers passionate adventure to 'homely quiet' and cannot be expected to find gratitude in a nation so idle and cowardly that it is frightened by a mere pen. Sidney's scorn for 'idle England' recalls Languet's reaction to the English court upon his visit in the winter of 1579: 'to speak plainly, the habits of your court seemed to me somewhat less manly than I would have wished.'[29] The notion that poetry has withered in England because there is no longer any heroism to praise occurs also in Spenser's 'October Eclogue' of *The Shepheardes Calender*. When 'mighty manhode brought a bedde of ease,' Cuddie sings, 'The vaunting Poets found nought worth a pease, / To put in preace among the learned troupe.'[30]

The most striking feature of Sidney's argument here is not his sarcasm about the ungrateful and cowardly English, about whom there is nothing for poets to celebrate, but his identification of poetry with Venus. The image of Venus caught making love with Mars, the boldness of which is barely contained by the qualifying parenthesis, is the most startling and paradoxical of Sidney's attempts to couple the 'effeminacy' of poetry with the 'masculinity' of war. The illicit union of Venus and Mars, which by heroic convention should represent the immoral and feminizing subjection of the god of war to the goddess of love, becomes a figure for the admirable daring of poetry. The attraction of Venus for Mars links poetry to the virility of war. Sidney thus assimilates into this single image the conventional criticisms of poetry – its appeal to the senses, its seductiveness, its connection with illicit love – and overcomes them though the alchemy of wit: if poetry is a dangerous seductress, then her target is Mars, and better his potency, even in a net, than the 'homely quiet of Vulcan.'

One consequence of the failure of England to appreciate poetry, according to Sidney, is that 'base men with servile wits undertake it, who think it enough if they can be rewarded of the printer' (111.3–5). In the absence of praise, monetary reward becomes the sole motive for writing, a motive that attracts men who are 'base' in several senses: in their motivation, their poetic capacity, and their social class. The intellectual and social elite are therefore driven to 'suppress the outflowings of their wit' rather than 'by publishing them, to be accounted knights of the same order' (111.15–16). Since Sidney immediately backs away from this sociological argument, admitting that 'the very true cause of our wanting estimation is want of desert' (111.19), his reason for including it, presumably, is to preclude any ambiguity about the class of poet he envisages. His preoccupation with titles recurs here in his desire not to be accounted a knight of the same order as those 'base men' who print their works. The restoration of England's heroic tradition depends upon a renewed respect for poetry, which in turn depends upon men like Sidney, true aristocrats by birth and ability, taking up the pen as if it were the sword. Sidney develops imaginatively some of the implications of this aristocratic conception of poetry, as we shall see in chapter 7, in his caricature of the 'poor painter' in the *New Arcadia*.

In defending his 'unelected vocation,' Sidney thus deflects the traditional attack upon poetry back onto the English court, which in its effeminacy and idleness inhibits the development of heroism in verse or war and encourages the proliferation of 'base' poets who demoralize the nation by writing for profit. England's problem is thus not poetry but a social enervation for which poetry is a cure. The review of contemporary writing with which Sidney concludes the *Defence* takes on political urgency by being set within this context.

Sidney's personal desire for military action, then, may be said to shape in subtle ways the argument of the *Defence*, transforming a treatise on poetry into a call for arms. To some extent this shaping may be unconscious, the result of Sidney's need to imagine himself in the role of warrior-prince, a role that would be unequivocally aristocratic and masculine. But the overall thrust of the argument, the attempt to use poetry to convert England from a passive and idle victim to a world military power, is surely conscious and consistent with many of Sidney's other writings. In *The Lady of May*, Sidney tried to entice Elizabeth to favour the bold and aggressive Therion over the passive Espilus. In the letter to the queen that partly precipitated his withdrawal from court in 1579, he urged her to overcome her timidity in the face of an unknown future and to refuse to marry Anjou. In the *Old Arcadia*, too, he pursued the implications of foolish withdrawals from an active life, both through Basilius, who abandons his responsibilities as duke, and, with a certain ambivalence, through the princes, who trade heroic action for love. The same work, as we have seen, includes Philisides' song of 'Ister Bank,' which ends with an appeal to the English aristocracy to recover their heroic past: 'know your strengths, and then you shall do well' (259.16). Seen in this light, the *Defence* becomes a continuation of Sidney's efforts to press for change not so much in specific policies but in the entire climate of the court. Perhaps the renewal of the aristocracy, effected through the persuasive power of poetry, could revitalize the nation; perhaps a revised and more fully epic *Arcadia* could serve this end. The image of Venus preferring entanglement with Mars to domestic tranquillity with Vulcan might be said to crystallize in a wish-fulfilment fantasy Sidney's hopes to seduce that other Venus, Queen Elizabeth, to favour his cause.

Sidney does not conclude the *Defence*, however, with an earnest appeal for national renewal through poetry. Instead, he circles back to the scepticism of the beginning, with a witty and self-mocking flourish. The *Defence* itself becomes at this point an 'ink-wasting toy' (121.1) and poetry a willing servant to the vanities of the court. To those who have no faith in poetry, Sidney gives a parting curse: 'while you live, you live in love, and never get favour for lacking skill of a sonnet; and, when you die, your memory die from the earth for want of an epitaph' (121.35–8). One can view this return to self-mockery, as several critics have done, as the result of a deliberate epistemological or rhetorical design. Margaret W. Ferguson, for example, sees the *Defence* as a text that 'establishes and undermines rhetorical authority,' that is at once 'an exercise of ambition and a contemplation of it.' Alan Hager finds the work a 'mock encomium,' in the tradition of Erasmus's *In Praise of Folly*.[31] As we have seen, however, its sources lie in deeper layers of thought. The rhetorical energy and complex poise of the *Defence* lies, paradoxically, in Sidney's imaginative commitment to heroic action. Although the *Defence* puts forward Sidney's hopes for poetry, it leaves no doubt that when an opportunity should arise, as it did in 1585, he would abandon poetry for the battlefield, meta-phoric horses for real ones. The *Defence*'s continuing rhetorical power springs in large part from a persona who aspires to make poetry itself a form of heroic action, resolving imaginatively a personal and cultural conflict that could not be resolved in practice.

From a formal perspective, the effect of this inner tension is paradoxi-cal. Admissions of self-interest or expressions of modesty are of course conventional rhetorical devices, and to a certain extent Sidney's ironic gestures in such directions can be explained by rhetorical tradition. Sid-ney's methods, however, as we have seen, go far beyond the convention. As persona, he himself is at the centre of his oration, not merely as orator but as subject of praise and defence, as poet celebrating poetry. Implicit in Sidney's self-representation as orator is the notion that the true value of poetry lies in its power to promote the ideals of a militant warrior class, ideals to which he is deeply committed. This very commitment, however, entails the subordination of poetry to specific cultural ends; any choice between poetry and military adventure can have only one outcome. Hence the traditional notion of the orator tends to dissolve in inner con-tradiction: the true defender of poetry is the warrior-poet, whose legiti-macy as a defence attorney derives from his ultimate allegiance not to poetry but to military action. The very persuasiveness of the oration depends upon its ambivalence.

In *The Crisis of the Aristocracy*, Lawrence Stone describes the process by which the Tudor monarchs, over the course of a century, gradually arro-gated to themselves a 'monopoly of violence' both public and private, that had previously been in the hands of the nobility.[32] Among the causes for this decline in aristocratic power, according to Stone, are the several 'prolonged periods of peace,' which reduced opportunities among the aristocracy for the military service that for many ultimately justified their exalted status. In particular, he notes the tremendous change during the period of Sidney's youth: 'About three-quarters of the peerage – which means virtually every able-bodied adult peer – had seen service in the wars of the 1540's, but by 1576 only one peer in four had had any military experience.' As their utility in war declined, Stone argues, the peerage attempted to retain their status imaginatively 'by a romantic and artificial revival of the chivalric ideal,' which was doomed by the technical changes in warfare and by changes in the concept of duty that made the nobility increasingly subservient to the state and crown.[33]

Stone's analysis provides an illuminating social and political context for the development of Sidney's persona in the *Defence*. Sidney's persona embodies the predicament of the generation that Stone describes. Trained for war yet reduced to writing poetry, he attempts to vindicate his new role as poet by projecting upon it the vanishing ideals of his class and holding the court responsible for their loss. Sidney's satiric attacks against the effeminacy of the court, moreover, inevitably imply criticism of Elizabeth, whose policies, practices, and influences were almost necessarily 'effeminate.' Sidney's aspirations towards aristocratic renewal, like those of his class as a whole, do not include a positive role for the queen, who had shown herself happier at home with Vulcan than in pursuit of Mars. Through the role of heroic poet Sidney could recover imaginatively both the lost promise of his youth and the lost status of the warrior-aristocracy to which he belonged.

The context provided by Stone places Sidney's self-representation in the *Defence* in a deeply ironic framework. Sidney's struggle lay in defining his role of poet in such a way as to justify it in relation to his true vocation, which he imagined as pre-eminently that of warrior. Hence his vocational commitment was to a form of aristocratic power that was becoming increasingly outdated. Throughout the *Defence* Sidney's self-mockery shows his constant awareness of the difficulty of reconciling poetry with this sense of vocation. His aristocratic ideal, however, is penetrated by none of the ironies revealed in Stone's analysis or in Languet's warning: 'You and your fellows, I mean men of noble birth, consider that nothing brings you more honour than wholesale slaughter.' The satire of the *Defence* leaves aristocratic idealism intact, focusing instead on the social environment of the court, which inhibits its political effect. Defending poetry as an aristocratic vocation may have been for Sidney a revolutionary act, but it was an act that reinforced rather than undermined the traditional aristocratic commitment to heroic action. What Stone sees as an outmoded cultural ideal remained for Sidney a powerful imaginative force, as it did for Fulke Greville when he celebrated the glory of Sidney's death – a death that was caused not by a chivalric weapon, such as a lance or sword, but by a bullet to the thigh.

7

Philisides in Andromana's Court: The *New Arcadia*

In Book II of the *New Arcadia*, Pyrocles, wooing the princess Philoclea by narrating his adventures, tells her the story of his imprisonment at the Iberian court. While describing the tournament during which he and Musidorus make their escape, he digresses from his own exploits to recount a brief episode involving a young Iberian knight whose 'manner' he found greatly pleasing. The youth in his story is Sidney's self-representation, Philisides, who participates in the tournament as a shepherd-knight. His fanfare is provided by bagpipes instead of trumpets; his page is a shepherd's boy; his attendants, also shepherds, carry lances that have been decorated to represent sheep hooks; his costume is decorated with wool and jewels; and his impresa is a sheep 'marked with pitch,' with the words, '"Spotted to be known."' Among the onlookers, it is said, is a lady identified as 'the "star" whereby his course was only directed.' His attendant shepherds, walking among the ladies in the audience, sing an eclogue, which questions why this shepherd has suddenly become a man of arms. Pyrocles remembers only six lines of the eclogue and repeats them to Philoclea.

Having described Philisides and his retinue, Pyrocles recounts the young knight's performance in the tilt. When the jousting begins, Philisides runs against his opponent, a Corinthian knight named Lelius. He soon discovers, however, that although he himself is breaking staves, Lelius is skillfully and deliberately missing him. Taking this as a sign of 'contempt of his youth,' Philisides becomes angry until Lelius, out of friendship, confesses that he has been bound by Philisides' mistress to spare him. His failure to score points against Philisides gives the Iberian side a temporary advantage. At this point Pyrocles and Musidorus enter the tournament, and Pyrocles resumes his own story with an account of their escape (254.35–256.34).

This brief description is all that remains of the role of Philisides in the *New Arcadia*. Although he is a minor character even in the *Old Arcadia*, Philisides is far more prominent in that work, particularly in the eclogues. He appears briefly in the body of the narrative, matching Pyrocles' cheerful love song with his own lament and aiding the princes in their fight against the rebels; he is also said to be the author of the song that flashes through Pyrocles' mind as he seduces Philoclea. He figures in each of the eclogues: engaging in a song contest with Geron, lamenting his fate with his answering echo, telling the beast fable he learned of Hubert Languet, narrating the story of his early years, and reporting his dream-vision and quarrel with Mira.

In the *New Arcadia*, all these events are either omitted or refashioned. The song that Pyrocles sings is no longer credited to Philisides, and although his dream-vision remains, it is reassigned to Amphialus, who believes that it represents his love for Philoclea. The original eclogues are omitted altogether. Although anticipations of eclogues at the end of books I and II show that Sidney intended to insert some into the *New Arcadia* at a later stage, these were unlikely to have included any by Philisides, whose role has been so radically altered. Even the editors of the 1590 *Arcadia*, who included some of the original eclogues in their version, reassigned those belonging to Philisides to an unnamed 'melancholy shepherd.'[1]

In revising his self-representation for the *New Arcadia*, then, Sidney dramatically reduced its scope. Why he did so is uncertain. The most likely reason is generic. The shift from tragiccomic romance to a kind of epic accounts for many of the major differences between the *Old* and the *New Arcadia* – among them, the increased stature of the heroes and heroines, the increased length and complexity of the narrative, and the elevation of the style. It probably also accounts for the new tendency towards authorial self-effacement. One of the distinctive changes in narrative mode between the two versions lies in the loss of the original's Chaucerian narrator, whose voice creates the impression of a strong authorial presence. In the *New Arcadia*, much of the narrative is either rendered by an omniscient narrator whose stance is largely impersonal and objective or by the princes themselves. Epic theory and such models as Aeneas's story to Dido provide precedents for the latter technique. Sidney's reduction of Philisides' role, then, and certainly his shift in narrative mode, may be explained in part by his desire to achieve a kind of epic dignity. The self-effacement represented by this shift in narrative mode distinguishes Sidney's conception of epic sharply from that of both Spenser and Milton, both of whom adopt the self-assertive convention of the inspired epic narrator.

The generic explanation serves better for the shift in narrators, however, than for the reduction of Philisides' role. A true desire for epic impersonality would have led, presumably, not to a reduction in the role of a persona but to complete erasure. As far as I am aware, Sidney had no precedent, in epic theory or practice, for this kind of self-representation. The only Elizabethan analogue, Spenser's appearance as Colin Clout in Book VI of *The Faerie Queene*, was published after the *New Arcadia* and may well have been influenced by Sidney's example. In creating even a small role for his former persona, Sidney was not following epic precedent but, like Spenser, assimilating a pastoral convention into a new epic design. This narrative merger of pastoral and epic modes in the *New Arcadia* enacts in structural terms the synthesis that Philisides himself represents in the role of shepherd-knight.

Assuming that Sidney saw the *New Arcadia* as a kind of epic, both the avoidance of the traditional epic voice and the innovative appearance of the persona Philisides imply an ironic view of the self in relation to traditional epic form. The decision not to develop the intrusive epic voice suggests Sidney's continuing ambivalence towards the role of poet, his unwillingness to identify the self with the full power of the poem; in this reticence, he is far removed from epic poets such as Spenser and Milton, whose commitment to the 'vocation' of poet was by no means 'unelected,' and whose narrative presence in their epic poems is deeply felt. Sidney's innovative insertion of the self in a radically different role, that of a minor figure in a single episode, suggests a desire not to express but to test a version of the self through epic. The representation of a miniaturized self within a vast epic context subjects both the self and the social world of the court to playful irony.

The reduction in Philisides' role in the *New Arcadia* precludes one of the most important functions of earlier self-representations, that of sustained self-exploration. In the *Old Arcadia* and *Astrophil and Stella*, Philisides and Astrophil are characterized both through action and expression, their narrative roles enabling a developmental analysis of their inner natures. The appearance of Philisides in Pyrocles' narrative in the later work is not only too brief to allow such insight but almost entirely externalized. We see this version of Philisides only through Pyrocles' eyes, and what we see is a public role, not its internal significance. In this version, moreover, the persona is divorced entirely from the plot, his existence reduced to the approving memory of Pyrocles as he narrates his own more important story. It is as if Sidney desired to include in his epic his own small signature; he plays the most insignificant of roles, but one that carries the approval of the greatest of heroes. Metafictionally, he is approved by his own creation.

If the role of Philisides is insignificant in relation to the narrative as a whole, it possesses, as we shall see, its own peculiar density and richness. The effect is reminiscent of that achieved by Ghiberti in placing self-portraits among the heroic biblical scenes of the North and East Baptistry doors in Florence.[2] Although the images are small and unobtrusive in appearance, their mere existence seems audacious, creating an ironical interplay between the artist and his representation, between personal experience and public story. Like Ghiberti's self-portraits, the role of Philisides represents an audacious authorial intrusion, all the more so because it challenges the conventions of heroic narrative. The role faces in two directions – outwards to the artist's life and inwards towards his fictional creation. The result is a perspective that fictionalizes life and makes fiction autobiographical.

Sidney's regular participation in tournaments at the Elizabethan court has prompted a number of scholars to attempt to identify a specific occasion for Philisides' appearance. Since Philisides' friend and opponent Lelius almost certainly represents Sir Henry Lee, the Queen's Champion, the most likely possibilities are the Accession Day tournaments of 1577 or 1581, in both of which Sidney and Lee ran against each other. As Katherine Duncan-Jones and Alan Young have shown, the evidence of the Ottley manuscript favors the 1577 event, which bears an especially close resemblance to that described in the *New Arcadia*.[3] On that occasion Sidney not only opposed Lee but appeared as a shepherd-knight, 'Philisides, the Shepherd good and true'; if it were his inaugural tournament, moreover, the event would have had special significance for Sidney, and would have been appropriately memorialized in the *New Arcadia* as a time of inexperience and youthful promise. If the event memorializes Sidney's first tournament, it would have had great psychological importance as a record of his initiation into a courtly role that had become increasingly significant for him. The evidence for this attribution is fragmentary, however, and it is quite posssible that the tournament in the *New Arcadia* fictionalizes recollections from more than one event.

As numerous recent studies have shown, the Accession Day tournaments and related chivalric pageants played an important political and social role at the Elizabethan court, particularly during the second half of the queen's reign. Such events were part of what Frances A. Yates has called 'an imaginative re-feudalization of culture' that was occurring throughout Europe at the time.[4] In the court of Elizabeth, chivalric pageantry played a complex role, enabling participants to express in nuanced symbolic action their relationships to each other and to the queen. As Richard C. McCoy observes, although such events as the Accession Day tournaments ostensibly celebrated the monarch, they were 'as much a celebration of the aristocracy's enduring "martial aspirations" and exalted social status as they were a tribute to Elizabeth.'[5] Through the rites of chivalry, the Elizabethan aristocracy attempted to assert its own military and political power in the face of the increasing dominance of the monarchy. For men of Sidney's generation, in particular, according to Arthur B. Ferguson, the chivalric tradition provided 'the means of romanticizing what they still considered the primarily military function of their class.'[6]

For Sidney in particular chivalric display had a rich significance. His uncle Leicester was a pivotal figure in the revival of chivalric pageantry under Elizabeth.[7] He himself excelled in all of the activities that tournaments required: the writing of poetry, the devising of imprese, the elaboration of symbolic action and costume, horsemanship, and the jousting itself. Duncan-Jones notes that by 1584 Sidney's reputation as a tilter was so high that Scipio Gentile, in dedicating a translation of twenty-five psalms to him, 'described his "most magnificent devising of shows and his equestrian feats" as the most striking achievement of his mature manhood.'[8] As Victor Skretkowicz observes, moreover, Sidney expressed his interest in imprese as early as 1573, and his contemporaries acknowledged his interest and skill throughout his career.[9] In his eulogy of Sidney, Edmund Molyneux, secretary to Sir Henry, singled out his role in tournaments and other 'roiall pastimes' for special attention: 'As time wrought alteration in his deepe and noble conceipt at iusts, torneis, triumphs, and other such roiall pastimes (for at all such disports he commonlie made one) he would bring in such a livelie gallant shew, so agreeable to everie point which is required for the expressing of a perfect devise (so rich was he in those inventions) as if he surpassed not all, he would equall or at least second the best.'[10] Sidney's role as participant and possible author of one tournament, known as the *Four Foster Children of Desire,* has received much recent critical attention. [11]

The skill that Molyneux highlights, interestingly, is not the physical performance of jousting but the imaginative performance of the 'conceipt,' as if the events were poems, as in some sense they were. Sidney could have rationalized his participation in such events with the same vocabulary he used to justify his role as an epic poet in the *Defence*: both the pageant and the poem could be said to inculcate virtue through the vicarious experience of heroic action. In drawing upon tournaments to memorialize his own role, then, Sidney was drawing upon an activity in which he excelled and upon one that was aligned to the new conception of the warrior-poet expressed in the *Defence*. In the tournament, Sidney seems to have found a means of self-representation that satisfied his needs as poet, courtier, and warrior. Unlike poetry, the symbolic action of the tournament needed no apology; it was aristocratic by nature and its end was war. It could be used to foster solidarity among the aristocratic class, to assert their privileges and special role, and to instruct, court, and celebrate the queen. Like epic poetry, the tournament was a kind of symbolic action that could lead to a renewal of the aristocracy. The significance of Sidney's appearance as Philisides extends well beyond its tiny narrative frame.

Sidney's devotion to the tournament thus carries forward the heroic work of the poet as described in the *Defence*. Both modes of symbolic action can be seen as imaginative attempts to reassert the waning power of the aristocracy, which, as Lawrence Stone has shown, was seriously eroded in the period.[12] As Yates makes clear, this 'romantic re-feudalization' was of European scope. Something of its political significance for those who attempted to reassert the power of the aristocracy is suggested by a description of such court ceremonies in *Vindiciae Contra Tyrannos*, a work generally attributed to Sidney's friend Du Plessis Mornay. The author urges the powerful magnates at court not to 'assume that they were created and ordained merely to appear at coronations and dress up in splendid uniforms of olden times, as though they were actors in an ancient masque playing the parts of a Roland, Oliver, Renaldo, or any other great hero for a day.' Such ceremonies, he asserts, 'are not celebrated for amusement; they are not *pro forma*, and they are not the games of children who, like Horace, create imaginary kings. Let the magnates remember, rather, that if the role which they receive brings honor, it carries many burdens also. The commonwealth has no doubt been committed and entrusted to the king as its supreme and principal protector, and yet to them also, as its co-protectors.'[13] In this view, the playing of a ceremonial courtly role was not a gesture of political escapism, as it may seem today, but a symbolic assertion of real political power. Sidney seems to have aspired towards such a conception of his role but to have recognized as well the ironic discrepancies between role and reality in the Elizabethan court.

Although grounded in the actual experience of Elizabethan tournaments, the episode in which Philisides appears alludes in complex ways to Sidney's more obviously literary self-representations. Its central image, that of the knight fighting in a tournament for his 'star,' recalls *Astrophil and Stella*, in which Astrophil not only woos a 'star' but, in sonnets 41 and 53, jousts in her presence. Although Stella has taken the place of Mira as Philisides' beloved, the role of shepherd carries forward the principal motif of the original Philisides, whose melancholy pastoral exile figures in the *Old Arcadia*. Sidney thus combines in the tournament of the *New Arcadia* two of his previous literary personas. The shepherd comes back to court and serves his queen, but he also serves his 'star.'

Philisides' new role as shepherd-knight recreates in more positive terms the role he played in the *Old Arcadia*. In the *Old Arcadia* Philisides plays a mere shepherd's role because he is a courtier in exile. In the *New Arcadia*, he is no longer an exile, and his identity as a shepherd, while retaining its conventional significance as a mark of unsuccessful love, is assimilated into his identity as a knight. His companions may be 'apparelled like shepherds,' but only in fashion; the garments themselves are of rich material. The lances may look like sheep hooks, but they are strong enough to 'give a lancely blow indeed.' And his own 'furniture,' though 'dressed over with wool,' is 'so enriched with jewels artificially placed that one would have thought it a marriage between the lowest and the highest.' This synthesis of knightliness and shepherdliness reaches its climax in the description of the impresa, a 'sheep marked with pitch, with this word: "'Spotted to be known'"' (255.7–14). The phrasing indicates that the sheep is not spotted in a negative sense – that is, tainted – but is marked only so that its owner can be identified. Skretkowicz suggests that the brand probably took the form of a star, since a 'star' is the owner (*NA*, 552.n.14).[14]

The pastoral imagery in the self-representation, then, is used not as a conventional means of representing love-melancholy and alienation from society but as a means of fusing values that are ordinarily in conflict, transforming love-melancholy into heroic virtue. Philisides is not merely a shepherd or a warrior but a shepherd-warrior. The image joins art and nature (wool and jewels); protection and aggression (sheep hooks and lances); abasement and exaltation (pitch and stars). It is in that sense similar to the image in Book I of the *New Arcadia* of the shepherds Strephon and Claius, whose love for the absent Urania is so ennobling that through it they become friends and scholars (3.1–5.30). The ideal of knightly service, which fails under the onslaught of sexual obsession in *Astrophil and*

Stella, is fulfilled in this figure of a young knight who transforms the conventional imagery of amorous rejection into the heroic imagery of amorous service. The assimilation of the pastoral role into that of chivalric warrior recalls the metaphoric sleight of hand in the *Defence*, whereby poetry itself becomes a form of heroic action.

The role of shepherd-knight alludes not only to the pastoral persona of the earlier Philisides but to the lyric persona of Astrophil, who had also wooed a 'star.' As part of the pageant, Philisides' companions walk among the observing ladies, playing recorders and singing an eclogue he has composed. Pyrocles recalls that the song was accorded 'great praise,' and he repeats the six lines he remembers, in which we are asked to imagine the reactions of the audience as they watch Philisides tilting:

> Methought some staves he missed – if so, not much amiss,
> For where he most would hit, he ever yet did miss;
> One said he brake across: full well it so might be,
> For never was there man more crossly crossed than he;
> But most cried, 'Oh, well broke!' O fool, full gaily blessed,
> Where failing is a shame, and breaking is his best!   (255.22–31)

The song achieves its comic effect by applying the technical language of the tilt to love. If it is true that Philisides missed his opponent several times, the song suggests, the failure is appropriate, for he has never hit his target in love. If he has struck an inferior blow, breaking his lance crosswise against his opponent, that too is just, for no man has been more crossed in love than he. Even if he has won points by breaking a lance well, however, he is none the less inept at love, where his worst performance brings the shame of failure, his best a broken lance.[15]

The suggestion of violent sexuality underlying these lines recalls Astrophil's ineffectual assaults upon Stella. Such imagery recurs often in Sidney and with a peculiar poignancy. As Duncan-Jones observes of the action of the *Four Foster Children of Desire*, in which the Fortress of Beauty is besieged, the 'sequence of violent sexual assault followed by painful retreat, self-reproach and repentance is close to the heart of Sidney's imaginative writings.'[16] In Philisides' eclogue, the violent sexuality that eventually undoes Astrophil becomes sublimated in ambiguous comic metaphor. The playful comparison of amorous and chivalric action gives phallic significance to the lance, but whether its breaking is a sign of success or failure is left uncertain. In *Shakespeare's Bawdy*, Eric Partridge asserts that 'even today' the phrase 'breaking a lance with' means 'to copulate' with a woman 'and thereby experience an orgasm'; he cites a line from *Troilus and Cressida,* '"The Grecian dames are sunburnt, and not worth the splinter of a lance."'[17] From another perspective, however, one more in keeping with the song's ironic treatment of Philisides as a lover, breaking one's lance in love might be taken as a sign of failure. Whatever the precise meaning of the phrase, the song as a whole creates a witty and ironic portrait of Philisides as a devoted but frustrated lover. As the presumed author of these verses, Philisides, like his own creator, achieves public success by depicting his ineffectuality in love.

The remarkable public image that Philisides represents as shepherd-knight-lover-poet, an image that attracts nothing but admiration up to this point in the narrative, is threatened with collapse once the tilt gets underway. While running against his opponent, Philisides notices that Lelius, 'who was known to be second to none in the perfection of that art,' is deliberately missing his head with each pass. Lelius's skill is such that he draws more admiration from missing than others do from hitting, 'for with so gallant a grace his staff came swimming close over the crest of the helmet, as if he would represent the kiss, and not the stroke, of Mars.' Although described as a gesture of love rather than war, the action angers Philisides, who believes that it indicates 'a contempt of his youth.' Philisides is mollified, however, when out of friendship Lelius explains that he has promised Philisides' 'star' that he would miss Philisides for 'so many courses' (255.34–256.9).

As a whole, the episode described by Pyrocles creates a complicated effect. On the one hand, it is deflationary, in the manner of the self-representations in the *Old Arcadia* and *Astrophil and Stella.* Philisides is represented as a comically unsuccessful lover and the unknowing victim of an affectionate joke undertaken by his beloved and his friend. As a warrior, he is youthful and inexperienced, opposed by a veteran so skillful that he creates admiration with his very misses. At the centre of the episode, moreover, is Philisides' quickness to anger; a more thoughtful knight might have been on the alert for a hidden significance in Lelius's actions. Lelius is his friend, after all, and his device, 'to come in all chained, with a nymph leading him' (255.3–4), provides a clue to his later actions. Philisides' angry response clearly mocks Sidney's own hot temper and impulsiveness, for which there is ample evidence throughout his career – in Moffet's comments on his treatment of servants, for example, in Languet's letter of warning, in Sidney's insulting letter to Edmund Molyneux, and in his challenge to the earl of Oxford.[18] In this respect the self-portrait remains consistent not only with the personality that Sidney's peers might have recognized but with his earlier depiction of Philisides in the *Old Arcadia*, whose temper flashes in his unjust abuse of old Geron. In each case, the anger is precipitated by an imagined insult to his youth.

Although the episode has to a certain extent a comically deflationary effect, the ironies directed against Philisides are much more muted than those directed against the earlier self-representations. Pyrocles includes the episode in his narrative because Philisides' 'manner' pleases him, and the description is largely a celebration. He is pitted against the best knight participating. His mistress cares enough for him to ensure that he is not injured, moreover, and his friend cares enough for him to explain his actions. Since the explanation is known to Pyrocles, the implication remains that others in the audience will know as well, and any threat to Philisides' reputation will be averted. Instead of shaming Philisides, the episode will presumably enhance his reputation as a knight who serves under the protection of a 'star.' Hence although the episode might seem to work ironically against Philisides in the worst possible way, by showing him publicly humiliated, the shame becomes metamorphosed into a public celebration of the power of love and friendship. In this sense, the episode is a microcosm of the forces that drive the protagonists of the work as a whole, with Philisides, Lelius, and the 'star' becoming epic protagonists in miniature.

Within the immediate context of the tournament, then, Philisides' performance memorializes Sidney as a promising young knight of the Iberian court. The attributes that are singled out for special attention are clearly those that were of great significance to Sidney himself. Pyrocles likes Philisides' 'manner,' and the word includes every aspect of his public performance. He is shown to be skilled in the pageantry of the tournament, designing a remarkable costume and impresa. He is shown as a poet, his eclogues entertaining the ladies with his rueful admission of failure in love. He is shown as a skillful tilter, 'breaking his staves with great commendation' (255.35). He is quick to anger, but only in the defence of his honour and reputation. And he is shown to be the beneficiary of friendship with the finest Corinthian tilter and of love from his protective if unyielding 'star.' Like Sidney's earlier self-representations, this one centres on the persona's youthful promise. For once, however, the promise seems on the verge of fulfilment, the unrequited love itself providing no bar to a potentially heroic role in the Iberian court. By telling his story, Pyrocles himself makes Philisides worthy of epic.

Since he was roughly twenty-eight years old when writing the *New Arcadia*, it is rather surprising that Sidney chose to represent himself as an

inexperienced young jouster. He should have been at his peak physically
and, as we have seen, he was known for his skill in such events. It seems
likely that the emphasis on youthfulness is deliberately nostalgic, a looking backwards at his earlier career, in keeping with a persistent tendency
in the self-portraits towards retrospection. In the *Old Arcadia*, Philisides
celebrates his youthful innocence and promise against the waste of his
present exile. In *Astrophil and Stella*, Astrophil sees his youthful promise
destroyed by his desperate love. In the *Defence*, the persona contrasts his
early studies in horsemanship with his present 'vocation' as poet.
Whether the tournament in the *New Arcadia* memorializes Sidney's first
joust is, as we have seen, uncertain; it conveys in any event an image of
youthful innocence and promise very similar to that presented in the
Defence. In the *Defence*, the promise of the young horseman is fulfilled metaphorically, if ambivalently, in the role of warrior-poet; in the *New Arcadia*, Philisides is a young warrior, whose courtly virtues include poetry and
heroic pageantry.

The relative optimism implicit in Philisides' new role seems to derive
less from any serious improvement in Sidney's position at court than
from his increased commitment to poetry. Although not estranged from
court during 1582–4, and certainly not idle, he none the less held no positions of any importance. He participated in the ceremonial activity at
court during the period, held a minor post in the Ordnance Office,
served as a member of Parliament, and arranged his marriage with
Frances Walsingham, but his literary activities must have absorbed most
of his attention: patronizing other writers, translating Du Plessis Mornay,
composing *Astrophil and Stella* and perhaps *A Defence of Poetry*, and revising
the *Old Arcadia*. Sidney's major commitments during the period were
thus imaginative, and both his revision of the *Old Arcadia* and his inclusion of a more positive self-portrait reflect a vindication of that kind of
commitment as potentially heroic.

To see the role of Philisides as simply an exercise in personal myth making, however, is to ignore the ironic framework in which the episode as a
whole is set. The personal context is not only celebratory but lightly and
familiarly ironic, recalling the playful mockery of Philisides in the *Old Arcadia*, whose melancholy paralysis is juxtaposed with the heroic vitality of the
princes, and whose very role is marginalized in the narrative. The young
jouster in the *New Arcadia* is mocked not only through his ineffectuality as
a lover and his quick temper but through his narrative irrelevance. His
story exists only because Pyrocles enjoys digressions; as soon as he resumes
his own story, Philisides disappears forever. Despite his worthiness as a

knight, moreover, and despite the temporary advantage given to the Iberians by Lelius's willful missing, Philisides fights for the losing side, for the Corinthians win the morning's round as they have won those of the preceding three days. Only in the afternoon, when Pyrocles, Musidorus, and Palladius enter, do the Iberians achieve a victory. The victory is itself ironic, for these three knights view the tournament not as a chivalric contest but as a means of escape from Iberia. While Philisides pursues honour in a pageant, Pyrocles and Musidorus are preparing to save their lives.

The subtlest and most significant irony in Philisides' performance lies in the overall nature of the tournament and the Iberian court in which it is held. The occasion receives a remarkable introduction from Pyrocles: '"The time of the marrying that queen was, every year, by the extreme love of her husband and the serviceable love of the courtiers, made notable by some public honours which did as it were proclaim to the world how dear she was to that people; among other, none was either more grateful to the beholders, or more noble in itself, than justs both with sword and lance, maintained for a seven-night together; wherein that nation doth so excel both for comeliness and ableness that from neighbour countries they ordinarily come, some to strive, some to learn, and some to behold"' (253.4–12). The passage clearly alludes to the custom at the Elizabethan court of honoring Elizabeth's Accession Day, 17 November, with jousts. The English aristocracy prided itself on its excellence in such chivalric display, which was often used to entertain visiting embassies. In 1554, for example, a tournament was held to celebrate the arrival of Philip II and his court to England; in 1581, as we have seen, the French ambassadors negotiating the Anjou marriage were similarly honoured. A manuscript in the possession of the earl of Leicester, Sidney's uncle, records the challenge from the tournament of 1554, a statement that captures the patriotic appeal of such events: '"Ever in cowrte of great Kynges are wont to com knights of dyvers nations and more to this cowrte of England where is mayntayned knyghthood and feates of armes ioyntly for the service of ladies in more higher degree than in any realme of the worlde."'[19] Iberia, like England, has an annual tournament in celebration of the queen, and is noted throughout the world for its devotion to chivalric display.

In itself, an allusion to Elizabeth's pageantry and Sidney's role in it might seem unexceptionable, an entirely appropriate way for him to memorialize himself and his role at court and to celebrate the queen. The allusion becomes highly problematic, however, when one considers the history of Andromana and her court. At first married to an Iberian nobleman, Andromana has an affair with the king's son, Plangus. When the affair is discovered, Plangus proclaims her innocence and, although he himself is banished, she attracts and eventually marries the king, producing two children – a daughter and Phalantus. Upon Plangus's return to court, she tries to seduce him, and when that fails she convinces the king that Plangus intends to murder him. Plangus is forced to flee to his cousins, Tiridates and Artaxia, thus provoking his father's undying hatred of all of them. Andromana's son, Phalantus, is appointed successor to the king.

Later, having rescued Pyrocles and Musidorus from Chremes's forces, the king of Iberia takes them to his court, where Andromana falls in love with them both. When they resist her advances, she imprisons them. Zelmane, a young lady of the court, has also fallen in love with Pyrocles, and persuades Phalantus, who loves her, to seek the freedom of both knights. Seeing an opportunity to escape during the tournament at which Philisides appears, Phalantus leads Pyrocles and Musidorus into the forest, where they are pursued by Andromana and her troops. In the fight, Phalantus is killed and Andromana, grief-stricken, kills herself.

With this summary in mind, it is not difficult to penetrate the ironies underlying the Iberian tournament. As McCoy observes, the festivities are a 'hypocritical sham';[20] they celebrate the wedding anniversary of an unfaithful queen governed by murderous lust. What Pyrocles delicately calls 'the extreme love' of the king for this queen has caused him to lose both of his sons and the control of his kingdom. In view of Andromana's sexual proclivities, Pyrocles' allusion to the 'serviceable love' of her courtiers also seems suspect. The 'honours' that 'proclaim to the world how dear she was to that people' are empty ceremonies, for nothing suggests that her people should or do hold her dear. The excellence of the kingdom in jousting, which leads knights from other countries to participate, to learn, or to watch, becomes itself ironical after the Iberians are defeated so handily by the Corinthians, who win three out of the four days. We have been informed earlier, moreover, that Andromana is not only morally reprehensible but middle-aged and of imperfect beauty: 'an exceeding red hair with small eyes did, like ill companions, disgrace the other assembly of most commendable beauties' (95.2–4). Sidney's own queen, interestingly, had reddish hair when she was young, and when she was old she wore what J.E. Neale calls 'a great reddish-coloured wig.'[21]

Behind Sidney's description of the annual tournament in honour of Andromana's wedding day is an obvious and outrageous satire upon Elizabeth and her Accession Day festivities. In the figure of Andromana,

Elizabeth is depicted not as a paragon of beauty and virtue, loved and honoured by her subjects, but as a middle-aged woman whose beauty is marred by red hair, who is unloved by her subjects, and who is driven throughout her life by murderous lust. If read in this way by the queen herself, the episode would have been extremely dangerous. Sidney disarms censorship, however, in two ways: first, by the very outrageousness of the parallelism (no one accused Elizabeth of devoting herself exclusively to sexual pursuits); and secondly, by the narrative juxtaposition of another portrait of Elizabeth, one that presents her with a familiar courtly idealism. At this same point in the narrative Sidney chooses to describe Helen of Corinth, whose knights are the principal challengers at Andromana's tournament.

Both Helen's personal attributes and manner of rule idealize the character and reign of Elizabeth. When Clitophon fights in an earlier tournament for Helen, his device is that of the ermine (101.21), an animal that appears as a symbol of virginity in the 'ermine portrait' of Queen Elizabeth.[22] Before he turns his attention to Andromana's tournament, Pyrocles describes Helen as more beautiful than any other woman (excepting Philoclea and Pamela, who are incomparable), and remarks that her government has 'been no less beautiful to men's judgements than her beauty to the eyesight.' Her career parallels that of Elizabeth. She was placed on the throne at an early age 'to govern a people in nature mutinously proud' and accustomed to harsh rulers, yet she has so carried herself that her people have found cause to admire, not condemn, the 'delicacy of her sex.' She has kept the realm at peace, turning the threats of war against those who threatened, and she has ruled with a 'strange' but 'well-succeeding temper,' the nature of which is described in terms often applied to Elizabeth: 'she made her people (by peace) warlike, her courtiers (by sports) learned, her ladies (by love) chaste; for, by continual martial exercises without blood, she made them perfect in that bloody art; her sports were such as carried riches of knowledge upon the stream of delight; and such the behaviour both of herself and her ladies as builded their chastity, not upon waywardness, but by choice of worthiness: so as, it seemed that court to have been the marriage place of love and virtue, and that herself was a Diana apparelled in the garments of Venus' (253.20–254.6). Helen's devotion to Amphialus, moreover, which keeps her grief-stricken throughout the narrative, seems almost certain to be the means whereby the story will achieve a harmonious resolution. Just before the narrative breaks off, she takes Amphialus to her court to cure his wounds, as she has earlier cured those of Parthenia.

The full context of Andromana's tournament, then, includes two portraits of Elizabeth – one satiric, the other idealistic. Sidney had used the same device in the *Old Arcadia*, in the contrast between the satirical treatment of Venus and Diana and the idealization of Mira, who deserves their crowns. The use of such a double portrait disarms censorship, for any questions about the negative image can be answered by an appeal to the positive. In the *New Arcadia*, moreover, the technique enables Sidney to develop what he must have seen as the latent potentialities within Elizabeth's reign – the negative towards 'effeminate' misrule, the positive towards a 'feminine' rule that would lead the realm towards heroic virtue. Neither the travesty of Elizabeth in Andromana nor the idealization in Helen is intended to reflect the actual nature of the queen. They are instead 'imitations' in a characteristically Sidneyan sense, assimilations and re-creations of the latent potential within actual experience for vice or virtue.

The most curious fact about the tournament in the *New Arcadia* is that Sidney chose to represent himself as a member of the Iberian court. If he wished to memorialize himself in his fiction, would it not have been more appropriate and more politic to do so as a member of Helen's court? In that case he would have complimented Elizabeth and registered his allegiance to her at the same time. This is the role he gives to Lelius, who fights for Helen of Corinth. Sidney chose not to depict his own relationship to Elizabeth's court in this manner. The synthesis of virtues represented by Philisides furthers those found in the description of Helen's rule, not Andromana's. His role in the tournament combines peace with war, learning with sports, and chastity with love. Although he himself seems naïvely unaware of it, his virtues are necessarily inhibited by being placed in the service of a corrupt court and queen. By representing himself in Andromana's service, Sidney reflects the subversive side of himself, his continuing sense of alienation. By representing himself as an embodiment of the virtues of the idealized reign of Helen of Corinth, however, he conveys a new and guarded optimism about his own imaginative role and about the potential within Elizabeth's court for true service.

The subtle dissociation of Philisides from Andromana conveys tensions in the role of courtier that Sidney himself certainly experienced and perhaps even articulated obliquely at tournaments before Elizabeth. In the tournament of 1581, for example, the *Four Foster Children of Desire*, Sidney's role included symbolic acceptance of the very marriage with Anjou that he had earlier fought so vigorously to prevent. Sidney's motto on that occasion – *Sic nos non nobis* ('thus we [do or are] not for ourselves') –

seems slyly cryptic and ambiguous. It can be read, among other possibilities, as a sign of noble disinterestedness or as a sign of muted opposition. As Montrose has demonstrated, court pageantry of the kind enacted in this tournament enabled courtier-participants to insinuate criticism into events that were ostensibly devoted to celebration.[23]

Sidney's celebration of Helen's tournaments illustrates the imaginative potential these chivalric displays had for him at this stage of his career. As described in the passage previously quoted, Helen's tournaments are the chivalric counterpart of epic poems. Both work through imagery to inspire and instruct aristocrats in the art of war. The making of men warlike through chivalric pageantry is essentially the same as making them Cyruses through reading epic: both activities work towards the perfection of the self through acts of imitation. By aligning Philisides' service with the Iberian court and his virtues with the Corinthian, Sidney was able to promote his political aesthetic without committing himself either to a dangerous satire on Elizabeth or to an unfelt idealization. Philisides, like the warrior-poet of A Defence of Poetry, is in the court but not of it, an insider whose virtues are not recognized but could lead to its renewal.

The complex balance that Sidney achieves in this self-representation as Philisides contrasts strikingly with the inner tensions that characterize the earlier version in the Old Arcadia, tensions that suggest Sidney's earlier difficulty in coming to terms with his recent exile from court. The sophisticated poise of the newer self-portrait may result in part from Sidney's own deeper integration into the world of the court.[24] It may also be related to a narrative decision, the creation of the character of Amphialus. With this new character, who dominates the final stages of the New Arcadia, the dark side of Sidney's self-representations is given full rein and yet dissociated from Sidney himself.[25] Although not linked to Sidney, as is Philisides, Amphialus's character and predicament might be said to recapitulate in tragicomic form the imagined biography that runs through the self-representations. Amphialus is a noble young man, full of promise, known for his courtesy and military valour. He is alienated from his proper role at court, having been groomed as a prince by his mother, whose political ambitions have thus far been foiled by Basilius's marriage and production of heirs. Amphialus's downfall is his passionate love for Philoclea, a love prompted by the inadvertent sight of her bathing, naked, in a stream. Because of this passion, he becomes complicit in his mother's rebellion against Basilius and the kidnapping of his daughters. Thrust by love into the position of a rebel, Amphialus devotes all his heroic energies to corrupt ends: his chivalric gestures in battle are rendered meaningless, his wooing becomes a coercive sham, and his political and rhetorical skills merely further his rebellious intrigue. The result, in short, is a loss of self that culminates in despair and attempted suicide. Amphialus's story thus converts into nightmare the anxieties about political alienation, the betrayal of a vocation, and sexual passion that disturb the sophisticated comic and ironic surfaces of the earlier self-representations.

From this perspective, Sidney's decision to reassign to Amphialus Philisides' dream-vision of Mira in the *Old Arcadia*, a vision that juxtaposes amorous passion and political estrangement, becomes richly suggestive. In the *Old Arcadia*, as we have seen, Philisides' unhappy love of Mira is a figure for his relations with Elizabeth, whose virtues are at the centre of his dream. In its new setting, the vision seems to have no political significance, for Amphialus understands the Mira of the dream to be Philoclea, the object of his desperate passion (346.26–352.5). As Victor Skretkowicz observes, however, Amphialus errs in his interpretation of his dream (*NA.* xxvii). He himself is loved by Helen of Corinth, whose quest for his love in return seems at the point of fulfilment when the story breaks off. Severely wounded by his assaults upon himself, Amphialus is taken into Helen's care, and Helen, we are told, has an 'excellent surgeon' (445.24). Although Amphialus does not know it, then, his 'real' Mira is Helen, who is a queen and an idealized version of Sidney's own queen, Elizabeth. A marriage between Helen and Amphialus would thus not only cure Amphialus but resolve the tensions that afflict the Philisides of the *Old Arcadia*. All of Sidney's self-representations, in short, the Philisides of the *Old* and the *New Arcadia* and the shadow-self represented by Amphialus, belong in Helen's court.

If Amphialus is a shadow of Sidney as warrior and lover, another character, a very minor 'poor painter,' represents his shadow as poet. Philisides' role as poet, as we have seen, is constrained by his social milieu; he may express his love for his star, but any public role for poetry, even the poetry of the tournament, is tainted by the corruption of Andromana and her court. Philisides' position as poet, then, caricatures that outlined by Sidney in *A Defence of Poetry*. In the *Defence*, Sidney aspires towards a view of poetry as a means to renew the court and aristocracy. One obstacle in the way of such renewal was the court's own 'effeminacy' and contempt of poetry; another, however, was the equally problematic emergence of bourgeois poets and dramatists, whose aesthetic standards threatened an aristocratic art. It is this threat that is represented by the curious figure of the 'poor painter' in the *New Arcadia*. A grotesque version of Sidney himself as epic poet, the painter becomes implicated in a foolish rebellion and loses his hands in the process. He thus represents what Philisides himself might become if he were to expose his poetry to politically subversive ends. Although not identified with Sidney as a self-representation, the painter travesties the role of the artist and thereby helps to clarify the relationship between Philisides' role as courtier and Sidney's as heroic poet.

The 'poor painter' appears only in the revised version of the rebellion of the commoners against Basilius in Book II. The broad outlines of the episode, however, are the same in both the *Old* and the *New Arcadia*. The insurrection begins innocently enough with the commoners celebrating the birthday of Basilius. As the wine flows, the revelers become increasingly disturbed by the events surrounding Basilius's retreat into pastoral isolation. Weapons in hand, they attack the court party, including Basilius, the princes, and the princesses. When the court party retreats into the palace, the rebels prepare to set fire to the building, but Pyrocles (disguised as Zelmane, an Amazon) confronts the mob, assuages their wrath, sows dissension among them with clever rhetoric, and persuades the majority to throw themselves upon Basilius's mercy (*OA*, 123–34; *NA*, 280–94).

Sidney made several changes to the rebellion when he revised the *Old Arcadia*, the most striking of which lies in the heightening of the grotesquely comic violence of the battle. In the original, the rebels are a faceless mob, described only as 'clowns.' In the revision they are both 'clowns and other rebels' and are categorized at length by occupation: among them are cooks, barbers, vine-labourers, apprentices, and merchants. Four, moreover, although not graced with names, are singled out for special attention. One, a tailor, 'a dapper fellow' who imagines himself a bit of a fencer, has his nose sliced off by Basilius; as the tailor reaches to the ground in hopes of reattaching it, Zelmane sends 'his head to his nose' with one blow. The tailor's friend, a butcher, after berating Zelmane with 'butcherly eloquence,' loses the top half of his head, leaving 'nothing but the nether jaw, where the tongue still wagged.' Seeing this, a half-drunk miller falls between the legs of Musidorus (disguised as Dorus, a shepherd), who thrusts 'his sword quite through from one ear to the other.' Leaving the miller to 'vomit his soul out in wine and blood,' Musidorus cuts another rebel in half at the waist, a rebel who had ironically dreamt the night before that he 'was grown a couple' and bragged all day that he was fated to be married (280.7–282.10).

The culminating event in this grotesque comedy of war is the attack upon the painter, who is momentarily paralysed at the sight of the rebel halved before his eyes: 'But that blow astonished quite a poor painter who stood by with a pike in his hands. This painter was to counterfeit the skirmishing between the Centaurs and Lapiths and had been very desirous to see some notable wounds, to be able the more lively to express them; and this morning, being carried by the stream of this company, the foolish fellow was even delighted to see the effect of blows – but this last happening near him so amazed him that he stood stock still, while Dorus with a turn of his sword strake off both his hands; and so, the painter returned well-skilled in wounds, but with never a hand to perform his skill' (282.10–20). This is for Sidney unusually savage comedy, made all the more so because the incipient sympathy in the opening reference to the 'poor' painter is so coldly undermined in the ironies that follow. How can we explain this brutally playful treatment of a revolt that culminates in the incapacitating of an artist, a figure who should have been for Sidney a kindred spirit?

In 'Murdering Peasants: Status, Genre, and the Representation of Rebellion,' Stephen Greenblatt offers an insightful reading of this scene and others like it. Placing Sidney's episode in the context of Renaissance representations of rebellion, Greenblatt focuses on the problem of genre posed by depicting aristocrats in conflict with peasants. Sidney solved this problem, according to Greenblatt, by disguising his heroes, thereby shielding them from a demeaning conflict with their social inferiors and robbing the inferiors of any glory they might have won from the battle. The defeat of the rebels, moreover, occurs not through violence but through the traditional weapon of Renaissance humanists: rhetoric. The figure of the painter, suggests Greenblatt, represents the threatened loss of status that might accrue to Sidney himself from portraying rebels. From this perspective, Sidney reaffirms his class status by attacking 'the professional as opposed to the amateur, cutting the hands off the artist who would allow himself to drift toward solidarity with the rebels.'[26]

Greenblatt's essay provides important insights not only into Sidney's depiction of rebellion but into the generic problems such depictions posed for Renaissance artists. The restrictions of his general theme, however, prevent Greenblatt from attending to other more distinctive aspects of Sidney's treatment of the painter. Examining the portrait in greater detail enables us to see more precisely just how it comments on Sidney's own 'drift toward solidarity' with rebels; more importantly, it enables us to see how the portrait comments on Sidney's own conception of art, establishing links between the theories of *A Defence of Poetry* and the act of self-representation in the *New Arcadia*. The autobiographical pressures underlying the portrait of the painter, moreover, help to explain its macabre and comically menacing tone.

Although Greenblatt suggests that the image of the painter standing idly on the battlefield mirrors Sidney's frustrations at his own enforced idleness at court, a more pointed connection exists between the painter's 'drift toward solidarity with the rebels' and Sidney's espousal of a rebellious political position during the Anjou affair. Sidney's opposition to Elizabeth's proposed marriage with Anjou, stated forcefully in his letter to her on the subject, resulted in his absence from court for about eighteen months from 1579 to 1581. The original version of the rebellion against Basilius, composed mainly during this period of exile, almost certainly alludes to that opposition. In the *Old Arcadia* the rebels accuse Basilius of being 'possessed' by a 'strange woman' (127.20–1) and portray their insurrection as an attempt to deliver their duke from 'foreign hands' (127.32). As W. Gordon Zeeveld has shown, the fear that Elizabeth might be 'possessed' by a corrupt and foreign prince dominated political opposition to her proposed marriage to Anjou.[27] In Sidney's revision of the episode in the *New Arcadia*, the motives of the rebels have been made innocuously vague: they complain that 'great treasures' have been spent, that none but 'great men and gentlemen could be admitted into counsel,' and that the duke's isolation causes uncertainty in their government (291.32–292.3).

Since the Anjou affair had blown over by the time of Sidney's revisions, the suppression of these political allusions might have resulted as much from Sidney's desire to elevate and depersonalize his narrative in the interest of epic universality as from any desire to avoid political reprisals; his critique of the painter's aesthetic views, as we shall see later, supports such an explanation. This very enhancement of the heroic in the *New Arcadia*, moreover, probably reflects, as Annabel Patterson suggests, Sidney's 'loss of confidence in indirect or covert discourse, or in messages accommodated to the forms of Elizabethan courtship.'[28] Sidney's erasure of his own earlier drift towards solidarity with a rebellious position at court in the Anjou affair seems much in line with his revision of the role of Philisides, who serves at Andromana's court but is dissociated from either protest or corruption, and his introduction of a poor painter, whose rebelliousness results in the loss of his hands.

The fate of the 'poor painter' is suspiciously similar to that of John Stubbs, who shared Sidney's opposition to the marriage with Anjou and published his views in *The Discoverie of a Gaping Gulf, whereinunto England is like to be swallowed by another French marriage, if the Lord forbid not the banes* (1579). Stubbs's protest in the *Gaping Gulf* provoked not only the burning of all copies of his book but the loss of his right hand for sedition. In 1581 a new 'Act against seditious words and rumours' (23 Eliz. Cap. II) was introduced in Parliament, with penalties that resemble the grisly symmetries of Sidney's battlefield.[29] Reporting malicious slanders against the queen was worth one ear, inventing them, two; writing them (Stubbs's offence) became a felony and therefore punishable by death. Sidney himself sat on the Parliamentary committee that lessened somewhat the rigour of this statute, but whatever his personal attitude towards Stubbs's punishment, his allusion to the affair suggests the folly of exposing one's art to political mutilation. The punitive and coarse tone of the passage, the social position of the painter, and the specific nature of his fate suggest that social satire is more at stake than self-parody.

The satiric basis of the episode becomes clearer, moreover, when we turn from its political to its aesthetic implications. The painter participates in the insurrection not because he opposes Basilius but because he wants to see 'notable wounds' (282.14) in order to enliven his depiction of the battle between the Centaurs and the Lapiths. The painter thus loses his hands not only because he has been swept along with a rebellious mob but because he holds a certain theory of art, a theory that Sidney holds up to ridicule in *A Defence of Poetry*. The painter loses his hands because he does not understand the doctrine of imitation.[30]

Although Sidney's overall conception of imitation is subject to debate, the episode involving the painter focuses on a reasonably straightforward distinction between two versions of the role of the artist. The painter assumes that the success of his art depends upon his ability to copy nature; he therefore wants to see real wounds on the battlefield. In the *Defence*, however, Sidney defines the true artist as independent of nature: 'lifted up with the vigour of his own invention, [he] doth grow in effect another nature, in making things either better than nature bringeth forth, or, quite anew, forms such as never were in nature' (78.23–6). In distinguishing between true and false poets, moreover, Sidney amplifies the notion of imitation in a way that points directly to the painter in the *New Arcadia*. The difference is the same as that between 'the meaner sort of painters, who counterfeit only such faces as are set before them, and the more excellent, who having no law but wit, bestow that in colours upon you which is fittest for the eye to see: as the constant though lamenting look of Lucretia, when she punished in herself another's fault, wherein he painteth not Lucretia whom he never saw, but painteth the outward beauty of such a virtue.' Artists of this latter sort, painters or poets, 'most properly do imitate to teach and delight, and to imitate borrow nothing of what is, hath been, or shall be' (80.30–81.6).

Sidney's painter in the *New Arcadia* is one of those who 'counterfeit only such faces as are set before them.' The phrase that Sidney applies to such artists, 'the meaner sort,' is ambiguous in the same way as that used to describe the painter, who is 'poor.' In both cases, aesthetic and social judgments are joined, as they are at the end of the *Defence*, when Sidney blames the poor state of contemporary poetry on the fact that 'base men with servile wits undertake it, who think it enough if they can be rewarded of the printer' (111.3–5). The quality of one's art depends not only upon one's freedom from nature but upon one's freedom from economic need. Poor men produce poor art.

Sidney's resistance to any notion of art that defines imitation as mere copying holds not only for the imitation of nature but of art itself. Among the contemporary abuses of writing he treats in the *Defence* is that of copying the styles of Cicero and Demosthenes. To counter such slavish reproduction, he urges his contemporaries not to keep 'paper-books' of the 'figures and phrases' of these authors but 'by attentive translation (as it were) [to] devour them whole, and make them wholly theirs' (117.25–8). This distinction between the copying and assimilation of ancient models also applies to the poor painter of the *New Arcadia*, for his ostensible subject, the battle of the Centaurs and Lapiths, has behind it a long poetic and artistic tradition.

Sidney's description of the rebellion in the *New Arcadia* makes this very point, for it parodies the same battle that his poor painter desires to depict. As narrated by Nestor in Ovid's *Metamorphoses*, the battle of the Centaurs and Lapiths takes place at the marriage of Pirithous and Hippodame, to which the Centaurs are invited. Inflamed by wine and the beauty of the bride, the fiercest of the Centaurs, Eurytus, seizes Hippodame and provokes a general mêlée. Ovid describes the battle at great length and with gusto. Hit in the face by Theseus with an antique goblet, Eurytus is described as 'drumming his heels on the sodden ground and vomiting from his shattered mouth gobbets of blood and wine and brains.' One combatant has his eyes gouged out by a stag's antlers; another has a flaming brand thrust into his mouth; another has his tongue speared to his chin and his chin to his throat. Although several heroes play prominent roles, the central figure among the Lapiths is Caeneus, who, impervious to attacks by the sword, is finally smothered by the Centaurs under a pile of trees and metamorphosed into a bird. This is Caeneus's second metamorphosis, for he began life as a girl, a fact that does not escape the Centaurs: 'We, a whole people, are worsted by a single man, and scarcely a man at that!'[31]

Sidney's parody of this episode from Ovid is of the kind that he himself recommends – not a copying but a devouring whole, resulting in a new creation. Yet his underlying dependency upon Ovid is clear. Both battles begin at a feast – a wedding feast in the *Metamorphoses*, a birthday feast in the *New Arcadia*. Both are incited by wine: 'Bacchus indeed it was which sounded the first trumpet to this rude alarum,' Clinias tells Basilius (290.35–6). Both pit representatives of high civilization against rude barbarians who are ruled by passion; Sidney's rebels attack the ladies 'like enraged beasts' (280.10). Both battles feature the heroism of a figure of ambiguous sexual status: Caeneus, the woman turned man, and Pyrocles, the man disguised as a woman. Both episodes, finally, revel in grotesque violence, with much graphic description of slicing, piercing, and bludgeoning the human (or animal) anatomy.

This parody of Ovid is the subtlest and wittiest of Sidney's attacks on the mistaken aesthetic of his poor painter, for it encircles the social satire with a metafictional irony. Within the fiction, the poor painter is victimized by his own foolish ideas of imitation, which lead him into the battle and to the loss of his hands. Within the metafiction, however, he is victimized by another artist, Sidney himself, who presents his own version of the battle between the Centaurs and Lapiths and places the painter inside it; Sidney thus imitates the scene his own creation desires to imitate, leaving him not only with no hands but with no subject.

Sidney's poor painter thus represents in several respects the obverse or the underside of his conception of the role of epic poet. The poor painter is a caricature of figures in Elizabethan society who threaten Sidney's aristocratic conception of art. He is 'poor' in several senses of the word. He is a commoner and therefore driven to see art as a commercial activity, like those poets who are tainted by the print shop in the *Defence*. He is also poor because he is wedded to an inferior conception of art, tied to copying rather than imitating nature. In his desire for verisimilitude, moreover, he exposes himself to political danger. Although he himself may be politically naïve, he endangers himself by being swept along with the mob. The painter's is a bourgeois art, representing class and commercial interests antithetical to those espoused by Sidney.

Sidney opposes to these new forces a vision of the aristocratic poet, whose epic conceptions answer to the values of his own class. Released from the taint of commercial interests, such a poet is able to serve a select audience of fellow aristocrats, with the capacity to translate his epic inventions into action. Unhampered by a foolish desire to copy reality, he imitates in the true sense, assimilating and re-creating previous models from life or art. Such a conception of imitation not only serves the goal of virtuous action, but, as in the case of Sidney's imitations of Elizabeth in Andromana and Helen, it protects the poet from a potentially dangerous involvement in political affairs.

Although tinged with self-satire, Sidney's portrait of Philisides translates these same political and aesthetic values into the pageantry of a tournament. As a courtier, Philisides is himself an artist. His art is not a commercial activity but one that integrates the various aspects of the courtier's role. It is an art of poetry, of love, of friendship, of service, of horsemanship, of tilting, of pageantry, of costume. In this version of art, as in Castiglione, the courtier himself becomes an aesthetic object and his various activities, whether at war or at court, become manifestations of his pervasive influence. In this sense, the figure of Philisides is similar to that of Sidney as author, for both re-present ideals that might be imitated. In the language of the *Defence*, Sidney as epic poet, Pyrocles as teller of stories, and Philisides as shepherd-knight are all potentially engaged in the making of Cyruses (*DP*, 79.13) by and through imitation. The making of Cyruses remains only potential, however, both in the *Defence* and in the *New Arcadia*, for both poet-figures are enclosed within a corrupt court; the challenge for both Sidney and Philisides is to direct poetry, and the poetry of the tournament, towards political renewal without losing a hand in the process.

Although the analogy between chivalric display and epic poems illuminates Sidney's commitment to both media, it is important to recognize that Sidney chose chivalry for his self-representation, not poetry. Had he chosen to accentuate his role as poet, he could have followed the main epic tradition, as did Spenser and Milton later, and enhanced rather than suppressed the distinctive authorial voice that narrates the *Old Arcadia*. The choice in favour of a chivalric miniature witnesses to Sidney's continuing ambivalence about the role of poet even as he attempted a work of epic scope.

The distinctive limitations of Sidney's self-representation as Philisides in the *New Arcadia* emerge forcefully if we compare it to that of Spenser's as Colin Clout in Book VI of *The Faerie Queene*. The episodes in which the two self-representations appear have much in common. Both involve the reintroduction of personas from earlier works – Philisides from the *Old Arcadia* and Colin Clout from *The Shepheardes Calender* and *Colin Clout Comes Home Again*. Both develop the personas in relation to a framing heroic action. And both deal with the same basic theme, courtesy, which is central to Philisides' role in Andromana's tournament, and the explicit topic of Book VI of *The Faerie Queene*. In view of the apparent uniqueness of Sidney's inclusion of a self-representation in an epic action, moreover, it is possible that Spenser's version is a general imitation. His concern with courtesy in the context of the pastoral life, moreover, suggests even a more telling link to Sidney's shepherd-knight, one that Frances Yates develops in her suggestion that Spenser's hero, Calidore, might commemorate Sidney.[32] Since my focus is on Sidney's conception of his persona, however, the affinities between the two episodes are less important than the differences, the most important of which lies in the radically different stance each author takes towards the poet's role.

Before I develop these differences, a brief summary of the Spenserian episode might be helpful. In Canto x, the hero of Book VI, Calidore, the knight of courtesy, interrupts his pursuit of the Blatant Beast for a pastoral interlude, in which he courts Pastorella, a beautiful shepherdess. While wandering alone one day, he comes across a mysterious scene. He sees on a secluded hill a hundred naked maidens dancing in a circle, accompanied by the piping of a shepherd; within their circle, dance three more maidens, who enclose a single maiden in the centre. Desirous of discovering who they are, Calidore steps forward. At his sudden appearance, however, the maidens all vanish and the shepherd, grief-stricken at their loss, breaks his pipe. The shepherd is Colin Clout, and, as Calidore learns after apologizing for his interruption, the maidens are Venus's Graces, dancing in celebration of Colin's beloved, who has herself been made another Grace. Although Calidore is tempted by the beauty of the scene to remain, his love for Pastorella draws him back to find her. He leaves, and Colin is never seen again.

As is clear from this brief account, Spenser represents himself as a pastoral poet, continuing the persona of Colin Clout that he had developed in his earlier eclogues, but placing it in a new context, that of the epic virtue of courtesy. Spenser thus provides in the persona of Colin Clout a continuation of his earlier self-explorations as pastoral poet. In the *New Arcadia*, Sidney, in contrast, disrupts the continuity of his persona, transforming the melancholy shepherd-exile of the *Old Arcadia* into an active courtier, a role that assimilates and extends not only the previous conception of Philisides as shepherd but the role of Astrophil as well: the Philisides of the *New Arcadia* is a shepherd-knight in love with a star. Sidney's self-representation is thus not only autobiographically more dynamic but more complex and concrete. The friend with whom he jousts is probably identifiable, as we have seen, as are at least parts of the tournament. Whereas Spenser simplifies and generalizes his self-representation, giving his reader an idealized image of himself in the role of poet, Sidney complicates and particularizes his portrait, displaying not only a more rounded personality but one that has developed over time. His self-portrait is more resonantly autobiographical.

The two writers differ, then, in their fictional identification with their roles as writers. Spenser identifies himself completely with an idealized image of the self as poet, Sidney with a concrete and partly ironic image of the self as courtier, whose role as poet not only enables him to celebrate his love for his star but to fulfil the social expectations of the courtly world. This difference becomes even more pronounced if we consider the roles of the narrators of both works. Sidney, as we have seen, dissociates himself both as author and as persona from his narrator. The episode in which Philisides appears is narrated by Musidorus, thus heightening its heroic potential, and the narrator of the epic as a whole is extremely impersonal. Spenser, however, prefaces Book VI with an epic invocation, blurring distinctions between himself as author and himself as narrator, and even concludes the book with an allusion to 'a mighty Peres displeasure' at one of his previous works as an example of the incessant raging of the Blatant Beast.[33] Hence Spenser emphasizes the continuity among his various selves, as author, narrator, and persona, all of which are manifestations of his overarching identity as poet.

This sense of continuity in the various manifestations of the role of poet becomes extremely important in the episode involving Colin Clout because its major thrust is towards a powerful celebration of the role of poet and an equally powerful critique of the court world, including, ambiguously, the queen. As Daniel Javitch observes, the proem to Book VI constitutes an audacious claim on Spenser's part, that he as epic poet has access through the Muse to the peculiarly aristocratic virtues that the book defines and celebrates. The bourgeois poet, ironically, thus becomes the teacher of courtesy to the court.[34] Spenser's treatment of the court makes it clear that such teaching is vitally necessary: not only is he openly satirical of courtly discourtesy, but throughout Book VI the positive examples of courtesy all come from outside a court environment. The Wild Man, Tristram, and Pastorella are all orphans, with no courtly experience; their courtesy is innate, springing from their noble blood. The celebration of Colin Clout's mere shepherd lass as another Grace, symbolically located at the source of all courtesy, is even more audacious, for neither she nor the poet has noble blood. In ironic contrast to this beautiful vision is Calidore's graceless interruption, which he himself sees as 'rash' (X.xxix), and which makes the most courteous of all Faery knights look foolish and inept before the grace of a shepherd poet and his shepherd lass.

Although Spenser attempts to distinguish between the corruption of the court and the virtue of the queen, his attempts are either illogical and half-hearted or, more likely, slyly ironical. In the proem, the narrator first contrasts the hypocritical courtesy of the contemporary court with the true courtesy of antiquity. He then praises Elizabeth as superior in courtesy even to antiquity and, with what is probably a calculated *non sequitur*, celebrates her as the source of the behaviour of her court, 'where courtesies excell' (VI.Proem.vii). Having criticized the court for feigned courtesy, Spenser praises the queen for instilling true courtesy into the court. The praise of Elizabeth is also undermined in Canto x by Colin's celebration of his own beloved, who, as one of Venus's Graces, seems to usurp a role more properly assigned to Elizabeth. Although the narrator attempts to discount this impropriety with an apology to the queen, the gesture is rather weak and the passage in which it occurs, Stanza xxviii, seems calculated to compound the problem by conflating the glory of Colin's beloved with that of the queen herself.

Spenser's development of the persona of Colin Clout thus enables him to assert his power as a poet, a visionary and teacher superior to even the most courteous of knights, and to arrogate to his beloved a position at the symbolic centre of the virtue of courtesy, a position that subtly challenges the image of the queen. Sidney's persona, too, is used for satiric effect, as we have seen, but his satire is directed in the first instance at his own persona – at Philisides' ineptitude at love and proneness towards anger – a target that corresponds to the more concrete and personal realization of the role that we have already observed. Sidney's secondary target is Elizabeth, whose portrait he surrounds, as does Spenser, with enough ambiguity to allow positive or negative interpretations. Although a satiric thrust against the court might be implied in the development of Andromana's tournament, court behaviour as such is clearly not Sidney's major target in this episode. For Sidney, the aristocratic insider at court, whose persona shines at pageantry, the culprit in his struggles for advancement is the queen herself, shadowed forth in Andromana; for Spenser, the bourgeois outsider, whose only claim to advancement is his poetry, the culprit is the more general environment of the court, an environment that becomes localized in the anger displayed in the final lines of Book VI at the slander that has caused a 'mighty Pere' to take offence at his poetry.

As the preceding analysis should have made clear, the centrality of Spenser's self-representation to the meaning of Book VI is far greater than that of Sidney's at Andromana's court. Musidorus narrates Philisides' role at Andromana's tournament as a digression in the story of his own adventures, and although the episode highlights values that are important to the narrative as a whole, its major role is to serve as a partly ironic and partly celebratory memorial of Sidney himself and his circle. In the case of Book VI, in contrast, the ostensible hero is diminished by his encounter with the mere shepherd-poet, whose vision he destroys, and the true hero becomes the poet, whose pipes express his concord with the mystical origins of courtesy.

The centrality of a mere shepherd's role in an epic narrative devoted to the courtly virtue of courtesy raises interesting generic questions about the relationship Spenser implies between pastoral and epic. These questions are explored not only through the roles of Colin and his beloved, whose alienation from court seems the source of their visionary purity, but through Calidore, whose attraction to Pastorella is treated by the narrator with considerable ambivalence. Although the pastoral idyll is a temptation, keeping Calidore from his quest, it is not to be 'greatly blamed,' according to the narrator, for the 'perfect pleasures' experienced there are not available in the merely 'painted show' of the court (X.iii). It may be significant that after Calidore captures the Blatant Beast nothing is said about his return to the Faery court. It is difficult to escape the conclusion that Spenser's sense of estrangement from the court at this stage led him to undermine the basic assumptions of the epic, assumptions that make courtly experience, not the life of shepherd-poets, the ultimate test of value. This is yet another way of calling attention to Spenser's heroic assertion of the power of poetry and his own identification with that power.

In the *New Arcadia*, in contrast, Philisides' roles as shepherd and lover are integrated, through his role as courtier, into the world of the court. Although his poetry expresses powerfully his personal love for his star, to whom he dedicates his heroic actions, it does not challenge but reinforces courtly values. The same is true of his role as shepherd, which, by being assimilated into that of knighthood, offers no critical vantage-point from which to survey the court. The attempt to synthesize pastoral and heroic values in the figure of the courtier is in some ways close to Spenser's treatment of Calidore, whose pastoral experience seems to make him a better knight and whose love of Pastorella might be taken to symbolize the wedding of the two disparate worlds. If something of the kind lies behind Spenser's narrative, however, the surface actions make the vision too problematic to sustain.

Spenser's venture into epic self-representation deserves extensive discussion in its own right, for it clearly engages his imagination deeply and produces some of the richest and most complex effects in *The Faerie Queene*. Our topic is Sidney, however, whose choices in the development of his persona are highlighted by contrast to Spenser's. To some extent, the differences may be generational. Sidney's persona belongs to the mid 1580s, Spenser's to the mid 1590s, when even Sidney's qualified optimism about courtly renewal might have seemed too rosy a view. Partly, too, the differences reflect different experiences at court. Despite Sidney's frustration with Elizabeth, through his activities in Parliament, in government office, and in pageantry, he was becoming increasingly integrated into courtly life; Spenser, whose frustration with the court is everywhere apparent in Book VI, seems to have resigned himself at this stage in his career to a position of permanent alienation.

More important than any of these differences, however, are differences in the two poets' commitments to their roles as poets, differences that probably originate in, although are not restricted to, differences in social rank. Spenser's self-representation crystallizes forcefully a commitment to the poet as visionary seer that is evident throughout his career and has no true counterpart until Milton. Sidney's self-representation, however, typifies his unwillingness to commit himself to such a role, and his attempt to integrate poetry into a broader conception of heroic social action. Simply put, Spenser, the bourgeois poet, invested his entire social identity in the moral power of poetry, a power that ultimately transcended the possession of social rank or noble blood; Sidney, the aristocratic courtier, poet by 'unelected vocation,' invested his identity in an ideal of service to the state and attempted to assimilate poetry, with due deference to rank and noble blood, into that ideal.

Hence Sidney's innovative mode of self-representation in the *New Arcadia*, which places him in the role of a promising young knight of Andromana's court, may be seen as a figure for Sidney's ironic and ambivalent attitude even to the epic form that so deeply engaged his imaginative energy. The poet who writes the *New Arcadia*, who might play the role of intrusive narrator – invoking the Muses, commenting on the action, alluding to his own experience – is an invisible presence, withdrawn and largely impersonal. In contrast, the poet who lives in the *New Arcadia*, Philisides, whose poetry is part of the world of the tournament, a world in which pageantry prepares the spirit for military action – this poet is slyly and wittily visible. And it is this poet whose pen drops at mid-sentence, leaving the epic unfinished and Sidney dead at Zutphen.

8

The Autobiographical Impulse: Conclusions

This study began by asking why Sidney might have been so preoccupied with the creation of literary personas. In chapter 1 we examined various biographical and cultural forces that contributed to such a preoccupation, including, most significantly, the sense of vocational crisis that continued throughout Sidney's career and the doctrine of imitation that shaped so profoundly both educational and literary practice in the period. Having explored in later chapters the way in which these forces play themselves out in Sidney's career, with particular attention to the letters to Languet, the *Old Arcadia*, *Astrophil and Stella*, *A Defence of Poetry*, and the *New Arcadia*, it seems appropriate to expand the original question and to consider from a broader perspective the significance of this tendency towards self-representation. As we have seen, the limited audience for which Sidney wrote and his literary independence from the queen give his self-representations an inwardness that distinguishes them from the more theatrical personas of a courtier like Ralegh. Hence it seems appropriate in this final chapter to consider that inwardness more deeply, to imagine from Sidney's point of view what personal functions his self-representations might have served throughout his career.

The variety of Sidney's personas makes generalization difficult. The self-representations differ greatly in their nature, their relative importance, and their generic frame. In the letters to Languet, the persona is not only friend to Languet but also a son, a student, an imitator of Cicero. Philisides, the melancholy exile of the *Old Arcadia*, is a lover, a courtier, and a feigned shepherd living in a pastoral world. Astrophil is lover, courtier, and sonneteer. The persona of *A Defence of Poetry* dominates the work as an orator, a poet, and a warrior. And the Philisides of the *New Arcadia* plays in miniature the various roles expected of a perfect courtier – lover, poet, warrior, and servant to the crown – in a world driven by epic conflict.

Not only do the roles and genres differ greatly; the relationship between author and persona changes with each new role. The relative naïveté of the device in the letters to Languet tends to collapse distinctions between author and persona, tempting the reader to ignore the notion of persona altogether and to assume a direct and unmediated relationship between literary voice and author. The same is true of the *Letter to Queen Elizabeth*. Such occasional writings, with their dependence upon a specific agenda and audience, are in any case difficult to include in a general discussion of this kind and will be invoked only on occasion. Even the far more sophisticated use of persona in *A Defence of Poetry* has a similar effect, however, blurring distinctions between oratorical and authorial voices. In the more obviously fictitious personas, the distinction between author and persona is more easily maintained: Sidney was never a shepherd, as is Philisides in the *Old Arcadia*, nor did he serve a queen named Andromana, as does Philisides in the *New Arcadia*. In *Astrophil and Stella*, as the critical tradition shows, the relationship between author and persona is so ambiguous as to have provoked antithetical readings – with some critics treating Astrophil as a mere fiction and others identifying him completely with Sidney himself.

The variety of Sidney's self-representations, then, frustrates generalization, making the efforts of this chapter necessarily tentative and exploratory. The variety is itself significant, however. It tells us, for one thing, that, although Sidney's drive towards self-representation was strong and sustained, it was not programmatic. His self-images are spontaneous and improvisational, each one a response, as we have seen, to a particular moment in his career and a particular genre of writing. In a letter of 1 March 1578, written to Languet in response to his frustrations at court, Sidney observed that 'thorough self-examination' is an 'employment' to which 'no labour that men can undertake, is in any way to be compared.'[1] Neither Sidney nor Languet would have appreciated at the time the role that literary creation was to play in this 'self-examination'; as Sidney's later letter outlining an educational program for his friend Edward Denny shows, self-examination meant conventionally the study of biblical and classical texts, not the production of pastoral romances, sonnets, or even translations of the psalms.[2] Upon his entry into court after his travels on the Continent, Sidney at first attempted to play a literary role as a courtier, writing *The Lady of May* and advising the queen on the match with Anjou. As his alienation from court increased, however, he turned towards a more private mode, in which self-representation, in particular, could become a playful yet serious means of examining the self.

In chapter 1 Sidney's tendency towards self-representation was characterized as an impulse towards autobiography in an age when the genre was just beginning to develop. In exploring the significance of Sidney's self-representations, it is useful to keep the genre of autobiography in mind, even if it was only emergent in Sidney's day and remains today notoriously ill-defined. To link Sidney's self-representations to the autobiographical forms of the sixteenth and seventeenth centuries is to become conscious of the distinctiveness of Sidney's interests. Despite his militant Protestantism, for example, he was not attracted to the inward spiritual probing that was to characterize much seventeenth-century autobiographical writing, as in Donne's *Devotions upon Emergent Occasions*. Nor did he attempt to create a new form for a sustained and unmediated journey of self-discovery, as did Montaigne; his images of the self are improvisational and placed within conventional forms. Nor did Sidney engage in an extended, 'factual' narrative of his life, as did Thomas Whythorne or, somewhat later, Lord Herbert of Cherbury. Sidney's autobiographical impulse manifested itself in spontaneous and fragmentary ways and was subordinated to other modes, including that of fiction. It is an outgrowth, one might say, of conventions found already in pastoral and Petrarchan poetry and in classical oratory. Sidney's improvisational approach to self-representation has something in common with that of Rembrandt, who traced his changing conception of himself over a lifetime by adopting a multiplicity of different costumes and roles for his self-portraits.[3] Although they are signs of an autobiographical impulse rather than full-scale autobiographies, Sidney's self-representations none the less fulfil at least two of the conventional functions of the genre: they provide complex vehicles for self-justification and for what might be called self-recreation.

The 'most secret purpose' in every autobiography, observes Georges Gusdorf, is 'personal justification.'[4] If so, then Sidney's self-representations are truly autobiographical. Underlying all of the self-representations, despite their many differences, lies a single, core motif, as if the various roles allowed the compulsive expression of a basic psychological need. The language that Sidney himself uses in characterizing the act of literary composition, as we have seen, makes such a continuity likely. Sidney says that he wrote because he was 'overmastered' with thoughts that demanded release, or because he was compelled to deliver 'monsters' that might otherwise have overwhelmed his brain; although playfully histrionic, these metaphors suggest considerable psychological urgency in the act of writing. The first evidence of this kind of psychological pressure occurs in a letter we have already examined, the letter of 21 April 1576 in which the young Sidney attempts to defend himself against Languet's charge that by not writing he has betrayed their friendship. Because of the insight they provide into Sidney's motivation for creating literary roles, the details of his response to Languet's attack, examined previously (42–7, above), are worth reviewing with some care.

Sidney's first impulse is to recoil in anger and resentment at the accusation of inconstancy, accusing Languet of betraying their friendship himself by an accusation of bad faith; since the ideal of friendship requires that it be based on the love of virtue, Sidney contends, an attack on a friend's virtue is tantamount to a 'wish to terminate our sacred friendship.' He continues by refusing to believe that Languet could have intended the additional charges of deceit and ingratitude and by accusing Languet himself of depriving him of letters. Finally, in a more temperate tone, he protests his love for Languet and pleads with him to desist from further accusations of betrayal. Attempting to deflect his anger with wit, he confesses himself willing to accept charges of laziness, idleness, or even stupidity, but not of a failure of love. He reminds Languet of his proneness to anger and expresses playfully the wish to answer his charges in 'the high tragic style,' a wish that is denied because the court has 'driven all my Latin into exile.'[5] In his first preserved letter to Languet, written on 5 December 1573, Sidney had answered a less serious attack of the same kind by defending himself against the charge of inconstancy and by wishing he had enough skill in Latin to make a 'scene.'[6] The image of the theatre ties both letters together.

The most intriguing feature of the letter of 1576 is the psychological pattern of Sidney's response. Feeling himself under attack for a betrayal of the ideal of friendship, an ideal that was central to his conception of self, Sidney is willing to admit partial blame indirectly, accepting the relatively minor faults of laziness, idleness, or, jokingly, mere stupidity. Anger and resentment dominate the letter, however, and find expression in spurious counterattacks upon Languet. The anger is brought under control, however, and deflected by self-mockery at the 'hornet's nest' of his temper, which, Sidney admits, is always there to be stirred up again. It is also deflected by the witty attack on the court, which has driven his Latin into exile and made it impossible for him to write in the 'high tragic style.' This latter notion, which appears in the earlier letter as the desire to create a tragic 'scene,' is particularly suggestive in connection with Sidney's comments about his motives for writing in the dedication to the *Old*

Arcadia and *A Defence of Poetry*. In both cases, broadly speaking, the common ingredient is the self-conscious compulsion to release internal pressure, to rid the brain of monsters, through the creation of fictions. The invention of a 'tragic' role provides a way of justifying the self. The play of wit provides a mode of self-defence.

Sidney's letter to Languet not only alerts us to the possibility of a specific psychological motive for his creation of fictions, including the fictional representations of himself; it also provides a paradigm for all of the later self-representations. Each of Sidney's personas is in some sense under attack, threatened by a force that calls in question the very foundations of the self. Each responds, as does the persona of the letter to Languet, with a mixture of playful self-mockery and aggressive self-justification.

In the *Old Arcadia*, Philisides is under assault from two directions: from the anger of the goddesses Diana and Venus, who seek revenge for his choice of Mira, and from the anger of Mira, whom he has somehow offended. The underlying problem, if we accept a political reading of the persona, is rejection as a courtier, disguised metaphorically as a rejection of love. The failure has made Philisides a melancholy exile, cut off not only from his appropriate social position but from his status as a man. It thus cuts deeply into his sense of self, expressed in nostalgia for a past time of innocence and youthful promise, marked by peaceful studies at Samothea and friendship with Languet. Although Philisides admits to some fault in his quarrel with Mira and seems conscious of overreaching himself in judging the goddesses, the power of the self-representation lies mainly in Philisides' anger and resentment, which are directed not only at Mira, whom he accuses of unfairness but, through Languet's beast fable and the satires of Venus and Diana, at the queen and the court.

The self-representation in the *Old Arcadia*, then, seems the kind of 'tragic scene' that Sidney wished he had Latin enough to create in his letter to Languet. Through it he could exorcize the monsters in his brain, giving voice, with a mixture of fact and fiction, self-defence and self-mockery, to the accumulated frustrations of his several unsuccessful years at court. Although the exercise may have been personally therapeutic, no hint of a successful outcome occurs in the work itself. Philisides ends as hopeless and paralysed as he began, and the fictional framework, which defines his predicament as the result of a divine curse, implies that no resolution is possible.

In *Astrophil and Stella* the assault comes from romantic, not political love, embodied throughout by the figure of Cupid with his bow. The force of love throws Astrophil into crisis, challenging his sense of self at first and eventually undermining it altogether. As does Philisides, Astrophil gives voice to strong feelings of nostalgia, pitting his new-found anguish against his youthful promise and 'great expectations.' As his love develops, however, turning increasingly to lust, it alienates him from his past: from any morality of his teachers, from his vocational commitment, from his aspirations towards a spiritual union. In the early stages of his love Astrophil's blame for his predicament turns partly inwards, towards his own betrayal of his ideals. As the sequence proceeds, however, all efforts at either self-defence or self-criticism are eroded by an increasingly mindless pursuit of passion. The story of Astrophil, like that of Philisides, ends with an unending commitment to a hopeless passion.

Summarized in such a way, the 'tragic scene' of Astrophil reads much like that of Philisides, except that the blame for Astrophil's predicament seems completely internalized. Astrophil is frustrated by Stella's refusal to yield but never seriously challenges her devotion to chastity; nor does he explore to any great extent the possibility of weaknesses in the traditional arguments for virtue that cause him so much anguish. Instead of seeking a rationale for his passion, a defence of sexuality, he simply yields to it, conscious of his folly but unwilling or unable to resist. If we take into account the differences in manner of presentation between Philisides and Astrophil, however, we may find in the latter self-representation a similarly satiric edge. Stella's virtue, as we have seen, is itself ironically empty, although Astrophil's moral blindness prevents him from realizing it. The satiric presentation of the court world, moreover, becomes by the end of the sequence so pronounced that both lovers seem to become representative victims of a corrupt society.

In contrast to the 'tragic scene' in the *Old Arcadia*, that in *Astrophil and Stella*, focusing as it does on Astrophil's multiple failures as a lover, seems to derive from a strongly internalized sense of guilt. The powerful current of self-satire that runs throughout the sequence, however, is qualified by the ironic distance between persona and author. The insistence that Astrophil both is and is not Sidney translates the love affair into a peculiarly self-conscious kind of comedy, with the authorial voice tempering self-satire with sympathy and evoking self-conscious delight in the representation of love itself. Self-justification is thus achieved, or at least attempted, through the comic and paradoxical representation of the self as flawed.

With *A Defence of Poetry*, the mode of self-representation changes sharply, from that of ironical fiction, with an implied distance between persona and author, to that of oratory, with an implied identity between the two. In this work too, however, the persona is presented as under attack, this time because he has lost his vocation and 'slipped into' the disreputable 'title' of a poet. Here, too, the persona expresses a powerful sense of nostalgia, beginning his discourse with an allusion to the training in horsemanship in Vienna that was so central to his promise as a man and aristocrat. Although Sidney acknowledges ruefully a certain complicity in his lapse into poetry – he has 'slipped' into a title that he never wanted – he attributes his lapse mainly to the effeminacy and corruption of the court, which has kept him idle. The self-critical tendencies that emerge as powerful self-satire in *Astrophil and Stella* are transformed into more positive energy in the *Defence*, as the figure of the poet becomes progressively identified with that of the warrior-aristocrat. The attack on the foundations of the self is answered by a demonstration that the 'unelected vocation' is to be imaginatively identified with the old. The self is constant. The continuing target of satire is the court itself, and by implication the queen, both of which misunderstand and devalue poetry, thereby perpetuating the court's destructive enervation and effeminacy.

In the *New Arcadia*, the persona is once again rhetorically dissociated from the author and recedes into a minor role in a single episode, the tilt in celebration of Andromana's wedding day. Philisides finds himself both literally and metaphorically under assault in this episode – by his friend, who jousts against him, and by his 'star,' who in his verses defeats his attempts to unhorse her in the combat of love. Both 'assaults' theaten the notion of the self. In the literal tilt, Philisides is angered by the thought that his opponent deliberately avoids striking him in order to insult his youth – the thought strikes at the core of his identity as courtier. In the metaphoric tilt, Philisides must come to terms once again with the reality of unrequited love. In both cases, however, the notion of assault is itself undermined, for both the friend and the 'star' act out of love for Philisides, who is gently mocked for his misunderstanding, and the threat to the self is ultimately illusory.

The absence of an inner conflict or sense of guilt in the portrait of Philisides makes this persona seem more like an exercise in self-celebration than in self-criticism or self-defence. Musidorus tells the story of Philisides' joust because 'his manner liked me well.' This persona inhabits a world in which assaults upon the self are illusory, and the persona finds fulfilment in the varied roles that mark the successful courtier – of lover, friend, poet, and warrior. The sense of nostalgia that so powerfully informs the other self-representations, creating an unnerving contrast between past promise and present waste, is in this case transformed into a positive force. If the episode celebrates Sidney's first entry into the world of the tournament, it does so in a way that keeps that memory alive, its meaning carried into the present; if the source is more immediate, then Sidney's present experience is itself given the energy and promise of his youth. In either case, the episode absorbs the previously negative or problematic roles of lover, poet, and courtier into a positive design, presented in such a way that the present self fulfils the promise of the past.

Even this essentially positive self-representation, however, contains a qualifying irony – the corrupt nature of the court that Philisides serves. The irony goes unnoticed by Philisides, whose portrait in any case is largely externalized, but also by Musidorus, who has himself been Andromana's victim. As a critique of Philisides, then, the irony seems muted. As a critique of the world in which courtiers must survive, however, the irony conveys considerable power. Even Sidney's most affirmative self-representation is thus set against the backdrop of a corrupt court and queen.

Although much of importance is necessarily omitted from a brief and sharply focused survey of this kind, the recurrent pattern it reveals, of a self in crisis attempting self-defence, tells us much about the psychological significance of Sidney's persistent interest in self-representation. Sidney had monsters developing in his brain as the result of his failure as a courtier, as he tells us, and he felt compelled to release them, drawing time and again, with a mixture of anguish and ironic wit, upon the same basic emotions – nostalgia for youthful promise, guilt at the loss of a vocation, and anger and resentment at the court and queen.

To explain Sidney's autobiographical impulse merely as a compulsive form of self-defence, however, is to dramatically oversimplify a complex series of literary and psychological manoeuvres. If the self-representations are in some sense self-defences, they are also playful self-attacks, teasingly oblique and sophisticated in their displacement of the pressures of court politics. The guardedly optimistic tone of the self-representations in the *Defence* and the *New Arcadia*, moreover, suggests the possible development of a more positive integration of self and social role, as we shall see later. Although the underlying drive of the self-representations may originate in a need for self-defence, its expression is thus complicated by self-consciousness, playfulness, and the development of Sidney's art. To understand this more positive and creative function of the self-representations, it is important to focus on their artifice, which makes them not merely defensive but re-creative autobiographical gestures.

Central to Sidney's artifice in the representation of self is his refusal to be bound by fact or fiction. For him, the veracity of a persona, a mask, lies both in the face it hides and the face it reveals. In some cases, as in the letters to Languet or *A Defence of Poetry*, we might be tempted to ignore the notion of persona altogether and to assume a direct and unmediated relationship between persona and author, fiction and fact. In other cases, as in *Astrophil and Stella*, we might be tempted to ignore the authorial self behind the persona, treating Astrophil as a character contained entirely within the fiction. In every case, however, Sidney mixes the rhetorical and real, treating his personas both as fictions and as literal self-images. Somewhat like the clowns of the Elizabethan theatre, Sidney's personas carry their offstage notoriety with them as they play their assigned roles, with the result that the boundaries between player and part, play-world and audience-world, are eroded.

This consistent refusal to respect the boundaries between fact and fiction challenges traditional definitions of autobiography as a genre, which often rely upon notions of historical truth. To place Sidney's self-representations against Philippe Lejeune's conventional, if rather restrictive definition of autobiography, indeed, is to become sharply aware of their evasion of traditional generic constraints. For Lejeune, autobiography is 'a retrospective account in prose that someone makes of his own existence, emphasizing his individual life and especially the history of his personality.'[7] Sidney's fragmentary versions of autobiography are both immediate and retrospective, poetic and prosaic, fictional and historical. The many discrepancies between this conventional notion of autobiography and Sidney's self-representations highlight not only the elusiveness of Sidney's autobiographical impulse, however, but the instability of generic definitions themselves. In recent years, indeed, both the theory and practice of autobiography have overturned traditional conceptions of the genre in ways that make Sidney seem almost postmodern.

The deconstructive turn in current autobiographical thought can be illustrated by a brief but highly influential essay by Paul de Man, 'Autobiography as De-Facement.' De Man asserts that traditional attempts to define autobiography as a genre 'founder in questions that are both pointless and unanswerable,' producing nothing of even heuristic value. He finds equally pointless and impossible any attempt to distinguish between autobiography and fiction. In the absence of a unitary self, moreover, he argues that the act of writing might be said to produce rather than represent the self: 'We assume that the life *produces* the autobiography as an act produces its consequences, but can we not suggest, with equal justice, that the autobiographical project may itself produce and determine the life ...?'[8] Postmodern autobiography, as exemplified by Barthes's *Roland Barthes by Roland Barthes*, resists efforts to contain autobiography generically, to separate it from fiction, to align it with a belief in a unitary self, and to treat identity as prior to the act of writing.[9]

Although Sidney's autobiographical fragments have certain affinities with postmodern autobiographical thought, they derive, as we have seen, from a very different conception of the world and self. Since the genre of autobiography did not exist for Sidney, he had no need to deconstruct it. The culturally pervasive notion of defining the self through imitation, moreover, enabled a sophisticated interplay between fictionality and historicity in the construction of identity that, for a writer like Sidney, did not undermine the essential reality of the self. Through imitation, the self was not created *ex nihilo* but re-created, shaped anew in response to new experience. Sidney's own doubts about a unitary self, as we have seen, were not philosophically or theologically based but grew out of the imagined loss of his civic vocation, which essentially defined his identity. What he feared was the dissolution of that self. In this regard writing represented for Sidney both a threat and an opportunity, a self-destructive lapse away from his true vocation and a means of exploring, testing, and reshaping the self in other terms. Writing was thus recreational in both senses of the word: an idle game, or 'toy,' and a making of something new. Hence the ambivalence towards writing that characterizes his career.

The kind of imaginative role-playing characteristic of Sidney's autobiographical fragments was an essential feature of Elizabethan culture, as we have seen earlier in the discussion of the theory of imitation. Through projecting oneself into a literary role, even a 'monstrous' one like that of the early Philisides, one could enlarge or redefine the self, becoming in imagination and, later, in actuality, a different person. This is the theory behind Sidney's own concept of imitation in *A Defence of Poetry*, where the poet's creation of heroes in imagination leads readers to heroic actions in life. In this way, by projecting himself into the role of Philisides, say, or the warrior-poet of the *Defence*, Sidney might not only re-create the self but the world at large. The process could be both cyclical and progressive, with imaginary and social roles interacting with each other over time and, through literary or personal circulation, expanding to encompass an entire community.

Although we know too little about the subjective experience or social environment of most writers in the Elizabethan period to observe this process in any detail, one exceptional writer, the court musician Thomas

Whythorne, provides an illuminating model of how it might have worked. The text, written about 1576, is his autobiography, the first of its kind in England. Addressed to a friend, the manuscript divides the story of Whythorne's life into three stages – childhood, adolescence, and old age – and mixes narrative, poems, and poetic commentaries. The title of the manuscript suggests its peculiar form: 'A book of songs and sonnets, with long discourses set with them, of the child's life, together with a young man's life, and entering into the old man's life, devised and written with a new orthography by Thomas Whythorne, gent.' Addressing himself to young readers in a prefatory poem, Whythorne offers his life to their judgment as a potential model for imitation, one from which they can derive 'learned lessons large.'[10]

More significant than this conventional preface for our purposes is the way in which Whythorne's narrative unfolds, with nearly every event in the life producing a poetic reaction. One example might make this process clear. At the beginning of adolescence, Whythorne tells us, he began to be troubled by Cupid and Venus, who turned his thoughts to love. In order to protect himself from Cupid, he 'remembered' a 'remedy,' which he put into effect. He devoted himself to Pallas, the goddess of wisdom, reading poetry and moral philosophy. He also turned to Apollo and Terpsichore, advancing his knowledge of music. Further, he sometimes wandered in the woods and groves of Diana, the goddess of chastity. On one such occasion, he wrote a poem, which he includes, celebrating the joy and solace he found in the scene. The poem begins, 'It doth me good in Zeph'rus rain / In Dian's walk for to disport,' and concludes with the prospect of future solace 'so oft as I this time may see,' the poem becoming a continuing source of joy, a future remedy against troubling thoughts of love. In this case, alas, the remedy was ineffective; Whythorne remained severely troubled by Venus and Cupid.[11]

The rhythm of this brief episode is characteristic of the work as a whole. Both experience and reading are assimilated into poetic form, which crystallizes a new insight, a new sense of self, and becomes a touchstone for later experience. The work as a whole becomes an imitative source for future readers, who might themselves assimilate their reading and experience into new poems. And so on. The process adapts to the autobiographical mode a central conceit of Sidney's *Defence*, that the making of a Cyrus in fiction can produce a world of Cyruses in fact. In creating his poems, the poet re-creates a self.

Although Sidney's autobiographical manner is more sophisticated and more oblique than Whythorne's, it too shows signs of this imitative spiral.

Sidney's pose as the melancholy shepherd-exile, Philisides, in the *Old Arcadia*, for example, grew naturally out of his own exile from court, as we have seen. It probably originated, however, in his much earlier role as the shepherd Philisides in the Accession Day tournament of 1577. The role also figures in the allusion in *The Lady of May* to the 'young courtiers' who become 'old shepherds,' singing of their despair in exile (28.26). Sidney's letter to his brother of 18 October 1580, moreover, shows that the role was not merely a literary but a social one: 'I write this to yow as one, that for my selfe have given over the delight in the world but wish to yow as much if not more then to my selfe.'[12] The role makes a final appearance in the *New Arcadia*, in the figure of Philisides, the shepherd-knight. It is thus possible to trace the role of shepherd through the vicissitudes of Sidney's career. The role begins with Philisides, a naïve worshipper of the queen in a tournament. His potential exile is then fantasized in the allusion to unsuccessful courtiers in *The Lady of May*. His melancholy exile is enacted at the time of writing the *Old Arcadia*, both as a social pose and as a literary role. And finally, in the *New Arcadia*, the role is transformed into that of shepherd-knight and integrated once more into the world of chivalry, this time in fiction. Upon his death, Sidney is memorialized as the shepherd-knight, and the image is assimilated into aristocratic culture at large. Such a spiral, in which life and art seem endlessly imitative of each other, epitomizes in many ways the life of a courtier-poet.

In a more general sense, the image of the melancholy shepherd might be said to haunt Sidney's imaginative life, for each of his self-representations involves to some degree an exploration of alienation. Philisides is an extreme case, estranged not only from the court but from the shepherd-world to which he has fled. Astrophil's alienation is of a different sort, internalized rather than literal, the result of his own feeling of separation from a world that does not understand his love. The persona of *A Defence of Poetry* begins with an admission of his alienation – he has 'slipped' into the role of poet, which makes him an outcast – but by the end of the work he has redefined his role as central to aristocratic culture. The Philisides of the *New Arcadia* seems perfectly integrated into his society as a courtier; yet in his case the notion of alienation is kept alive in the ironic estrangement between his values and those of Andromana's court. His true home, one might say, like that of his shadow, Amphialus, is with Helen. This recurrent posture of withdrawal gives literary form to an attitude that appears as well throughout the personal correspondence.

In *Renaissance Self-Fashioning*, Stephen Greenblatt notes that each of the figures he studies achieves self-fashioning 'in relation to something per-

ceived as alien, strange, or hostile. This threatening Other – heretic, savage, witch, adulteress, traitor, Antichrist – must be discovered or invented
in order to be attacked and destroyed.'[13] In Sidney's self-representations,
a threatening external force of this kind is difficult to define because the
struggle to imagine the self is from the first internalized. The central
threats to the identity of Sidney's various self-images are generally represented by the court and queen, on the one hand, and poetry itself on the
other. Since Sidney defined himself as a courtier, however, and since the
very act of representing the self defined him as a poet, these destabilizing
forces could not be demonized in the way that Thomas More, say, could
imagine heretics or Tyndale the Pope. Perhaps this difference helps us to
understand why Sidney so often represented himself in the role of alien.
His real enemy was not the court or queen or poetry but his own potential emptiness, a loss of self through a loss of social role.

Another example of the continuing interaction between Sidney's life
and art can be found in the recurrence in the personas of a single
attribute, that of anger. Biographically, Sidney's proneness to explosive
anger is well documented: it appears, for example, in his letter to
Languet defending himself against the betrayal of their friendship; in his
harsh and accusatory letter to Edmund Molyneux, his father's secretary;
and in Greville's account of his challenge to the earl of Oxford. The challenge to Oxford, as we have seen, probably contributed to the estrangement from the queen and exile that prompted the creation of the *Old
Arcadia*. Not surprisingly, then, Philisides is shown with a churlish and
angry disposition, especially in his relations with the old shepherd,
Geron. Whether this literary displacement of an acknowledged fault produced a change in behaviour we cannot tell. The literary acknowledg-
ments of anger continue, however, in Astrophil's vengeful sonnets against
Stella after she has refused him, and, in the *New Arcadia*, in Philisides'
wrath when he believes that his friend is intentionally insulting him for
his youth and inexperience as a tilter.

The witty and playful acknowledgment of this fault in the literary personas must have enhanced their social appeal, especially to audiences who
knew Sidney well. As early as the letters to Languet, one can see Sidney
bringing his faults to the surface with wry self-mockery. The preoccupation with anger, however, probably also reflects an attempt to come to
terms with this tendency, to exorcize or at least discipline it imaginatively.
As early as July 1574, Languet had warned Sidney of the need to control
his temper: 'From your last letter ... you appear to have thought better of
your anger, and to have let yourself be mollified, so that what could not

be changed you yourself smoothed over. And this is a method you will have to use again and again before you arrive at my age, unless you perhaps wish to spend your life in never-ending quarrels.'[14] Since the most common metaphor for imitation was that of digestion, the bee transforming pollen into honey, perhaps we may say that Sidney's imitations of an angry self were imaginative attempts to follow Languet's advice and digest his wrath.

The recurrence of wit and irony in the self-representations is of considerable interest, since these attributes are crucial to Sidney's literary reputation. The first recorded reference to wit that affects Sidney occurs, as we have seen, in the first letter his father sent to him when he was a young student at Shrewsbury School. The exhortation to imitate his father in merriness clearly had an impact on Sidney, for an explicit acknowledgment of the importance of wit occurs in one of the early letters to Languet (28 May 1574). A later letter, written on 21 April 1576, attempts to deflect Languet's anger by means of a self-conscious resort to wit. Only one of Sidney's self-representations lacks wit altogether, the Philisides of the *Old Arcadia*, but in his case the absence of wit is itself playful, part of the underlying and controlling irony of the author. Astrophil's wit sparkles during the early part of the sequence, lessening as he becomes more and more enmeshed in his hopeless lust, but even at his wittiest he too is mocked by authorial ironies. Persona and author merge in *A Defence of Poetry*, with the result that the playfulness and irony of the argument are compressed into a single self-consciousness, which is one reason for the extraordinary energy and complexity of the work. Finally, in the *New Arcadia*, Philisides expresses considerable wit and self-conscious irony in his poem and impresa, but is himself mocked by his ignorance of the meaning of the attacking knight's actions and by the nature of the monarch he serves. Such social gestures as the presentation of a jeweled whip to the queen and the wearing of the slashed motto 'speravi' to symbolize his lost inheritance suggest that Sidney enacted at court the ironic postures he displayed in his literary personas.

Sidney's wit may not have come naturally. Duncan-Jones notes that Languet felt Sidney 'to be too solemn for his years,' an attitude that may have encouraged Sidney's self-conscious efforts at wit in the letters. Fulke Greville reports that 'though I lived with him and knew him from a child, yet I never knew him other than a man, with such staidness of mind, lovely, and familiar gravity as carried grace and reverence above greater years.'[15] Thomas Moffet observes that Sidney did not like games and that he allowed himself recreation from his studies only to protect his health.[16] There is little evidence of playfulness, moreover, in the personas adopted for court affairs, as in the letter chastising Molyneux, the *Letter to Queen Elizabeth*, and the *Defence of the Earl of Leicester*. Even in the more literary personas, the ironic and self-deprecating wit gives way on occasion, as we have seen, to anger or resentment. One might explain the conflicting evidence and the complexity of Sidney's own attitude as the result of an imposed persona. Sidney may have been encouraged by his father's exhortation and example to cultivate a 'merriness' that was not natural to him. If so, then the self-representations, both social and literary, might reflect a continuing inner tension between earnest passion and ironical detachment.

Anger and wit are not the only attributes that might be used to suggest the continuing reciprocity between Sidney's actual life, his personality and experience, and the fictional or rhetorical roles developed in art. Many personal characteristics recur in the self-representations with considerable frequency: among others, idealism, a love of horsemanship, a tendency towards aggression, an identification with the aristocracy, a proneness to sexual passion, a questioning of sexual identity, a commitment to friendship, ambivalence or even hostility towards the queen, and a strong commitment to the idea of vocation. The list could easily be enlarged, but it is probably long enough to suggest the underlying continuity of personal self-examination and development that runs throughout the various self-portraits and links them to the historical 'person' that biographers are able to construct from much more varied historical evidence. The self-representations offer a rich resource for psychological studies of Sidney, a network of recurrent attitudes, values, and anxieties.

Similar continuities can be detected in the repetition of certain general roles, as we have seen in the persona of the melancholy exile. In the early letters, Sidney appears as friend to Languet; in the *Old Arcadia*, as friend to Languet and Coredens; in *Astrophil and Stella* as friend to an anonymous adviser; in the *Defence* as friend to Edward Wotton; and in the *New Arcadia* as friend to his challenger at the tilt. He is a melancholy lover in the *Old Arcadia*, a frustruted wooer in *Astrophil and Stella*, a rueful witness to love's power in the *Defence*, and an ardent but unsuccessful wooer of a 'star' in the *New Arcadia*. As a warrior, he makes only a momentary appearance in the *Old Arcadia*, but *Astrophil and Stella* and the *Defence* are rich in military metaphors, as we have seen, and the tilt in the *New Arcadia* is designed to highlight Philisides' military potential. The role of poet appears only implicitly in the *Old Arcadia* but becomes increasingly prominent in *Astrophil and Stella* and the *Defence*, and surfaces as well in Philisides' lines to his 'star' in the *New Arcadia*. With the exception of the letters to Languet, each of the personas also places Sidney in the role of courtier. As one might expect, in view of the course of Sidney's development and the nature of the imitative process, the literary personas tend to build upon one another cumulatively, with the final role, that of Philisides in the *New Arcadia*, providing, in miniature, a synthesis of the varied roles played up to that point.

In Sidney, then, as in Whythorne, we can detect signs of the imitative spiral, the process by which the self is constantly recreated through literary imitation. For Sidney, however, unlike Whythorne, the process is invariably displaced through the self-conscious creation of a persona, such as Astrophil and Philisides, and through the situating of the personas within a variety of fictional or rhetorical genres. Whythorne writes poems in which he is the speaker; Sidney writes letters, prose fictions, poems, and orations, and peoples them with self-representations. This difference calls attention not only to Sidney's recurrent preoccupation with 'fictions' of the self but with the generic frames within which that self is forced to play a role. Whereas most autobiography places the subject within a recognizable historical world, that of the author's own environment, Sidney's autobiographical fragments place the subject within a recognizable literary world, one dictated by generic norms and conventions. Sidney uses his self-representations, then, not merely to explore his self in relation to his immediate social environment but in relation to an environment shaped by literary tradition. As we have seen in earlier chapters, this dynamic interaction between persona and genre works in complex ways, sometimes holding the persona up to ridicule, sometimes the generic frame: in the *Old Arcadia* Philisides remains with the shepherds while the world of heroic romance swirls around and above him; in *Astrophil and Stella*, the conventions of the sonneteers do not meet the test of Astrophil's experience. Genre serves Sidney, as Claudio Guillén suggests it serves writers generally, as 'a problem-solving model on the level of form.'[17]

This testing, however, was in Sidney's case not limited to genre alone. Each of the self-representations after the letters to Languet involves an effort to imagine the self as poet. The melancholy shepherd of the *Old Arcadia*, Philisides, laments his misfortunes in songs of Mira. The unsuccessful wooer, Astrophil, prides himself on his mastery of the sonnet form even as he uses it to seduce Stella. The persona of the *Defence* confesses that his only 'title' is that of poet. The Philisides of the *New Arcadia* assimilates his role as poet into the pageantry of Andromana's court, serving,

poetry its conventional sphere of significance within the broader role of courtier. As we have seen, moreover, that role, with its synthesis of poetry, pageantry, and war, seems the symbolic equivalent of the conception of the poet's role put forward in *A Defence of Poetry*. The glorification of this role implicit in Musidorus's approval, however, is qualified by the satire of Andromana's court, which cannot help but taint the idea of Philisides' service. Like all the other self-images, therefore, that of Philisides involves a probing critique of the containing form: the ideal of courtly service is central to that of epic. Any restoration of the epic ideal in the *New Arcadia* seems to depend upon the role of queen Helen, who rules over a court where poetry and pageantry are virtuous arts of war.

The development of Sidney's fictional autobiography thus allows us to see not only versions of the self but versions of self-making; the self is always placed in tension with a generic frame. The commitment to genre, like Sidney's commitment to poetry itself, is always provisional and temporary. In the *Defence* and the *New Arcadia* there are signs of an increasing acceptance of the role of poet, marked especially by imaginative attempts to assimilate poetry into an aristocratic model of service to the state. It is tempting to view the portrait of Philisides in the *New Arcadia* as a playful affirmation, in miniature, of a conception of the role of poet that fulfils completely Sidney's conception of his identity. It is important to recognize, however, not only the ironies within the *New Arcadia* that prevent such a reading but the ironies within the life itself. Despite his tendency towards idealism, Sidney never allowed his attraction to the role of poet to alter fundamentally his conception of himself or his public role. He did not leave the court to become a poet; nor did he make a single gesture towards the printing of his literary works. Nor are his varied literary self-representations experiments in a new conception of the self, of the kind that Montaigne was to undertake in his *Essays*; they are a means, instead, to test and define the self against a traditional vocational ideal. Sidney's impulses were ultimately conservative, driving him to retain the sense of vocation into which he had been born and educated, assimilating into it the role that he had 'slipped into' for want of better activity at court. A potent symbol of that conservatism, and of the ultimate choice it implied, is the unfinished *New Arcadia*, which breaks off at mid-sentence. An even deeper scepticism is disclosed when, on his deathbed, according to Fulke Greville, Sidney bequeathed 'no other legacy but the fire to this unpolished embryo.'[18]

Sidney's ongoing commitment to political action points to another ironic limitation in the development of the personas and the works as a whole. As we have seen, Sidney's final two self-portraits imply a conception of poetry not as a mode of contemplation but as an act of political engagement. For poetry to serve as an agent of social reform, however, even in Sidney's terms, it would have to be circulated beyond a small circle of family and friends. Sidney's estrangement from the court and queen, however, led him away from courtly genres such as *The Lady of May* or the letter on the Anjou marriage, cutting off literary access to the centre of social and political power. His apparent resistance to publication, moreover, precluded circulation of his works to a more widespread and popular audience. If Sidney saw in poetry the possibility of national renewal, then he seems to have based that hope on a small inner circle – what Milton might have called, in quite another sense, 'fit audience though few.'

From a modern political perspective, Sidney's struggle to define his vocation through fictions of the self may seem merely escapist. Sidney himself inclined towards such a view, as we have seen. Within the terms of the imitative tradition, however, these fictions may have played a more positive role, enabling Sidney not only to work through courtly frustrations or enact heroic fantasies but to move towards meaningful enactments of an imagined social role. The ultimate purpose of imitative fictions was virtuous action, and Sidney's last role before Zutphen was that of the young jouster, Philisides, whose appearance in a tournament was preparation for war. Conceived in these terms, Sidney's self-representations might be considered what Kenneth Burke calls '*equipments for living*,' strategies that not only compensate for the vicissitudes of life but enable writers to 'fight' on their own terms, defining attitudes that may translate into action.[19] If so, then Sidney's role as a young jouster equipped him, ironically, not for living but for death.

With the publication of Sidney's works after his death, his self-representations were subjected to yet other ironies. Although the example of his life and writings did inspire the aristocracy to which Sidney appealed, it also inspired the very publishing poets he condemned, whose poetic role could be sanctioned by his own heroic precedent.[20] In the development of Sidney's reputation, moreover, his self-representations tended to be absorbed into a single heroic image and conflated simplistically with the man himself. In the commemorative poems printed in the 1580s and 1590s, for example, the names 'Philisides,' 'Astrophil,' and 'Philip' are used interchangeably, and the varied attributes he himself explored in distinctive individual personas blend to produce a single, idealized 'Sidney,' the representative figure of the perfect courtier. The ambivalence, the irony, the continuing struggle to identify the self in a medium that mixes fact and fiction, all are lost in the single-minded pursuit of the perfect hero. The image of Sidney that survived was essentially that of idealizing poets and biographers, such as Fulke Greville, Thomas Moffet, and Sidney's sister, the countess of Pembroke, not the image, or series of images, provided by Sidney himself in his fictional autobiography.[21] The creators of the Sidney legend invented a fictional self less interesting and perhaps less 'true' than the fictional selves that Sidney had created before them.

Whatever the ultimate 'truth' of these fictional autobiographies, the picture of imaginative activity they provide helps us to understand not only Sidney himself but the complex cultural environment that produced him and within which he sought to play a meaningful role. Whether Sidney ever succeeded in assimilating his aristocratic values into the role of poet remains an open question, appropriately symbolized by the gap between Philisides' joust and Sidney's death at Zutphen. If we consider the fictional autobiography as a whole, the composite image that emerges is of a self in continuing crisis, in a continuing search for definition and vocation. For Sidney, this is the ultimate meaning of the imitative spiral. The image is not that of a perfect Elizabethan courtier; the tensions within the image, however, provide a complex picture of the imaginative life of a major aristocratic writer who aspired to serve the state.

Notes

Preface

1 Stephen Greenblatt, *Renaissance Self-Fashioning* (Chicago: Univ. of Chicago Press, 1980), 2.

1: Imitation and Identity

1 *Renaissance Self-Fashioning: From More to Shakespeare* (Chicago: Univ. of Chicago Press, 1980).
2 For useful accounts of Renaissance portraiture and self-portraiture, see Lorne Campbell, *Renaissance Portraits* (New Haven: Yale Univ. Press, 1990) and John Pope Hennessy, *The Portrait in the Renaissance* (New York: Bollingen Foundation, 1966). The allusion to Whythorne's autobiography occurs in Campbell, 214. The Hilliard self-portrait is reproduced in Mary Edmond, *Hilliard and Oliver* (London: Hale, 1983), 64.
3 *Sidney and Spenser: The Poet as Maker* (Univ. Park: Pennsylvania State Univ. Press, 1989), 439, 440, 484.
4 Greenblatt, *Sir Walter Ralegh: The Renaissance Man and His Roles* (New Haven: Yale Univ. Press, 1973), 57.
5 Helgerson, *Self-Crowned Laureates: Spenser, Milton, and the Literary System* (Berkeley: Univ. of California Press, 1983), 29.
6 *Poetry and Courtliness in Renaissance England* (Princeton: Princeton Univ. Press, 1978), 68.
7 *Sir Philip Sidney: Courtier Poet* (London: Hamish Hamilton, 1991), 233.
8 *The Elizabethan Courtier Poets* (Columbia: Univ. of Missouri Press, 1991), 97–8; chapters 2–4 of May's study provide a useful context for Sidney as a courtier-poet.

9 'Tudor Aristocrats and the Mythical "Stigma of Print,"' *Renaissance Papers 1980* (1981): 11–18; I am also indebted to an unpublished paper by Jean R. Brink, 'The Stigma of Print: Sidney and Shakespeare.'

10 Several recent studies show that, in sixteenth- and seventeenth-century England, the widespread and often professional production and circulation of manuscripts constituted a kind of 'publishing' comparable to the production of printed books: see Harold Love, *Scribal Publication in Seventeenth-Century England* (Oxford: Clarendon Press, 1993); Arthur F. Marotti, *Manuscript, Print, and the English Renaissance Lyric* (Ithaca, NY: Cornell Univ. Press, 1995); and, especially, H.R. Woudhuysen, *Sir Philip Sidney and the Circulation of Manuscripts 1558–1640* (Oxford: Clarendon Press, 1996). Woudhuysen, whose study illuminates Sidney's entire social milieu, attributes Sidney's preference for manuscript publication largely to his 'fear of the so-called "stigma of print"' (211). He also shows, however, that although Sidney published his manuscripts, their restricted circulation ensured a very small audience; Sidney allowed eight copies to be made of the *Old Arcadia* within two years but restricted access to the later works much more severely (8, 386).

11 *The Elizabethan Prodigals* (Berkeley: Univ. of California Press, 1976), 130.

12 For self-portraiture, see Campbell, *Renaissance Portraits*, and Pope Hennessy, *The Portrait in the Renaissance*; in addition, H. Perry Chapman provides a useful account of Rembrandt's motives in *Rembrandt's Self-Portraits: A Study in Seventeenth-Century Identity* (Princeton: Princeton Univ. Press, 1990). For the origins of British autobiography, see Paul Delany, *British Autobiography in the Seventeenth Century* (London: Routledge and Kegan Paul, 1969).

13 'The Rewriting of Petrarch: Sidney and the Languages of Sixteenth-Century Poetry,' in *Sir Philip Sidney and the Interpretation of Renaissance Culture*, ed. Gary F. Waller and Michael D. Moore (Totowa, NJ: Barnes and Noble, 1984), 76.

14 In emphasizing the introspective quality of Sidney's self-representations, I depart from Alan Hager, whose book, *Dazzling Images: The Masks of Sir Philip Sidney* (Newark: Univ. of Delaware Press, 1991), also deals with Sidney's use of persona throughout his career. For Hager, Sidney's adoption of various roles is a completely conscious rhetorical device, designed to entrap readers into an ironic awareness of the paradoxical nature of human experience. While Hager's view of Sidney as a master ironist has much to recommend it, I believe that it overstates the case and oversimplifies both the personal and rhetorical functions of the self-representations. Rhetorical irony and inner conflict, as I hope to show, are not mutually exclusive.

15 *Sir Philip Sidney: The Maker's Mind* (Oxford: Oxford Univ. Press, 1977), 52–90; Connell cites, among other studies, the most influential attempt to define this courtly state of mind, Huizinga's *Homo Ludens* (53).

16 The two most useful biographies are Malcolm W. Wallace, *The Life of Sir Philip Sidney* (1915; rpt New York: Octagon Books, 1967), and Katherine Duncan-Jones, *Sir Philip Sidney: Courtier Poet*; I am especially indebted to Duncan-Jones throughout this study.

17 *Life*, 68–70.

18 *Prodigals*, 16–43.

19 *The Family, Sex and Marriage in England, 1500–1800* (New York: Harper and Row, 1977), 105–14.

20 *The Prose Works of Sir Philip Sidney*, ed. Albert Feuillerat, 4 vols. (Cambridge: Cambridge Univ. Press, 1962) III, 125.

21 William H. Woodward, *Desiderius Erasmus concerning the Aim and Method of Education* (New York: Teachers College, Columbia Univ., 1964), 187.

22 *Prodigals*, 20.

23 *De Officiis* I.xxi and vi; quoted in Kenneth Charlton, *Education in Renaissance England* (London: Routledge and Kegan Paul, 1965), 29.

24 Thomas M. Greene, *The Light in Troy* (New Haven: Yale Univ. Press, 1982), 1.

25 'Latin Language Study as a Renaissance Puberty Rite,' *Studies in Philology* 56 (1959): 103–24.

26 *Autobiographies* (London: Macmillan, 1955), 477; *Mythologies* (London: Macmillan, 1959), 333–4.

27 *Vives: On Education*, trans. Foster Watson (1913; rpt Totowa NJ: Rowman and Littlefield, 1971), 64.

28 Woodward, *Erasmus*, 189.

29 *English Works*, ed. William Aldis Wright (Cambridge, 1904), 206–20.

30 Ibid., 183.

31 Ibid., 200.

32 Woodward, *Erasmus*, 164.

33 *Institutio Oratoria*, trans. H.E. Butler (Cambridge, MA: Loeb Classical Library, 1958), I.ix.1–3, and II.vii.1–5.

34 *Th'overthrow of Stage-Playes* (London: 1599), 19. For a penetrating study of Puritan opposition to the stage, see Jonas Barish, *The Antitheatrical Prejudice* (Berkeley: Univ. of California Press, 1981), 80–131.

35 George William Fisher, *Annals of Shrewsbury School* (London: Methuen, 1899), 18.

36 Wright, ed., *English Works*, 267–8.

37 *Timber, or Discoveries*, ed. Ralph S. Walker (Syracuse NY: Syracuse Univ. Press, 1953), 86–7. For excellent studies of Jonson's conception of imitation, see Richard S. Peterson, 'Imitation and Praise in Ben Jonson's Poems,' *English Literary Renaissance* 10 (1980): 265–99, and chapter 13 of Greene's magisterial survey of literary imitation in the Renaissance, *The Light in Troy*. General

surveys of the literary idea of imitation are provided in Harold Ogden White, *Plagiarism and Imitation during the English Renaissance* (1935; rpt New York: Octagon Books, 1965), and J.W. Pigman III, 'Versions of Imitation in the Renaissance,' *Renaissance Quarterly* 33 (1980): 1–32.

38 Woodward, *Erasmus*, 173.

39 I quote Pigman's translation in 'Versions of Imitation,' 24; a more formal translation is provided by Izora Scott in *Ciceronianus* (1908; rpt New York: AMS Press, 1972), 58.

40 Watson, trans., *Vives: On Education*, 197–8.

41 See especially his study of Shakespeare, *A Theater of Envy* (New York: Oxford Univ. Press, 1991). While I am unconvinced by Girard's overall theory, I find his attention to the psychology of emulation in Shakespeare suggestive. Since he sees 'mimetic desire' as a universal phenomenon, Girard does not relate it specifically to Elizabethan culture.

42 *Role-playing in Shakespeare* (Toronto: Univ. of Toronto Press, 1978), 11–20.

43 Fulke Greville, *The Prose Works of Fulke Greville, Lord Brooke*, ed. John Gouws (Oxford: Clarendon Press, 1986), 76–7. Greville's description of the misadventure at Zutphen insinuates some doubts about the judgment of the English 'leaders' (77), but their vagueness serves to deflect any potential criticism away from Sidney himself. Gouws quite appropriately calls the work as a whole a 'biographical panegyric' (xvii).

44 Quoted in Wallace, *Life*, 208.

45 Ibid., 201.

46 *Chronicles* (1808; rpt New York: AMS Press, 1965) IV, 880.

47 *The VIII Bookes of Xenophon*, trans. William Bercker (1567), Sig. A4.

48 Although I believe he overstates the importance of the Calvinistic strand in Sidney's thought, Andrew D. Weiner provides useful information about the religious context of Sidney and his works in *Sir Philip Sidney and the Poetics of Protestantism* (Minneapolis: Univ. of Minnesota Press, 1978).

49 *A Treatise of the Vocations or Callings of Men*, in *The Work of William Perkins*, ed. Ian Breward (Appleford, Eng.: Sutton Courtenay Press, 1970), 446–7.

50 Ibid., 451, 459.

51 Quoted in Helgerson, *Prodigals*, 124.

52 James M. Osborn, *Young Philip Sidney: 1572–1577* (New Haven: Yale Univ. Press, 1972), 538, 540.

53 *Prodigals*, 37.

54 *Cicero: De Officiis*, trans. Walter Miller, Loeb Classical Library (London: Heinemann, 1928), I.xxvi.92.

55 *Prodigals*, 37.

56 *Prose Works*, 5.

57 *The Aspiring Mind of the Elizabethan Younger Generation* (Durham, NC: Duke Univ. Press, 1966).

58 *The Crisis of the Aristocracy, 1588–1641* (Oxford: Clarendon Press, 1965).

59 Claudio Guillén, *Literature as System* (Princeton: Princeton Univ. Press, 1971), 109, 120.

2: Friend to Hubert Languet

1 Quoted in John Buxton, *Sir Philip Sidney and the English Renaissance* (London: Macmillan, 1954), 43.

2 Quoted in James M. Osborn, *Young Philip Sidney: 1572–1577* (New Haven: Yale Univ. Press, 1972), 36.

3 *The Prose Works of Sir Philip Sidney*, ed. Albert Feuillerat, 4 vols. (Cambridge: Cambridge Univ. Press, 1962), III, 125.

4 Katherine Duncan-Jones, *Sir Philip Sidney: Courtier Poet* (London: Hamish Hamilton, 1991), 170.

5 For a survey of Elizabethan travel books and some accounts of travellers, see Clare Howard, *English Travellers of the Renaissance* (1914; rpt New York: Burt Franklin, 1968); for a general discussion of Elizabethan adolescent rites, see Edward Berry, *Shakespeare's Comic Rites* (Cambridge: Cambridge Univ. Press, 1984), 1–32.

6 Lawrence Stone, *The Crisis of the Aristocracy, 1588–1641* (Oxford: Clarendon Press, 1965), 701.

7 Buxton, *Sidney*, 51.

8 *The Prose Works of Fulke Greville, Lord Brooke*, ed. John Gouws (Oxford: Clarendon Press, 1986), 6.

9 The correspondence is entirely in Latin. Unless otherwise indicated, the letters will be identified henceforth by date only and taken from the translation of Charles S. Levy in 'The Correspondence of Sir Philip Sidney and Hubert Languet, 1573–1576,' (PhD diss., Cornell Univ. 1962). Readers without access to this edition can find many of the letters, arranged chronologically, in Feuillerat and in Steuart A. Pears, trans., *The Correspondence of Sir Philip Sidney and Hubert Languet* (1845; rpt Westmead, Eng: Gregg International, 1971). For a brief overview of my use of the letters throughout this book, see the preface (xii).

10 Neil L. Rudenstine, *Sidney's Poetic Development* (Cambridge MA: Harvard Univ. Press, 1967); Richard Helgerson, *The Elizabethan Prodigals* (Berkeley: Univ. of California Press, 1976); Louis Adrian Montrose, 'Celebration and Insinuation: Sir Philip Sidney and the Motives of Elizabethan Courtship,' *Renaissance Drama*, n.s., 8 (1977), 3–36; and Richard C. McCoy, *Sir Philip Sidney: Rebellion in Arcadia* (New Brunswick, NJ: Rutgers Univ. Press, 1979).

11 Quoted in Malcolm W. Wallace, *The Life of Sir Philip Sidney* (1915; rpt New York: Octagon Books, 1967), 69.
12 Helgerson, *Prodigals*, 38.
13 See T.W. Baldwin, *William Shakspere's Small Latin and Lesse Greeke*, 2 vols. (Urbana: Univ. of Illinois Press, 1944), vol. 2: 253–62. For a stimulating and wide-ranging account of the letter in the Renaissance, see Claudio Guillén, 'Notes toward the Study of the Renaissance Letter,' in *Renaissance Genres: Essays on Theory, History, and Interpretation*, ed. Barbara Kiefer Lewalski (Cambridge MA: Harvard Univ. Press, 1986), 70–101; Guillén comments on the ideal of friendship that characterized the humanist epistolary tradition of the sixteenth century (91).
14 *Cicero: De Senectute, De Amicitia, De Divinatione*, trans. William A. Falconer, Loeb Classical Library (London: Heinemann, 1930), xiv.49; further citations will be indicated in parentheses.
15 The phrase 'a morsel for mockery' derives from Terence, *Eunuch*, 1087.
16 *Sir Philip Sidney*, 240–2. For thoughtful discussions of some of the issues surrounding the interpretation of homosexuality in the sixteenth century, see Bruce R. Smith, *Homosexual Desire in Shakespeare's England* (Chicago: Univ. of Chicago Press, 1991), esp. 3–29; Jonathan Goldberg, *Sodometries* (Stanford: Stanford Univ. Press, 1992); and Casey Charles, 'Heroes as Lovers: Erotic Attraction between Men in Sidney's *New Arcadia*,' *Criticism* 34 (1992): 467–96.
17 Levy, 'Correspondence,' 72, notes that the quotation is 'perhaps an inaccurate recollection of *De Amicitia* 18.66, "a certain pleasantness of speech and behavior, a by no means ordinary spice of friendship" (*condimentum amicitiae*).'
18 Wallace, *Life*, 69.
19 This letter appears only in Osborn, *Sidney*, 419–21.
20 McCoy, *Rebellion*, 10.
21 Osborn, *Sidney*, 418.
22 *Sir Philip Sidney*, 98.
23 Ibid., 23.

3: Self-Portrayals at Court, 1575–9

1 For an insightful account of the role of the courtier as itself a text, see Roger Kuin, 'Sir Philip Sidney: The Courtier and the Text,' *English Literary Renaissance* 19 (1989): 249–71. Kuin argues that Sidney's writing of fiction begins only after his 'self-written text' as courtier fails, and that he thereby 'ceases to be a text and becomes an *auctor*' (270). The habit of self-representation, however, blurs this distinction; to adopt Kuin's terms, one might say that Sidney's textual self simply moves from the court into fiction.

2 In a recent study of this portrait, which exists in five versions, Strong concludes that the original is the one now held at Longleat House in Wiltshire, and that it was executed in 1578 as a gift for Mary, countess of Pembroke; see 'Sidney's Appearance Reconsidered,' in *Sir Philip Sidney's Achievements*, ed. M.J.B. Allen, Dominic Baker-Smith, and Arthur F. Kinney (New York: AMS Press, 1990): 3–31. Katherine Duncan-Jones, however, points to evidence that suggests the painting was done in 1577; see *Sir Philip Sidney* (London: Hamish Hamilton, 1991), 113–14. The evidence either way is inconclusive, and my argument depends upon neither date. My interpretation of the portrait owes much to Duncan-Jones's brief but insightful remarks.

3 See *Tudor and Jacobean Portraits*, 2 vols. (London: Her Majesty's Stationery Office, 1969), I, 189–90 and II, plate 375; future references are indicated parenthetically by plate number.

4 *Renaissance Portraits* (New Haven: Yale Univ. Press, 1990).

5 Francis M. Kelly and Randolph Schwabe, *A Short History of Costume and Armour*, 2 vols. (1931; rpt New York: Benjamin Blom, 1968), II, plate v.

6 *Sir Philip Sidney*, 114.

7 Ralph M.Sargent, *The Life and Lyrics of Sir Edward Dyer* (1935; rpt Oxford: Clarendon Press, 1968), 24.

8 Philippa Berry, *Of Chastity and Power: Elizabethan Literature and the Unmarried Queen* (London: Routledge, 1989), 61–82.

9 'Sidney's May Game for the Queen,' *Modern Philology* 86 (1989): 252–64.

10 Stephen Orgel was the first critic to note the incongruity of the ending; see 'Sidney's Experiment in Pastoral: *The Lady of May*,' *Journal of the Warburg and Courtauld Institutes* 26 (1963): 44–57. For a challenge to the standard interpretation that privileges the role of Therion, see Catherine Bates, *The Rhetoric of Courtship in Elizabethan Language and Literature* (Cambridge: Cambridge Univ. Press, 1992); Bates suggests that Sidney 'could not afford to be seen to steer her [the queen] one way or the other' and therefore devised a form that reflected 'his own ineffectualness' (67).

11 *The Prose Works of Fulke Greville, Lord Brooke*, ed. John Gouws (Oxford: Clarendon Press, 1986), 41.

12 Duncan-Jones, *Sir Philip Sidney*, 164.

13 *Prose Works*, 37–8.

14 'Sidney and His Queen,' in *The Historical Renaissance: New Essays on Tudor and Stuart Literature and Culture*, ed. Heather Dubrow and Richard Strier (Chicago: Univ. of Chicago Press, 1988), 177. Quilligan provides an insightful analysis of various rhetorical strategies, including what might be called an aggressive humility, that Sidney uses to assert his specifically male power against the female monarch.

15 Historical Manuscripts Commission, *Salisbury MSS.*, II, 308–10.

16 Ibid., 245.

17 For a useful account of Sidney's ironic method in the letter see Alan Hager, *Dazzling Images: The Masks of Sir Philip Sidney* (Newark: Univ. of Delaware Press, 1991), 52–6. Although Hager finds the letter 'a model of tactful indirection' (53), he acknowledges that it was 'undoubtedly a frank letter by contemporary standards' (52).

18 James M.Osborn, *Young Philip Sidney: 1572–1577* (New Haven: Yale Univ. Press, 1972), 209, 420.

19 Steuart A. Pears, trans., *The Correspondence of Sir Philip Sidney and Hubert Languet* (1845; rpt Westmead, Eng.: Gregg International, 1971), 147, 137, 154.

20 *Sir Philip Sidney*, 114.

21 For a description of the portrait, see Strong, *Portraits*, I, 194.

22 *Sir Philip Sidney*, 113.

23 Daniel Javitch, *Poetry and Courtliness in Renaissance England* (Princeton: Princeton Univ. Press, 1978), 18–49.

4: Philisides in Exile: The *Old Arcadia*

1 Quoted in Katherine Duncan-Jones, *Sir Philip Sidney: Courtier Poet* (London: Hamish Hamilton, 1991), 192. Duncan-Jones observes that 'there is no doubt that this was a gesture of submission, for in his revised *Arcadia* Sidney made Musidorus, who had deeply offended Pamela, wear in his helmet "a whip to witness a self-punishing repentance."' Duncan-Jones does not comment on the way in which the analogy with Musidorus implies aggression as well as submission in Sidney's own gesture: Elizabeth, not Sidney, was to wear the whip as an emblem of 'self-punishing repentance.' By merely giving such an object, moreover, Sidney aggressively seized the initiative in defining the relationship between the two parties.

2 Other critics have also commented on the similarity between the opening of the *Old Arcadia* and the issues Sidney engaged in the Anjou affair. See, for example, Duncan-Jones, *Sir Philip Sidney*, 177–9, and Leonard Tennenhouse, 'Sidney and the Politics of Courtship,' in *Sir Philip Sidney's Achievements*, ed. M.J.B. Allen et al (New York: AMS Press, 1990), 206–9.

3 In his persuasive account of the conflict between autonomy and obedience that underlies the *Old Arcadia*, Richard C. McCoy provides a useful survey of interpretations of the ending; see *Sir Philip Sidney: Rebellion in Arcadia* (New Brunswick NJ: Rutgers Univ. Press, 1979), 132–7.

4 *Sir Philip Sidney*, 215.

5 In reading the letter as a private communication from Sidney to his sister

regarding the *Old Arcadia*, I follow the editor of the work, Jean Robertson (418).

6 In a stimulating essay on the Renaissance association of the creative imagination with the female body, Katharine Eisaman Maus suggests – rather surprisingly, given the complex tensions within her topic – that Sidney is merely playful in this passage, 'unconcerned about the authorial masculinity that his deliberate scrambling of maternal and paternal attributes might seem to compromise'; see 'A Womb of His Own: Male Renaissance Poets in the Female Body,' in *Sexuality and Gender in Early Modern Europe*, ed. James Grantham Turner (Cambridge: Cambridge Univ. Press, 1993), 270.

7 *Sir Philip Sidney*, 168.

8 The full text of the letter is in *The Prose Works of Sir Philip Sidney*, ed. Albert Feuillerat, 4 vols. (Cambridge: Cambridge Univ. Press, 1962), III, 130–3; the letter is dated 18 October 1580.

9 Quoted in *Sir Philip Sidney*, 189–90.

10 George Puttenham, *The Arte of English Poesie*, ed. Gladys Doidge Willcock and Alice Walker (Cambridge: Cambridge Univ. Press, 1936), 158.

11 'Of Gentlemen and Shepherds: The Politics of Elizabethan Pastoral Form,' *English Literary History* 50 (1983), 429.

12 Jorge de Montemayor, *The Diana*, trans. RoseAnna M. Mueller, *Hispanic Literature*, vol. 4 (Lewiston, NY: Edwin Mellen Press, 1989) and Jacopo Sannazaro, *Arcadia and Piscatorial Eclogues*, trans. Ralph Nash (Detroit: Wayne State Univ. Press, 1966); page references to Nash's edition of Sannazaro are indicated parenthetically within the text. For useful surveys of Sidney's sources, see *OA* xix–xxix and A.C. Hamilton, *Sir Philip Sidney* (Cambridge: Cambridge Univ. Press, 1977), 42–50. David Kalstone provides an illuminating discussion of Sidney's treatment of Sannazaro in *Sidney's Poetry* (Cambridge MA: Harvard Univ. Press), 9–101; although Kalstone does not deal with the issue of self-representation, his view of Sidney's critique of Sannazaro complements my own.

13 See Richard Helgerson's insightful discussion of Spenser's response to the Virgilian model in 'The New Poet Presents Himself: Spenser and the Idea of a Literary Career,' *PMLA* 93 (1978): 893–911.

14 For another, generally complementary interpretation of Philisides that focuses on Sidney's critique of the pastoral and Petrarchan traditions, see S.K. Heninger, Jr, *Sidney and Spenser: The Poet as Maker* (University Park: Pennsylvania State Univ. Press, 1989), 439–43. Heninger does not deal with the way in which the self-representation implies a critique of the pastoral version of the poetic career or of the use of pastoral as social commentary.

15 *The Life of Sir Philip Sidney* (1915; rpt New York: Octagon Books, 1967), 226.

16 For an insightful treatment of the relationship between the letters and the *Old Arcadia* in general, see Neil L. Rudenstine, *Sidney's Poetic Development* (Cambridge MA: Harvard Univ. Press, 1967), 3–45. Rudenstine, who spends little time on Philisides, finds far less guilt and inner tension in Sidney's development of these themes than I.

17 See, for example, Languet's letter of 3 December 1575, in James M. Osborn, *Young Philip Sidney: 1572–1577* (New Haven: Yale Univ. Press, 1972), 390 and his letter of 2 May 1578, in *The Correspondence of Sir Philip Sidney and Hubert Languet*, trans. Steuart A. Pears (1845; rpt Westmead, Eng.: Gregg International, 1971), 147–8.

18 *Sidney's Poetic Development*, 38.

19 Ralph M. Sargent, *The Life and Lyrics of Sir Edward Dyer* (Oxford: Clarendon Press, 1935), 186.

20 For illuminating studies of this function of pastoral, see Montrose, 'Of Gentlemen and Shepherds: The Politics of Elizabethan Pastoral Form,' *English Literary History*, 50 (1983), 415–59 and, in a broader context, Annabel Patterson, *Pastoral and Ideology: Virgil to Valéry* (Berkeley: Univ. of California Press, 1987).

21 Although Ringler categorizes the poems as 'wrongly attributed' (*P*, 356–8), Peter Beal provides convincing evidence of their authenticity; see 'Poems by Sir Philip Sidney: The Ottley Manuscripts,' *The Library*, 5th series, 33 (1978): 284–95. For accounts of the tilt, see Duncan-Jones, *Sir Philip Sidney*, 143–6, and Alan Young, *Tudor and Jacobean Tournaments* (London: George Philip, 1987), 154–8.

22 *The Life and Lyrics of Sir Edward Dyer* (1935; rpt Oxford: Clarendon Press, 1968), 207, 24, 55, 66–8.

23 See Annabel Patterson, *Censorship and Interpretation* (Madison: Univ. of Wisconsin Press, 1984), especially chapter 2.

24 For an interesting treatment of the relationship between the political and sexual meanings of the word 'courtship,' see Catherine Bates, *The Rhetoric of Courtship in Elizabethan Language and Literature* (Cambridge: Cambridge Univ. Press, 1992).

25 The most convincing approach to the question of Mira's identity, I find, is that of Dennis Moore, who links her to the queen; see *The Politics of Spenser's Complaints and Sidney's Philisides Poems*, Salzburg Studies in English Literature 101 (Salzburg: Institut für Anglistik und Amerikanistik, Universität Salzburg, 1982), 63–174. Sargent identifies Mira with Sidney's sister (*Sir Edward Dyer*, 68–71). Steven W. May, following Ringler, identifies her as one of Elizabeth's ladies-in-waiting; see *The Elizabethan Courtier Poets* (Columbia: Univ. of Missouri Press, 1991), 77. For the linkage between Mira and the queen in the *New Arcadia*, see *NA* xxvii.

26 The quotation is from Peter Lindenbaum, *Changing Landscapes* (Athens GA: Univ. of Georgia Press, 1986), 29. Although he deals only incidentally with Philisides, Lindenbaum provides an insightful account of Sidney's critique of pastoral traditions in the *Old Arcadia.*

27 *Censorship and Interpretation*, 38.

28 Ibid., 24–43; *Faire Bitts* (Pittsburgh: Duquesne Univ. Press, 1984); *Sidney's Arcadian Poems*, Salzburg Studies in English Literature 1 (Salzburg: Institut für Englische Sprache und Literatur, Universität Salzburg, 1973), 210–25; *Politics of Spenser's Complaints*, 139–54; 'The Politics of Sidney's Pastoral: Mystification and Mythology in *The Old Arcadia*,' *English Literary History* 52 (1985): 795–814; *The Sound of Virtue* (New Haven: Yale Univ. Press, 1996), 266–94, 347–54. Worden provides an especially rich personal and political context for his interpretation.

29 Quoted in James M. Osborn, *Young Philip Sidney* (New Haven: Yale Univ. Press, 1972), 538. Raitiere takes the concluding lines of the beast fable to be a straightforward exhortation to patience; see *Faire Bitts*, 65–70. Worden, more convincingly, assigns patience to the common people and strength to the nobles (292). As indicated above, I take the allusion to patience to be ironic.

30 *Censorship and Interpretation*, 40.

31 For an account of Sidney's source for Samothea, see Katherine Duncan-Jones, 'Sidney in Samothea: A Forgotten National Myth,' *Review of English Studies*, n.s. 25 (1974): 174–7, and W.L. Godshalk's comments in *Review of English Studies*, n.s. 29 (1978): 325–6.

32 Duncan-Jones, *Sir Philip Sidney*, 115–16.

33 *England's Eliza* (Cambridge MA: Harvard Univ. Press), 136.

34 *Sir Philip Sidney*, 147.

35 *Renaissance Pastoral* (Oxford: Clarendon Press, 1989), 251–2.

36 '"Eliza, Queene of shepheardes," and the Pastoral of Power,' *English Literary Renaissance* 10 (1980): 180; see also Wilson's treatment of pastoral celebrations of the Queen in *England's Eliza*, 126–66.

5: Astrophil and the Comedy of Love

1 'Sequences, Systems, Models: Sidney and the Secularization of Sonnets,' in *Poems in Their Place*, ed. Neil Fraistat (Chapel Hill: Univ. of North Carolina Press, 1986), 68. See also Anne Ferry, *The 'Inward' Language: Sonnets of Wyatt, Sidney, Shakespeare, Donne* (Chicago: Chicago Univ. Press, 1983), 16–18. Ferry notes that although some inconsistencies in reference show that 'sixteenth-century English writers did not always equate author and speaker ... they had

not formulated a distinct conception of the relationships possible between them, or of their significance' (16).

2 For insightful and wide-ranging discusssions of Sidney's complex relationship to Petrarch and the Petrarchan tradition, see Gary F. Waller, 'The Rewriting of Petrarch: Sidney and the Languages of Sixteenth-Century Poetry' (69–83) and Marion Campbell, 'Unending Desire: Sidney's Reinvention of Petrarchan Form in *Astrophil and Stella*' (84–94), in *Sir Philip Sidney and the Interpretation of Renaissance Culture*, ed. Gary F. Waller and Michael D. Moore (London: Croom Helm, 1984). Although both of these essays deal suggestively with the fragmentation of self in *Astrophil and Stella*, they do so without specific attention to Sidney's innovative split between the poet-lover and the authorial voice.

3 *Sir Philip Sidney: Rebellion in Arcadia* (New Brunswick NJ: Rutgers Univ. Press, 1979), 72.

4 'The Politics of *Astrophil and Stella*,' *Studies in English Literature* 24 (1984): 53–68. The notion of 'displacement' developed by Jones and Stallybrass provides an attractive middle ground between the views of McCoy, who sees the politics of the sequence as 'exclusively sexual' (*Sir Philip Sidney: Rebellion*, 72) and Arthur F. Marotti, who sees the sexuality of the sequence as a metaphor for politics ('"Love Is Not Love": Elizabethan Sonnet Sequences and the Social Order,' *English Literary History* 49 [1982]: 396–428). In 'A Woman's Touch: Astrophil, Stella and "Queen Vertue's Court"' (*English Literary History* 63 [1996]: 555–70), Sally Minogue offers a useful corrective to political interpretations of the sonnets that ignore the sexuality of Elizabeth; I am unconvinced, however, by her argument that Elizabeth herself is the subject of sonnets 9 and 83. For an interesting treatment of the interconnections between love and politics as related to the development of the word 'courtship,' see Catherine Bates, *The Rhetoric of Courtship in Elizabethan Language and Literature* (Cambridge: Cambridge Univ. Press, 1992).

5 See Robert L. Montgomery's subtle and balanced account of this issue in 'The Poetics of Astrophil,' in *Sir Philip Sidney's Achievements*, ed. M.J.B. Allen, Dominic Baker-Smith, and Arthur F. Kinney (New York: AMS Press, 1990), 145–56.

6 For a concise account of the biographical and textual background of *Astrophil and Stella*, see *P*, 435–58.

7 See *P*, 436; *DP*, 103.35–6; and Jean Robertson, 'Sir Philip Sidney and Lady Penelope Rich,' *Review of English Studies*, n.s. 15 (1964): 297. The account of Sidney's deathbed repentance for his love of Lady Rich gains support from the suggestive although by no means definitive version provided by Thomas Moffet, an intimate member of the Pembroke circle. According to Moffet, the

dying Sidney expressed rage at 'the eyes which had one time preferred *Stellas* so very different from those given them by God'; 'blushed at even the most casual mention of his own Anacreontics,' begging his brother not to allow 'this sort of poems' to 'come forth into the light'; and asked forgiveness of God, 'bewailing the lubricity of his adolescence.' See *Nobilis and Lessus Lugubris*, trans. Virgil B. Heltzel and Hoyt H. Hudson (San Marino CA: Huntington Library, 1940), 91–2. For a view that denies the significance of the deathbed allusion to Lady Rich and dissociates Sidney completely from Astrophil, see Thomas P. Roche, Jr, 'Autobiographical Elements in Sidney's *Astrophil and Stella*,' *Spenser Studies* 5 (1985): 209–31. Roche interprets the sequence as a negative moral exemplum in *Petrarch and the English Sonnet Sequences* (New York: AMS Press, 1989). 193–242. For an account of the relationship between Sidney and Penelope as merely a playful literary friendship, see S.K. Heninger, Jr, 'Sequences,' 78.

8 *Sir Philip Sidney* (London: Hamish Hamilton, 1991), 179.

9 The Oxford editors indicate a preference for 1579–80 (*DP*, 62); one of the editors, however, Katherine Duncan-Jones, apparently now prefers 1582–3 (see *Sir Philip Sidney*, 230–1).

10 '*Astrophil and Stella:* Pure and Impure Persuasion,' *English Literary Renaissance* 2 (1972): 111; *Dazzling Images* (Newark: Univ. of Delaware Press, 1991), 82. For a useful review of biographical and fictional approaches to the sonnets, see J.G. Nichols, *The Poetry of Sir Philip Sidney* (Liverpool: Liverpool Univ. Press, 1974), 52–79.

11 For a useful review of the methods of structuring sonnet sequences, see Carol Thomas Neely, 'The Structure of English Renaissance Sonnet Sequences,' *English Literary History* 45 (1978): 359–89.

12 *Faultlines* (Oxford: Clarendon Press, 1992), 201; Sinfield shows that Sidney's attitude towards love poetry in this passage is 'more puritan than the standard currency of Elizabethan critical thought' (201).

13 The image of Hercules with the distaff as a comic emblem of love figures also in the revised version of the *Arcadia*. In the *Old Arcadia*, Pyrocles, in love with Philoclea and disguised as an Amazon, wears a brooch with an eagle covered with the feathers of a dove, preyed upon by a dove (27.6–14); in the *New Arcadia*, the brooch represents Hercules with a distaff and a word in Greek, to be interpreted as ' "Never more valiant" ' (69.5–9). Nancy Lindheim suggests, persuasively, that in the context of the *New Arcadia* the addition of the phrase 'Never more valiant' marks Sidney's attempt to reconcile reason and love; see *The Structures of Sidney's Arcadia* (Toronto: Univ. of Toronto Press, 1982), 51.

14 Philip Sidney, *Apology for Poetry*, ed. Geoffrey Shepherd (London: Thomas Nelson, 1965), 223–5.

15 See, for example, the discussions by Margreta De Grazia, 'Lost Potential in Grammar and Nature: Sidney's *Astrophil and Stella*,' *Studies in English Literature* 21 (1981): 21–35; Alan Sinfield, *Literature in Protestant England 1560–1660* (London: Croom Helm, 1983); and Roche, *Petrarch and the English Sonnet Sequences*. In a wide-ranging and insightful essay on Sidney's relation to the English Petrarchan tradition, Germaine Warkentin argues that Sidney's ethical stance in *Astrophil and Stella* represents a sophisticated response to the rather severe moralism of mid-Tudor love poets; see 'The Meeting of the Muses: Sidney and the Mid-Tudor Poets,' in *Sir Philip Sidney and the Interpretation of Renaissance Culture*, 17–33.

16 For a moralistic reading of *Astrophil and Stella* against the background of Sidney's theory of comedy in the *Defence*, see Daniel Traister, 'Sidney's Purposeful Humor: *Astrophil and Stella* 59 and 83,' *English Literary History* 49 (1982): 751–64.

17 Thomas Nashe, *The Works of Thomas Nashe*, ed. Ronald B. McKerrow, (Oxford: Basil Blackwell, 1958), III, 329, 333.

18 In *Squitter-wits and Muse-haters* (Detroit: Wayne State Univ. Press, 1996), Peter C. Herman argues convincingly that in this sonnet, and throughout the sequence, Sidney subjects Astrophil to the conventional moral judgments of Protestant anti-poetic discourse; although Herman attributes ambivalence about poetry to Sidney, he tends to ignore the complex effects of the self-representation, focusing instead on the Protestant critique of Astrophil (95–122).

19 De Grazia concludes that Astrophil's poems provide 'a negative example to the poetics of the *Defence*, an oblique line ... by which the straight is to be known'; see 'Lost Potential,' 35. Where they overlap, my account differs from De Grazia's in finding Sidney's representation of the debasement of theory by practice ruefully self-engaged and self-critical rather than detached and morally didactic.

20 'Politics of *Astrophil and Stella*,' 56.

21 For a useful analysis of Astrophil against the background of Petrarchan idealization, see S.K. Heninger, Jr, *Sidney and Spenser: The Poet as Maker* (University Park: Pennsylvania State Univ. Press, 1989), 479–87; Heninger suggests that *Astrophil and Stella* is Sidney's 'final, nostalgic analysis of platonist assumptions' (486).

22 The sequence is astonishingly rich in puns of this kind; see Alan Sinfield, 'Sexual Puns in *Astrophil and Stella*,' *Essays in Criticism* 24 (1974): 341–55. This pun is common in Shakespeare; see Eric Partridge, *Shakespeare's Bawdy* (London: Routledge and Kegan Paul, 1968).

23 Geoffrey Shepherd notes the pun on 'tale' and 'tail' in this passage; see his edition of the *Apology for Poetry*, 198n.7.

24 'Politics of *Astrophil and Stella*,' 59.
25 I am unconvinced by those critics who find evidence of sexual consummation at the end of this song; see, for example, Clark Hulse, 'Stella's Wit: Penelope Rich as Reader of Sidney's Sonnets,' in *Rewriting the Renaissance*, ed. Margaret W. Ferguson, Maureen Quilligan, and Nancy J. Vickers (Chicago: Univ. of Chicago Press, 1986), 283.
26 *English Poetry of the Sixteenth Century* (London: Longmans, 1986), 146.
27 'The Emergence of Stella in *Astrophil and Stella*,' *Studies in English Literature* 25 (1985): 5, 17.
28 *Petrarch and the English Sonnet Sequences*, 230. See also Katherine J. Roberts, *Fair Ladies* (New York: Peter Lang, 1993), 81–3; Roberts finds nothing but virtue in Stella's response in song viii but acknowledges her later inconstancy in song xi.
29 The word 'self' also represents the soul in opposition to the body in Argalus's expression of love for the disfigured Parthenia in the *New Arcadia*: 'But it was Parthenia's self I loved ...' (44). In *The 'Inward' Language*, Ferry reviews sixteenth-century usage of the word 'self,' including Sidney's (39–45).
30 For a contrasting view of this song, see Anthony Low, *The Reinvention of Love* (Cambridge: Cambridge Univ. Press, 1993), 24–5. Although Low's interpretation of Sidney as a poet of desire has much to recommend it, he occasionally overstates Sidney's 'Petrarchan' qualities; in this instance he identifies Sidney with Astrophil, neglecting the ironic humour of the use of Petrarchan clichés for seductive ends and the sharp shift in voice in the final line.
31 *Sidney's Poetic Development* (Cambridge MA: Harvard Univ. Press, 1967). See also the perceptive essay by Hulse in *Rewriting the Renaissance*, 272–86; Hulse observes that Stella's invocation of honour 'is a mere social pretense, of no more weight than a king's covenant, and so it is no argument of refusal at all' (284).
32 McCoy, *Rebellion*, 109. Richard B. Young also notes that from the point of his rejection Astrophil 'is transformed into the Petrarchan lover' ('English Petrarke: A Study of Sidney's Astrophel and Stella,' in *Three Studies in the Renaissance: Sidney, Jonson, Milton* [New Haven: Yale Univ. Press, 1958], 81).
33 Sidney is not atypical in avoiding direct imitation of Petrarch. For a discussion of the influence of Petrarch on sixteenth-century English poets, see George Watson, *The English Petrarchans: A Critical Bibliography of the 'Canzoniere'* (London: Warburg Institute, 1967); noting the rarity of direct imitation, Watson concludes that 'in Renaissance England Petrarch was a name rather than a book' (3).
34 'The Unauthorized Orpheus of *Astrophil and Stella*,' *Studies in English Literature* 35 (1995), 29; although Prendergast somewhat overstates the case for Stella as a figure of moral authority, her treatment of the question of originality in the series is stimulating and insightful.

35 'The Poetics of Astrophil,' 155.

36 See Leonard Forster, *The Icy Fire* (Cambridge: Cambridge Univ. Press, 1969).

37 Ferry, *'Inward' Language*, 127. Paul Allen Miller provides an illuminating account of the ways in which Sidney uses Ovidian sexuality to overturn Petrarchan idealization in *Astrophil and Stella*; see 'Sidney, Petrarch, and Ovid, or Imitation as Subversion,' *English Literary History* 58 (1991): 499–522.

38 In an instructive account of Sidney's relation to the sonnet tradition, Michael R. G. Spiller observes that what distinguishes Sidney's sequence from all others 'is not its relative sexual explicitness ... but the fact that it is, lightly and pervasively, funny' (*The Development of the Sonnet* [London: Routledge, 1992]), 107.

39 'Sidney, Petrarch, and Ovid,' 506.

6: The Poet as Warrior: *A Defence of Poetry*

1 *Trials of Desire: Renaissance Defenses of Poetry* (New Haven and London: Yale Univ. Press, 1983), 10. I am much indebted to Ferguson's brilliant analysis of the *Defence*. My essay mainly complements hers, I believe, by developing in a specific direction the biographical and social context to which she briefly alludes (160–1). For another stimulating essay that focuses on the power of the self in the *Defence*, see Clark Hulse's chapter, 'Sidney and Hilliard,' in *The Rule of Art* (Chicago: Univ. of Chicago Press, 1990). Hulse sees the *Defence* as 'a sort of aesthetic *coup d'état* in which Sidney explicitly figures the rules of art in political terms and sees himself as escaping their oppression into that golden world where he can exercise *virtù* and power' (125); Hulse neglects, however, the ironic ambivalence that characterizes the self-representation.

2 James M. Osborn, *Young Philip Sidney 1572–1577* (New Haven: Yale Univ. Press, 1972), 537.

3 Charles S. Levy, 'The Correspondence of Sir Philip Sidney and Hubert Languet, 1573–1576' (PhD diss., Cornell Univ., 1962), 59.

4 See Levy, 'Correspondence'; Osborn, *Young Philip Sidney*, 537–40.

5 For the inferior position of poetry in humanistic education, see Richard Helgerson, *The Elizabethan Prodigals* (Berkeley: Univ. of California Press, 1976), 31–5; for poetry's role at court see Baldesar Castiglione, *The Book of the Courtier*, trans. Charles S. Singleton (Garden City NY: Doubleday, 1959), 70. For Sidney's commitment to moral philosophy, see the letters to his brother and Edward Denny already cited; for his commitment to history, see Elizabeth Story Donno, 'Old Mouse-eaten Records: History in Sidney's *Apology*,' *Studies in Philology* 72 (1975): 275–98.

6 For an insightful interpretation of the *Defence* as an attempt to assert the

masculinity of poets and readers against a conventional view that saw both as effeminate, see Mary Ellen Lamb, 'Apologizing for Pleasure in Sidney's *Apology for Poetry*: The Nurse of Abuse Meets the Tudor Grammar School,' *Criticism* 36 (1994): 499–519. See also Peter C. Herman, *Squitter-wits and Muse-haters* (Detroit: Wayne State Univ. Press, 1996), 61–93; Herman places Sidney's concern with effeminacy within the broad context of traditional Protestant attacks upon poetry.

7 *The Elizabethan Courtier Poets* (Columbia: Univ. of Missouri Press, 1991), 48.

8 *The Arte of English Poesie*, ed. Gladys Doidge Willcock and Alice Walker (Cambridge: Cambridge Univ. Press, 1936), 63; see also 4 and 247–8.

9 *Sir Philip Sidney: Courtier Poet* (London: Hamish Hamilton, 1991), 230–1.

10 In 'Sidney's *Defence of Poesie*: The Politics of Pleasure' (*English Literary Renaissance* 25 [1995]: 131–47), Robert Matz argues that Sidney attempts to reconcile protestant utilitarianism with a courtly ethos of pleasure, thus reconciling as well 'middle-class' and aristocratic values; in emphasizing the 'middle-class' status of militant Protestants such as Stephen Gosson, however, Matz understates the importance of the courtly Protestantism manifested by such figures as Walsingham and Leicester. Alan Sinfield also interprets the *Defence* as representing Sidney's desire to 'establish a courtly culture' that was 'a vehicle for earnest protestantism'; see *Faultlines* (Oxford: Clarendon Press, 1992), 207. Sinfield's argument, although often persuasive, leaves little room for internal conflict within Sidney himself.

11 Osborn, *Young Philip Sidney*, 209, 420.

12 *Correspondence of Sir Philip Sidney and Hubert Languet*, trans. Steuart A. Pears (1845: rpt Westmead, Eng.: Gregg International, 1971), 171n.

13 Ibid., 147, 154, and 137.

14 See *The Prose Works of Fulke Greville, Lord Brooke*, ed. John Gouws (Oxford: Clarendon Press, 1986), 46–71, and Mark L. Caldwell, 'Sources and Analogues of the *Life of Sidney*,' *Studies in Philology* 74 (1977): 279–300.

15 See Lawrence Stone, *The Crisis of the Aristocracy, 1588–1641* (Oxford: Clarendon Press, 1965) 715–21.

16 Ferguson, *Trials*, 11. Ferguson's view of the *Defence* as a generic hybrid is supported indirectly by earlier controversies, in which critics unsuccessfully tried to relegate the work simply to one oratorical kind or another. See, for example, Kenneth Myrick, *Sir Philip Sidney as a Literary Craftsman* (Cambridge MA: Harvard Univ. Press, 1935), chapter 2, and Robert M. Coogan, 'The Triumph of Reason: Sidney's *Defense* and Aristotle's *Rhetoric*,' *Papers in Language and Literature* 17 (1981): 255–70.

17 *The Prose Works of Sir Philip Sidney*, ed. Albert Feuillerat, 4 vols., (Cambridge: Cambridge Univ. Press, 1962), III, 133.

18 Duncan-Jones, *Sir Philip Sidney*, 194.

19 Ibid., 267–8.

20 Feuillerat, III, 125.

21 Levy, 'Correspondence,' 62.

22 Feuillerat, III, 132.

23 *Sir Philip Sidney: A Study of His Life and Works* (Cambridge: Cambridge Univ. Press, 1977), 110.

24 For a generally complementary account of Sidney's conscious appropriation of the argument of the *Defence* to 'earnest protestant activism,' see Alan Sinfield, 'The Cultural Politics of the *Defence of Poetry*,' in *Sir Philip Sidney and the Interpretation of Renaissance Culture*, ed. Gary F. Waller and Michael D. Moore (Totowa NJ: Barnes and Noble, 1984), 124–43.

25 Morris Bishop observes that Petrarch wanted to 'restore the broken tradition, standing on the very spot hallowed by the great poets of the Roman past' (*Petrarch and His World* [London: Chatto and Windus, 1964]), 160.

26 Quoted in *An Apology for Poetry*, ed. Geoffrey Shepherd (London: Thomas Nelson, 1965), 168n.

27 See George W. Fisher, *Annals of Shrewsbury School* (London: Methuen, 1899), 43.

28 Pears, *Correspondence*, 143.

29 Ibid., 167.

30 *The Works of Edmund Spenser: A Variorum Edition*, ed. Edwin Greenlaw et al, 11 vols. (Baltimore: Johns Hopkins Press, 1943), VII, 97.

31 Ferguson, *Trials of Desire*, 162; Hager, *Dazzling Images* (Newark: Univ. of Delaware Press, 1991), 103. See also Ronald Levao, 'Sidney's Feigned Apology,' *PMLA* 94 (1979): 223–33, and Martin N. Raitiere, 'The Unity of Sidney's *Apology for Poetry*,' *Studies in English Literature* 21 (1981): 37–57.

32 Stone, *Crisis*, 200.

33 Ibid., 266.

7: Philisides in Andromana's Court: The *New Arcadia*

1 See Ringler's commentary on the poems in the *Old Arcadia* (*P*, 372, 378).

2 See Kenneth Clark and D. Finn, *The Florence Baptistry Doors* (London: Thames and Hudson, 1980).

3 *Sir Philip Sidney: Courtier Poet* (London: Hamish Hamilton, 1991), 144–6; *Tudor and Jacobean Tournaments* (London: George Philip, 1987), 154–8. See also Henry Woudhuysen, *Sir Philip Sidney and the Circulation of Manuscripts 1558–1640* (Oxford: Clarendon Press, 1996); Woudhuysen mentions the identifica-

tion of Lelius as 'Mounseur' (the name Elizabethans gave to the duke of Anjou) in a 1605 folio of Sidney's works, but he acknowledges that 'the circumstances of his fighting Philisides-Sidney do not fit' (274–5).

4 *Astraea* (London: Routledge and Kegan Paul, 1975), 108.

5 *The Rites of Knighthood* (Berkeley: Univ. of California Press, 1989), 18; I am much indebted to McCoy's insightful treatment of Elizabethan chivalry throughout this chapter.

6 *The Chivalric Tradition in Renaissance England* (Washington DC: Folger Shakespeare Library, 1986), 71.

7 McCoy, *Rites*, 28–54.

8 *Sir Philip Sidney*, 271.

9 See his introduction to the *New Arcadia*, xxi–xxii; see also his discussion of the role of Philisides, '"A More Lively Monument": Philisides in *Arcadia*,' in *Sir Philip Sidney's Achievements*, ed. M.J.B. Allen, Dominic Baker-Smith, and Arthur F. Kinney (New York: AMS Press, 1990), 194–200.

10 Raphael Holinshed, *Chronicles* (1808; rpt New York: AMS Press, 1965) 4.883.

11 See especially Louis Adrian Montrose, 'Celebration and Insinuation: Sir Philip Sidney and the Motives of Elizabethan Courtship,' *Renaissance Drama* n.s. 8 (1977): 3–36; Young, *Tudor and Jacobean Tournaments*, 158–60; McCoy, *Rites*, 35–40; Arthur F. Kinney, 'Puritans Versus Royalists: Sir Philip Sidney's Rhetoric at the Court of Elizabeth I,' in *Sir Philip Sidney's Achievements*, ed. M.J.B. Allen et al, 42–56; Philippa Berry, *Of Chastity and Power* (London: Routledge, 1989), 103–7; and Catherine Bates, *The Rhetoric of Courtship in Elizabethan Language and Literature* (Cambridge: Cambridge Univ. Press, 1992).

12 *The Crisis of the Aristocracy, 1558–1641* (London: Clarendon Press, 1965), 199–270.

13 *Constitutionalism and Resistance in the Sixteenth Century: Three Treatises by Hotman, Beza and Mornay*, ed. and trans. Julian A. Franklin (New York: Pegasus, 1969), 191–2. McCoy discusses this passage in *Rites*, 26.

14 For a discussion of this device, see D. Coulman, ' "Spotted to Be Known," ' *Journal of the Warburg and Courtauld Institute* 20 (1957): 179–80. See also Dennis Kay's suggestion that the spots may represent the actual smallpox scars that marred Sidney's face as well as that of his mother, who contracted the disease while nursing the queen ('"She was a Queen, and therefore beautiful": Sidney, His Mother, and Queen Elizabeth,' *Review of English Studies*, n.s. 43 [1992], 28); the trauma of this disfigurement, as Kay persuasively argues, may well underlie Sidney's troubled relationship with the queen throughout his career.

15 For the method of scoring that lies behind the poem, see Young, *Tudor and Jacobean Tournaments*, 46–8.

16 *Sir Philip Sidney*, 207.

17 *Shakespeare's Bawdy* (London: Routledge and Kegan Paul, 1968), 132.

18 *Sir Philip Sidney*, 22–3.

19 Quoted in McCoy, *Rites*, 40.

20 Ibid., 68.

21 J.E. Neale, *Queen Elizabeth I* (1934; rpt Garden City NY: Doubleday, 1957), 28, 356. For the association of both Helen and Andromana with Queen Elizabeth, see James Holly Hanford and Sara Ruth Watson, 'Personal Allegory in the *Arcadia*: Philisides and Lelius,' *Modern Philology* 32 (1934): 1–10. See also Clare R. Kinney, 'Chivalry Unmasked: Courtly Spectacle and the Abuses of Romance in Sidney's *New Arcadia*,' *Studies in English Literature* 35 (1995): 35–52; Kinney provides an excellent account of Sidney's critique of Elizabethan chivalry throughout the *New Arcadia*.

22 Roy Strong, *Gloriana: The Portraits of Queen Elizabeth I* (London: Thames and Hudson, 1987), 113–15.

23 'Celebration and Insinuation,' 3–36; see also McCoy, *Rites*, 35–40. Duncan-Jones surveys possible meanings of the motto in her treatment of the tournament (*Sir Philip Sidney*, 208–9).

24 Evidence discovered by Steven May suggests that Elizabeth may have shown increasing signs of favour towards Sidney at this stage of his career; see 'Sir Philip Sidney and Queen Elizabeth,' *English Manuscript Studies 1100–1700*, II (1990): 257–67. May argues persuasively that Elizabeth supported Sidney throughout his career more generously than is usually appreciated by Sidney scholars; he acknowledges, however, that 'Sidney and his friends continued to believe that Elizabeth did not appreciate his capacity for service to his country' (265).

25 As Joan Rees observes, the invention of Amphialus also enables Sidney to dissociate the princes, Pyrocles and Musidorus, from the moral ambiguity that compromises their heroic roles in the *Old Arcadia*: 'the propensities to sensuality and the improper use of force' are now located in Amphialus, not in the princes. See Rees, *Sir Philip Sidney and Arcadia* (Rutherford NJ: Fairleigh Dickinson Univ. Press, 1991), 40. For an insightful treatment of Amphialus as a literary 'scapegoat' for the princes, see Nancy Lindheim, *The Structures of Sidney's Arcadia* (Toronto: Univ. of Toronto Press, 1982), 80–6.

26 *Representations* I (1983): 18.

27 'The Uprising of the Commons in Sidney's *Arcadia*,' *Modern Language Notes* 48 (1933): 209–17.

28 *Censorship and Interpretation* (Madison: Univ. of Wisconsin Press, 1984), 41. Patterson's treatment of Sidney's intentions is extremely persuasive.

29 For an account of Stubbs's role in the Anjou affair, see *John Stubbs's Gaping Gulf*, ed. Lloyd E. Berry (Charlottesville: Univ. of Virginia Press, 1968); for a

general account of the sedition act, see J.E. Neale, *Elizabeth I and Her Parliaments* (London: Jonathan Cape, 1953), 393–8.

30 Sidney's theory of imitation is complicated and controversial. For some useful discussions, see Geoffrey Shepherd's introduction to his edition of *An Apology for Poetry* (London: Thomas Nelson, 1965); D.H. Craig, 'A Hybrid Growth: Sidney's Theory of Poetry in *An Apology for Poetry,*' *English Literary Renaissance* 10 (1980): 183–201; John C. Ulreich, Jr, '"The Poets Only Deliver": Sidney's Conception of Mimesis,' *Studies in the Literary Imagination* 15 (1982): 67–84; S.K. Heninger, Jr, *Sidney and Spenser: The Poet as Maker* (Univ. Park: Pennsylvania State Univ. Press, 1989); and Clark Hulse, *The Rule of Art* (Chicago: Univ. of Chicago Press, 1990), 115–56. Although Hulse does not discuss the 'poor painter' episode, his fascinating contrast between the views of Sidney and Nicholas Hilliard, the miniaturist, raises the suspicion that Sidney may have been engaging in an indirect caricature of Hilliard's position. Hulse makes clear that Hilliard was actually 'involved in something much more complex than naive naturalism,' but he notes that 'one is tempted to contrast Hilliard and Sidney through the polar opposition of literal and transformative imitation' (134).

31 *Metamorphoses*, XII.189–535; I quote from *The Metamorphoses of Ovid*, trans. Mary M. Innes (Baltimore: Penguin, 1955). Skretkowicz remarks that 'the five drunken rebels are placed in an anti-heroic parody of the battle between the Centaurs and Lapiths,' and he notes verbal allusions to Ovid's descriptions in the *Metamorphoses*; see *New Arcadia*, xxxix and the footnotes on 555.

32 *Astraea*, 92.

33 *The Works of Edmund Spenser: A Variorum Edition*, ed. Edwin Greenlaw et al (Baltimore: Johns Hopkins Press, 1938), VI.xii.46; further citations to this edition are indicated in parentheses.

34 Daniel Javitch, *Poetry and Courtliness in Renaissance England* (Princeton: Princeton Univ. Press, 1978), 141–5. In my treatment of Colin Clout as Spenser's persona, I am much indebted to Javitch and to Richard Helgerson, whose *Self-Crowned Laureates* (Berkeley: Univ. of California Press, 1983) places the episode in Book VI in the context of Spenser's continuing commitment to the exalted role of poet laureate.

8: The Autobiographical Impulse: Conclusions

1 *The Correspondence of Sir Philip Sidney and Hubert Languet*, ed. Steuart A. Pears (1845; rpt Westmead, Eng.: Gregg International, 1971), 143.

2 James M. Osborn, *Young Philip Sidney 1572–1577* (New Haven: Yale Univ. Press, 1972), 537–40.

3 See H. Perry Chapman, *Rembrandt's Self-Portraits: A Study in Seventeenth-Century Identity* (Princeton: Princeton Univ. Press, 1990).

4 'Conditions and Limits of Autobiography,' trans. James Olney, in *Autobiography: Essays Theoretical and Critical*, ed. James Olney (Princeton: Princeton Univ. Press, 1980): 28–48.

5 Osborn, *Young Philip Sidney*, 419–20.

6 'The Correspondence of Sir Philip Sidney and Hubert Languet, 1573–1576,' ed. and trans. Charles S. Levy, PhD diss., Cornell Univ., 1962, 15.

7 'Nous appelons autobiographie le récit rétrospectif en prose que quelqu'un fait de sa propre existence, quand il met l'accent principal sur sa vie individuelle, en particulier sur l'histoire de sa personnalité': *L'Autobiographie en France* (Paris: Librairie Armand Colin, 1971), 14.

8 'Autobiography as De-Facement,' in *The Rhetoric of Romanticism*, ed. Paul de Man (New York: Columbia Univ. Press, 1984), 68–9.

9 For useful discussions of the most recent tendencies in autobiographical theory, see the introduction to James Olney, ed., *Autobiography*, and Laura Marcus, *Auto/biographical Discourses* (Manchester: Univ. of Manchester Press, 1994). Paul Jay's *Being in the Text* (Ithaca: Cornell Univ. Press, 1984) contains a stimulating discussion of *Roland Barthes by Roland Barthes* (174–83).

10 Thomas Whythorne, *The Autobiography of Thomas Whythorne*, ed. James M. Osborn (Oxford: Clarendon Press, 1961), 1–2 ; I have modernized the 'new orthography.'

11 Ibid., 20–2.

12 *The Prose Works of Sir Philip Sidney*, ed Albert Feuillerat, 4 vols. (Cambridge: Cambridge Univ. Press, 1962), III, 132.

13 *Renaissance Self-Fashioning* (Chicago: Univ. of Chicago Press, 1980), 9.

14 Levy, 'Correspondence,' 234.

15 *Sir Philip Sidney: Courtier Poet* (London: Hamish Hamilton, 1991), 72; *The Prose Works of Fulke Greville, Lord Brooke*, ed. John Gouws (Oxford: Clarendon Press, 1986), 5.

16 *Nobilis, or A View of the Life and Death of Sidney, and Lessis Lugubris*, ed. Virgil B. Heltzel and Hoyt H. Hudson (San Marino CA: 1940), 71, 73.

17 Claudio Guillén, *Literature as System* (Princeton: Princeton Univ. Press, 1971), 120.

18 *Prose Works*, III, 11.

19 *The Philosophy of Literary Form*, 3rd ed. (Berkeley: Univ. of California Press, 1973), 304, 298; see Richard McCoy's development of Burke's view in *The Rites of Knighthood* (Berkeley: Univ. of California Press, 1989), 1–8.

20 See in particular Raphael Falco, 'Instant Artifacts: Vernacular Elegies for Philip Sidney,' *Studies in Philology* 89 (1992): 1–19. Falco shows how elegists of

Sidney gradually shifted their attention from his roles as soldier and patron to his role as poet, thereby creating for themselves a 'strictly poetic precursor from whom to descend' (19). In the introduction to their reprint of the earliest elegies, A.J. Colaianne and W.L. Godshalk note that the poems 'uniformly stress Sidney's heroism at Zutphen, his bravery in battle and in the court, his loyalty, intelligence, political abilities, oratorical skills, and above all, his patriotism' (*Elegies for Sir Philip Sidney* [1587; facs. rpt Delmar NY: Scholars' Facsimiles and Reprints, 1980], ix).

21 In *Philip's Phoenix: Mary Sidney, Countess of Pembroke* (New York: Oxford Univ. Press, 1990), Margaret P. Hannay describes the countess's 'campaign to present the works and life of Sir Philip Sidney as a notable image of virtue, encouraging the hagiography that has developed into the Sidney legend' (60). For a perceptive general study of the creation of the Sidney legend, see Richard Lanham, 'Sidney: the Ornament of His Age,' *Southern Review* 2 (1967): 319–40; for an interesting account of its later development, see John Gouws, 'The Nineteenth-Century Development of the Sidney Legend,' in *Sir Philip Sidney's Achievements*, ed. M.J.B. Allen, Dominic Baker-Smith, and Arthur F. Kinney (New York: AMS Press, 1990), 251–60.

Index